WE WERE ALWAYS HERE

A MEXICAN-AMERICAN'S ODYSSEY

WE WERE ALWAYS HERE

A MEXICAN-AMERICAN'S ODYSSEY

Ricardo Chavira

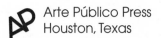

Arte Público Press
Houston, Texas

We Were Always Here is made possible through a grant from the National Endowment for the Arts. We are grateful for their support.

Recovering the past, creating the future

Arte Público Press
University of Houston
4902 Gulf Fwy, Bldg 19, Rm 100
Houston, Texas 77204-2004

Cover design by Mora Des!gn

Library of Congress Control Number: 2021930219

21 22 23   4 3 2 1

For the love of my life, Yoli, and our two sons, Fernando and Gabriel, ages 13 and 10 respectively.

For my two beautiful and exceptional children, Ricardo and Marlena, who have given me a lifetime of joy and special moments of laughter and pride.

For my two grandchildren, Lucía and Félix.

Table of Contents

Introduction

ONE DAY IN 1870, a teenaged orphan saddled a mare and left San Francisco Javier de Satevó in southern Chihuahua. He traveled northeast across 225 miles of desert to Fort Davis, Texas. Jesús Chavira, my great grandfather, unimpeded by American officials or anyone else, crossed the border in search of economic survival.

He found work as a stable boy at the Fort Davis US cavalry post. In time, Jesús would marry Estefana Molina, and they would have eight children, all just outside of Shafter, Texas. José, my paternal grandfather, was the eldest. He was born in 1896. Jesús and his family put down roots that would spread across Texas and California as he and Estefana's offspring had children and grandchildren of their own.

This book tells their story, and my own as a third-generation American. I have contended with the same inequality, poverty and withering racism my ancestors did. Mexicans of my generation typically took the path of acculturation, adapting to the ways of mainstream America. In the process, some of them distanced themselves from Mexican culture, failed to learn Spanish and came to view Mexico as a foreign land rather than as their ancestral homeland.

In Mexico, they were derisively called *pochos,* because many of them spoke little or no Spanish and had been cut off in their education from Mexican culture. They were proud Americans, yet they were conscious of the fact that they were of Mexican origin.

I was a considered *pocho* during much of my childhood. In the following pages, I recount how my career as a journalist helped me understand who I am and where I came from. In fact, it was my cultural hybridity that allowed me to flourish as a journalist, as I told the stories of the United States and Latin America from a profound and rare perspective.

My story is a tale of reconnection with Mexican culture and the retention of my American identity. I became fully bicultural and bilingual, but over time I became more at home in Mexico than in my native country.

I identify as American in the broadest and truest sense of the term: America is a hemisphere and not just the United States. My odyssey led me to all parts of my native land and most of Latin America, as well as other regions. This book took me many years to write because I was reticent to talk about myself. It struck me as presumptuous to assume that anyone would find my life interesting. My wife Yoleinis, my son Ricardo Jr. and daughter Marlena Medford Chavira ultimately convinced me that I had a story worth sharing. So, here it is.

CHAPTER ONE
Running with the Rebels

DESPERATELY, the heavily armed guerrillas and I scaled a steep, verdant hill in northern Nicaragua. In withering afternoon heat, the very fatigued twenty-seven rebels, my colleague and I pressed on at a grueling pace, often slipping and stumbling on loose soil. For the last hour, the muffled boom of Nicaraguan military artillery told the fighters their enemies were close. Vastly outnumbered, the guerrillas had to keep moving.

The group's mustachioed 29-year-old commander, Alfa, looked over his shoulder, his face tightened in fear and anger. "They are bombing where we just were. If we don't hurry and get out of here, they'll be on top of us."

Alfa and his young, American-trained and -armed Nicaraguan peasants were Contras, that is *contrarevolucionarios*, or counterrevolutionaries. They were locked in a three-year-old war with the leftist Sandinista government. The group included two women combatants, photographer Bob Nickelsburg and me. Both Bob and I were on assignment for *Time* magazine.

Weeks earlier, Alfa and his fellow combatants had engaged in a raid from their Honduran base into Nicaragua's

Nueva Segovia Department, blowing up electrical power lines, mining roads, fighting Sandinista troops and murdering two civilian government collaborators. Now, on Good Friday, 1984, the Contras were again in Nueva Segovia being chased by insurgents with murderous intent. The rules of this war dictated that captured fighters were immediately often executed.

I was terrified yet focused on returning to the safety of the Honduran border, some twenty miles to the north. Strangely, I was struck by the improbability of my dire situation. I thought of the great physical, intellectual and emotional distance I had traveled to be at this torrid, dangerous spot in Nicaragua. To this day, I don't understand why such thoughts came to me. My journey had begun some twenty-five years earlier as a poor Mexican boy in Southern California.

That journey would imbue me with a strong sense of dual identities, one Mexican, the other American. This biculturalism would enable me to navigate and understand the very different worlds and cultures of Mexico and the United States. As a journalist, I would view and interpret the world from the perspective of the poor, and my long immersion in Mexican culture allowed me to perceive Latin America as few Americans could.

When I was in Latin America, my Latino appearance allowed me to blend in. Then, as now, American journalists were overwhelmingly Euro-Americans, or we can say, simply middle-class white people, who grew up with the privileges afforded to those who lived in mainstream America. They could not see the world as I did. I found this was true even of white reporters who spoke fluent Spanish.

My experience would be filled with journalistic adventures in dozens of nations, including the Soviet Union, Vietnam and much of the Middle East. I would enjoy a first-hand view of historic events.

That years-long voyage would demand that I overcome the obstacles of poverty, racism and a dysfunctional family. I had struggled through high school, rejected gang affiliation, avoided committing serious crimes, evaded the Vietnam war draft and earned bachelor's and master's degrees. In my early twenties, I sometimes let myself dream of becoming a foreign correspondent for a top-tier American periodical. But I could not truly believe I would realize that dream.

Mine was an uncommon odyssey, since most Mexicans in the United States of my generation typically did not attend college. Sometimes I felt my goal of becoming a professional journalist was unrealistic. I was discouraged because there were only a handful of Latinos in mainstream English-language journalism. Institutional racism was an imposing barrier for those of us who were not white men. Even after I made my way into a newsroom, I fought to keep from being pigeon-holed as a "Hispanic" reporter. I was a journalist who happened to be Mexican—a mestizo comprised of European, indigenous Mexican and African ancestry—fully capable of reporting any story, including those that benefited from my Latino perspective and intimate knowledge of my American homeland.

I eventually earned the respect and trust of my colleagues and bosses at several news organizations and took on stories ranging from Los Angeles city hall to Mexico's *Palacio Nacional*, the US-Mexico border, Central American wars, historic summits and American diplomatic affairs in Washington, DC. As I reported and edited stories of every sort, traveling to more than forty nations, I would earn awards, including the 1994 Pulitzer Prize for international reporting.

I found that my profound identification with my Mexican heritage and the poor set me apart from most American journalists of my time, who I saw as privileged white people. Of course, I could not know that my Nicaraguan predicament would provide a dramatic chapter in my growth as a journalist. Nor could I imagine Central America and its poor would remain a US foreign policy concern well into the 2000s. I would witness how Washington's support for repressive regimes would set in motion the current mass exodus of Central Americans to the US-Mexico border.

⋘⊚⊚⋙

Our Good Friday escape began festively. At dawn, we arrived at a small hilltop farm. The family who lived there told us they were preparing to commemorate Good Friday, and so they generously shared with us coffee, sweet biscuits and fatty duck soup. The family knew several of the adolescent fighters who were from the area. As pop music from the local Sandinista radio station blared, a party was in the making. Then at about 8 am, Alfa used his binoculars to scan a valley from our perch. He muttered, "*piricuacos*," a disparaging term for the Sandinistas that meant "rabid dogs." I borrowed the binoculars and saw East German IFA trucks disgorging hundreds of troops. The Sandinistas were launching a sweep. Quickly, the fiesta ended as the Contras grimly hoisted US Army-issue backpacks, Belgian FAL assault rifles and Soviet AK-47s. There was an oppressive sense of urgency and apprehension as we set off.

Alfa decided we should move along a route toward the Honduran border that arced beyond the Sandinistas' flank. Alfa's outnumbered fighters had to avoid detection. We would march as much as possible where vegetation afforded us coverage. The next fifteen hours were an exhausting and frightening ordeal. We stumbled along the rocky creek beds, often clawing our way in darkness through dense vegetation. Mindful of the Sandinistas scouring the area, we hustled relentlessly.

By mid-afternoon, a Sandinista patrol was not far behind. Pelón, whose dark indigenous features and gold-capped teeth made him look fierce, greeted the news enthusiastically. He raised his rifle and shouted, "*Piricuacos*, sons of whores! We're ready!"

Just then, two Contra scouts who trailed behind to detect Sandinistas in pursuit confirmed by radio that the force was much larger than Alfa's. A battle, Alfa reasoned, would be too risky. Scouts in advance of the group radioed that there was no sign of government troops ahead.

Alfa was more convinced than ever that we should dash for the safety of the Honduran border, still many hours ahead.

Pelón was disgusted. "We could ambush them, then slip out of here," he told Alfa.

"No," Alfa replied, "now's not the time to fight."

Just as he said that, we could hear distant artillery fire behind us. I, for my part, was nearing the limits of my endurance. Almost from the start of our foray into Nicaragua six days earlier, my feet had become blistered; the blisters quickly turned into deep lacerations on my heels that burned with intense pain. Compounding my misery was the pace of the hours-long trek with no more than a periodic few-minutes rest. Throughout the trip we had to traverse steep hills, through patches of dense brush, while subsisting on little food. A few mouthfuls of red beans and a couple of tortillas were all we ate most days. One day we had only a hardened cone of brown sugar to deaden our hunger. The combined effect of having my feet painfully injured, nearly a week of arduous marching, scant food and now the frantic pace left me near collapse.

Gasping, I sank to one knee. I told Roberto, an adolescent Contra who always walked beside me, attentive to my well-being, "I'll stay here. You guys go on without me. When the Sandinistas get here, I'll explain that I'm a journalist and ask them to take me to Managua."

I was certain I couldn't walk any further. It was time to extricate myself from this awful misadventure. I was stupid to have undertaken the assignment, I thought. Nickelsburg was several yards ahead of me and unaware of my decision. Roberto pointed out that I was wearing American army fatigues—clothes I thought would make me less conspicuous—and the Sandinistas might not believe I was not a Contra or in some way collaborating with them.

"They will probably kill you," he said.

And so, I rose and pressed on, energized by the realization that I was no longer a neutral participant, but the quarry in a brutal war.

We marched all night, feeling our way sometimes. I slowed the group with my frequent need to pause to gather strength. At about midnight, Alfa said it was safe to rest because we were far ahead of the Sandinistas. We collapsed on a hilltop. I fell asleep as soon as I hit the ground.

An hour later, we were on the march again. We came to the unpaved road called the Ocotal Highway, the region's main thoroughfare. Crossing it dangerously exposed us, so we ran across. The road, I learned, had become the de facto Honduras-Nicaragua border, and it was also the site of many Sandinista ambushes. The Contras had a heavy and permanent presence beyond the road.

By noon we were back at the Contras' Camp Nicarao, just inside Honduras. Comandante Mack welcomed us. A former Nicaraguan National Guard Sargeant whose real name was Benito Centeno, he oversaw operations in Nueva Segovia. Centeno was eager to hear about the trip. He was just as eager to argue that without American aid, their war would go nowhere. Congress was debating whether to continue aiding what had become a controversial war to topple a government.

"Legislators might think that helping us will cost them votes," said Centeno, stocky, dark-skinned and clad in pressed fatigues. "They should also look ahead five or six years. If we are not around by then, the United States will have to send Marines into Nicaragua. This is not something we would like to see. With American help, we Nicaraguans can save our nation."

Next, Centeno offered me and Nickelsburg what seemed like a banquet: canned tuna with scrambled eggs, tortillas and a Coca-Cola. I had lost nearly twenty pounds during the foray, and I ached all over. By late afternoon, Nickelsburg and I were in Tegucigalpa, where I would write my story for *Time* and reflect on my trip.

A month earlier, I had pitched my idea to Edgar Chamorro, a top official of the Honduras-based Contras, known as the Nicaraguan Democratic Force, or FDN. A few weeks later, he phoned me in Mexico City, cryptically suggesting I visit Tegucigalpa. Once in the Honduran capital, trip details were worked out. Nickelsburg and I went to a Contra house a few blocks from the US embassy on the morning of Friday, April 17, 1984. Soon we were on our way aboard an SUV to a Contra base camp sixty miles southeast of the capital. As we tore down a stretch of road, Honduran peasants glared at us. Youths bathing in a river shouted insults as we passed. Honduran soldiers had made large stretches of the border with Nicaragua off-limits to ensure the Contras' security. This arrangement bred peasant resentment at what was viewed as an occupying force.

Before noon we were at Camp Nicarao, named for a sixteenth-century indigenous chief famous for his wisdom and courage. The camp, just two miles from Nicaragua, was a cluster of olive-green US Army tents. A few hundred Contras were in the camp. A clinic, a mess hall, an armory and several tent warehouses covered a few acres. Mule trains left there for Nicaragua carrying weapons, ammunition, mines and other supplies. I saw a man who appeared to be an American or European in one of the tents operating a lathe. He ducked when he spotted me. Most likely he was a CIA agent or operative. I also discovered several dozen landmines stored next to a large earthen wall. The Contras had denied ever planting the devices.

The base commander, Alfredo Peña, who looked more like an accountant than a warrior, greeted us. In briefing us on our trip, he predicted that the Contras would be the first insurgency to overthrow a communist government.

Some five hours after our arrival, we heard exploding mortar rounds. As the steady thuds grew louder, Peña revealed that the Contras and Sandinistas were battling a few miles over the border. Some fifty Contras headed out to the fight; an hour or so later, about a dozen adolescents arrived. They lined up and a Contra gave them tips on how to shoulder their weapons and fire: "Make sure you keep several paces apart when you are marching, and when the shit starts, hit the ground. And then don't be afraid to fire back."

We expected to leave for Nicaragua at dawn the next day, but the fighting had only just ended, and conditions were still unsafe. No one would disclose to me the battle's outcome. At around noon, we set out. A sinewy gray-haired mulatto named Armando and five armed adolescent Contras were to guide Bob and me into Nicaragua. Within the first few hours, I began to regret making the trip. Much of the walking was up 45-degree mountain trails, with the temperature exceeding 90 degrees. Late that afternoon we arrived at a Contra hilltop outpost in Nicaragua's Nueva Segovia Department. Several contras, including two women, welcomed us. I was drenched in sweat, bone-tired, my heels lacerated by the stiff, new boots I wore. We were asleep by nightfall.

Over the next several days, we would march deeper into Nicaragua—some twenty-five miles in all—as a test of Contra military prowess and civilian support. Alfa told us he had orders to only engage in combat if attacked, this to help ensure Nickelsburg's and my safety.

In the dim light of dawn of our second day, we approached the Ocotal Highway. We crouched and scurried across. A few hundred yards further on, one of the Contras shouted for us to halt. He had spotted a landmine firing mechanism, a small metal cylinder less than an inch above the ground. In all, Contras and Sandinistas would plant 180,000 mines, mostly in northern Nicaragua.

Later that day, we arrived at a farm where the residents happily greeted the group. "We are Contras," said "the grandmother," the code name for an elderly supporter. Smiling and clasping one of the young Contra's arm, she added: "These are our people. They are from here. We are in the same struggle. They fight with arms, and we support them with food and shelter."

We marched on in the early afternoon along a dry creek bed. Suddenly a peasant leading a mule hurried toward us. Alfa tensed and ordered the man to halt. The man was talking excitedly. Alfa said the peasant warned that a large Sandinista patrol was headed in our direction. We hid in the brush that lined the creek bed. About thirty minutes later, on a path about fifteen feet above us, we heard boots tromping on rocky soil and loud chatter. I scarcely dared breathe. It was a surreal few minutes. I thought our predicament was very much like one torn from a war movie.

When the apparently large patrol moved on, we quietly resumed our own march. We trudged on for the next few days, stopping at farms for rest and provisions. Unfortunately, the farmers had little food. Bob was holding up better than I was. My feet were a mass of bloody sores that soaked my socks, and I was constantly tired. All the peasants I interviewed told of being oppressed by the Sandinistas, thus driving them to back the Contras.

At one farm, the Contras gathered twenty or so peasants for a town-hall-style meeting. The men were clad in tattered clothes and rubber boots.

"I took my son—he is thirteen—to one of the *piricuaco* schools so he could learn to read and write," said one of the men. "They put a uniform on him and had him carrying a rifle. They brag about their literacy campaign but say nothing about making the boys soldiers."

Others said state security agents persecuted them. A farmer named Don Víctor said agents had threatened him days earlier. "They know the Contras could not exist here without our support, so we are threatened. One of the men who came to my farm said, 'We know you sons of whores are with the Contras. One of these days we are going to murder you and be done with the problem.'"

The Contra movement began in 1979 when former national guardsmen launched an armed anti-Sandinista insurgency. Initially, almost all Contras were linked to the deposed regime. Eventually, disillusioned Sandinistas joined their ranks, as did many peasants. Some were fighting because a relative had joined the FDN while others were drawn by the $100 they were paid monthly. Others said they were fighting solely out of the heartfelt conviction that Nicaragua would be better without the Sandinistas in control, although they did not know what sort of government should replace the one in power.

Years earlier, Alfa had worked as a radio repairman in his native Nueva Segovia. He told me that he lived peacefully—even during the revolution that overthrew the dictator, American ally Anastasio Somoza. But in the revolutionary fervor following their triumph, the Sandinistas rounded up suspected Somoza supporters. Alfa said that his three brothers were executed on the false charge of being counterrevolutionaries.

"That made me see we couldn't have that kind of government," he said.

Roberto was eighteen, short, with sharp, indigenous features. Several months later he and Alfa would be killed in combat. The adolescent guerrilla told me he had been with the FDN for a year and been in countless battles. Roberto had become a Contra after Sandinista security agents arrested and imprisoned his brother for denouncing the government. He told me about Manuelito, a spirit said to inhabit an abandoned farm. "If you have enough faith, he will speak to you," said Roberto. "He tells us where the *piricuacos* have ambushes."

Late on the afternoon of our sixth day in Nueva Segovia, Alfa announced a change in plans. We were to have linked up with more than a hundred Contras to the south, but now an even larger Sandinista force had moved between us. With the Sandinistas near, we maintained silence. Before dawn the next day, Good Friday, we began a trek that hours later would become our headlong dash to escape the Sandinistas in hot pursuit.

My trip demonstrated that while many peasants supported the FDN cause, organized support was spotty and often came without food and intelligence on Sandinista movements. I would learn in a future trip with leftist guerrillas in El Salvador that solid civilian support required a ready supply of food, information and even armed combat, much in the way the Viet Cong aided the North Vietnamese regulars.

During the Ronald Reagan Administration, wars in Guatemala and El Salvador and with the Sandinista government were top foreign-policy issues. They were key to the

Reagan Doctrine of "rolling back" global communism. He described it on February 6, 1985: "We must not break faith with those who are risking their lives—on every continent from Afghanistan to Nicaragua—to defy Soviet-supported aggression and secure rights which have been ours from birth."

Reagan was determined to topple Nicaragua's government. "The consensus throughout the hemisphere," he said in a July 18, 1983 speech, "is that while the Sandinistas promised their people freedom, all they've done is replace the former dictatorship with their own: a dictatorship of counterfeit revolutionaries who wear fatigues and drive around in Mercedes sedans and Soviet tanks and whose current promise is to spread their brand of 'revolution' throughout Central America."

It was true that Central American revolutionaries received some Soviet, Eastern Bloc and Cuban support. But the Sandinistas were not hardened communists. They adhered to mild socialism. Critics alleged that the Contras were nothing more than terrorists and that the United States immorally had sided with murderous regimes in El Salvador and Guatemala.

At the 1986 White House Correspondents' Dinner, an annual gala that brings together journalists with the powerful and famous, I sat next to CIA Director William Casey. Someone must have told him about my Contra trip, because in the course of a chat with me, he asked what I thought of the rebels.

"They are not a true insurgency," I replied. "From what I saw, they do not have broad popular support."

Casey nodded and said, "That's what I thought."

The Reagan Doctrine would lead to the Iran-Contra Scandal. White House officials, among them National Security Council staffer Oliver North, illegally procured funds to arm the Contras. The efforts included the secret sale of TOW missiles to Iran during that nation's war with Iraq.

The Contras were a Reagan Administration creation. They would not have existed without US support. All fighters drew monthly pay, and CIA agents armed and trained them. Some of the leadership had been soldiers during the Somoza years. The Contras operated almost exclusively from bases in Honduras. That country, in exchange for allowing the Contras to operate unmolested, received substantial American aid.

After covering the war against Nicaragua by talking to Contra and American officials in Tegucigalpa, I had to have a first-hand look at this conflict that was being fought in remote areas of Nicaragua. There was no other way to accurately judge the truth of claims that the Contras were quickly developing as a potent military and political threat to the Sandinista government. But the theater of combat was not only remote but shrouded in CIA-imposed secrecy.

Traditionally a backwater, Tegucigalpa had with the war on Nicaragua become thick with intrigue. The CIA was in town to run the war, and middle-aged American men wearing cowboy shirts were everywhere. They hung out together at the Honduras Maya Hotel, speaking in hushed tones. Who were they? Other journalists and I guessed they were CIA agents or operatives. I would learn that Tegucigalpa had also attracted mercenaries and arms dealers.

The American embassy added heightened intrigue and mystery. American diplomats hinted that the war was to a large extent being run out of the mission, with Ambassador John D. Negroponte at the helm. Negroponte was a staunch Cold War warrior who had rendered diplomatic service in Vietnam. Officially, the United States was not running the Contras or the war. The implausible line was that the Contras were an indigenous force that Honduras decided to support. In fact, US military aid to Honduras jumped from $4 million to $200 million between 1980 and 1985. The aid was payment for Honduran collaboration and hosting of the Contras, who relished the intrigue. They met journalists only at places they deemed secure, supposedly to avoid Sandinista agents known to operate in Tegucigalpa. All in all, it made for a banana republic Casablanca.

The Contras, who demobilized in 1990 after the Sandinistas lost a presidential election, focused on soft targets, such as farms, clinics and civilians. A 1989 Human Rights Watch report called them ". . . major and systematic violators of the most basic standards of the laws of armed conflict, including by launching indiscriminate attacks on civilians, selectively murdering non-combatants. . . ." The Sandinista revolution and the Contra war together killed some 30,000 combatants and civilians.

A former Sandinista supporter, Edgar Chamorro concluded that the revolutionaries were anti-democratic. He was appointed as an FDN director and the group's press attaché. Chamorro would lose a power struggle, leave the FDN and become a vocal Contra critic. In a 1987 interview, he said that the CIA dictated what he should say publicly.

"I was told to speak about bringing democracy to Nicaragua, but we all knew that our purpose was to overthrow the Nicaraguan government," said Chamorro. "The CIA gave us a list of things to say about the Sandinistas to make them look like communists. And we were told to deny working with the CIA, that all our funding came from private sources."

The Contras would for years be a Reagan Administration foreign policy obsession, one that demanded media coverage. So, in early November 1986, I briefly left my Washington bureau duties and traveled to the Honduran-Nicaraguan border. *Time* editors reasoned that my recent on-the-ground reporting in Honduras would give me enhanced insight into the Contra war. Indeed, no one in the Washington bureau had ever been to Central America.

My reporting at the State Department and Capitol Hill suggested that the Contras were weaker militarily than they had been two years earlier, when I had traveled with them. This was significant because starting in October 1986, US military aid had, after a two-year prohibition, begun to flow once more. In addition, the Contra ranks had increased from 8,000 fighters in 1984 to 11,000 in 1986.

Immediately after arriving in Honduras, I headed for "The Road of Death." The dirt highway and surrounding area close to the Nicaraguan border had experienced a surge in combat. Significantly, Sandinista troops had crossed into Honduras to fight the Contras and, whenever possible, disrupt their logistical structure.

Despite its ominous appellation, the dirt road in southern Honduras' El Paraíso Department cut through pine-covered mountains and offered scenic views of grassy meadows, a majestic valley and flocks of tropical birds. In places, the road ran only yards from Nicaraguan territory. El Paraíso Department was where most of the Contras had several bases. The bases were used for training and as staging grounds for incursions into Nicaragua.

The road had earned its nickname following the 1983 deaths of American journalists Dial Torgeson and Richard Cross. They were killed when their car hit a landmine that Sandinista troops had planted to disrupt Contra supply lines. I saw the burned-out hulk of a truck that was used to ferry supplies to the Contras at a base called El Paraíso. A month earlier, Sandinista soldiers had slipped across the border and fired an RPG round into the supply-filled vehicle.

A string of Honduran army bunkers manned by young soldiers was spread along the road. Their M-16 rifles jutted over the edge of the protective shelters. Several hundred yards to the south of the border, Sandinista soldiers looked back from behind their own sandbags. "Sometimes they greet us," quipped a Honduran private, making light of the gunfire that erupted from the other side.

The day I was there, just a few hours later, there was a 45-minute firefight. While no one was killed or injured, the road and the surrounding Honduran territory were being dragged into the Contra-Sandinista war.

Two years earlier, the Contras had for the most part been taking the war to the Sandinistas. Now, Sandinista troops had taken up fixed positions in Honduras. Hundreds of Contras had clashed repeatedly with the invaders but failed to dislodge them.

This was an ominous development for the Contras and Honduras alike. Already the consequences were apparent, and nowhere was this clearer than in Las Trojes, a bustling farming town of some 40,000 right against the border with Nicaragua. The intermittent fighting in the surrounding countryside had driven about 2,000 farmers off their land and into Las Trojes.

"Before we lived in tranquility," said Jacoba Torres, a sixty-year-old farmer with a deeply wrinkled and weathered brown face. "Now, we hear bombs and gunfire all the time. We know that the Sandinistas are all around us. They have put mines in the ground, and many people have stepped on them."

She and her husband had fled from their farm. "We were not the only ones," Torres said. "There was too much fear. The Sandinistas took a whole family away; nobody knows why. People thought they would kidnap all of us, so now the area is abandoned."

American and Contra officials said the Sandinista strategy was to choke off shipments to the Contras in Nicaragua.

Las Trojes was an important resupply point, where the Contras would be back on their heels.

Adolfo Calero, head of the FDN and the most powerful of the Contras, told me that American military aid had arrived slowly. After Congress learned of the CIA's role in mining Nicaraguan ports, it ended Contra funding. Reagan on October 16, 1986, signed into law some $70 million in military aid and $30 million in humanitarian aid. In what would prove to be the tip of the Iran-Contra scandal, there was clear evidence that a clandestine network was arming the Contras. The network, it would be revealed, was, in fact, an illegal, American operation that had been delivering arms to the Contras even when US law prohibited it. Between 1984 and 1986 the NSC staff had raised $34 million for aid to the Contras from third parties, such as Saudi Arabia and Brunei; millions more were raised from donors at conservative fundraisers. Oliver North spearheaded the covert funding, depositing funds in Swiss bank accounts. North and Contra leaders had access to the funds.

While I was based in the region from January 1984 to January 1986, fellow journalists and I heard persistent rumors of an off-the-books Contra supply operation based at El Salvador's Ilopango airfield. But the facility was closed to journalists, and sources denied the rumors.

A downing of a C-123 supply plane over Nicaragua on October 5, 1986 was noteworthy because the crash's lone survivor told his Sandinista captors that he was working for the CIA. Eugene Hasenfus was sentenced to thirty years but then pardoned and released. I interviewed Elliot Abrams, Assistant Secretary of State for the Bureau of Inter-American Affairs, soon after the incident. He assured me repeatedly that Hasenfus was not working for or in any way connected to the American government. Abrams stated he was simply unaware of any such relationship, that he knew of all activity and so he could authoritatively assure me that Hasenfus was not connected to the Reagan Administration. It was just one of many lies Abrams would tell when the scandal broke.

The Hasenfus incident helped uncover the Iran-Contra crimes. Hasenfus's capture brought to light the fact that during a period when lethal aid to the Contras was banned, the National Security Council, with North in the lead, kept the arms and equipment flowing. The official line was that the Contras had been left to fend for themselves.

The black resupply operation, according to FDN official Indalecio Rodríguez, was poorly managed. "We didn't know how to get the supplies to where our troops were," he said. In Nicaragua's north-central Matagalpa Department, Rodríguez claimed, "We had 500 of our armed men who had to protect 1,500 who had no arms. We had no way to deliver them. Another time, we bought a lot of jungle boots, but they were poorly made. In a week, we had our people barefooted."

Abrams blamed Washington's aid cut-off for the Contras' loss of territory. Echoing Rodríguez, he claimed the lack of expert American administration made for the poor distribution of this purportedly private funding. Of course, Iran-Contra would reveal that there was never a time when the CIA and other Reagan officials had removed themselves from the supply efforts. In truth, the Contras had been put on the defensive because the Sandinistas had benefited from improved counterinsurgency training and ample Cuban and Soviet supplies, including the feared Hind combat helicopters.

Two years earlier, Contra and American officials insisted that the rebels were a force to be reckoned with. Now, the line was that the Contras had to make a comeback and then push on to final victory. The words lacked conviction.

Several weeks after my visit to Las Trojes, the Iran-Contra affair burst into the public arena, marking the beginning of the end of American efforts to overthrow the

Nicaraguan government. The war would end without so much as a whimper.

Certainly, of all the reporting assignments I had held, none excited me as much as covering Central America and Mexico. I already had several years of reporting experience in Mexico and the Mexican-American borderlands for *The San Diego Union*. But I was hungry for more. At first, I was absorbed by Mexico's economic turmoil. That proud nation's painful and distressing decline with its obvious implications for the United States was a major news story. I also felt a strong personal connection with Mexico.

In March 1982, a Tijuana leftist, José Luis Pérez Canchola, told me that hundreds if not thousands of Guatemalan indigenous people had in the last few weeks fled into the jungles of Mexico's Chiapas state. Pérez explained they were survivors of a Guatemalan army genocidal campaign. At that time, the Central American nation was in its second decade of armed conflict with leftist rebels. Most of the fighting was in the northern Guatemalan provinces of Quiché and Huehuetenango. Leftist rebels had been at war with the government since 1960. The Guerrilla Army of the Poor, or EGP, in 1982 had sizeable support among the nation's Mayan people.

Pérez said he did not know exactly where refugees were arriving, but he gave me the name of a Catholic priest in San Cristóbal de las Casas, Chiapas, who likely knew the location. I convinced my editors that photographer Ian Dryden and I would find the refugees. No news organization had reported on what was a little-known refugee crisis.

During the 2,000-mile trip south, I began thinking that my chances of finding the refugees were uncertain. The journey would prove to be one of my greatest journalistic challenges. Failure to confirm the story would have been a major professional blow. But I had faith in my judgment. Pérez was a sober and careful man. I trusted him.

We stopped for a day in Mexico City, where I interviewed an interior ministry official. He claimed there were no refugees. However, he said Guatemalan troops and guerrillas had infiltrated the area, requiring the Mexican government to declare it off-limits. I was forbidden to travel there, he said. While I said I would respect the ban, I decided to go, convinced that the Mexican government was hiding something.

Ian and I arrived in San Cristóbal de las Casas, a city high in the mountains of Chiapas. Inhabited for several hundred years by highland Mayans, the Spanish arrived to build the first church in 1547. I met with the priest who reportedly knew where the refugees were, but it turned out that he was unsure. He believed it was either Motozintla, a town on the Guatemalan border, or a jungle clearing called Puerto Rico on the Usumacinta River. The priest told me that Catholic priests and nuns were deeply concerned about the crisis but had no uncomplicated way to travel away from San Cristóbal.

In Motozintla, I went to a church on the hunch that priests or nuns would have information. An Irish nun who received us confided that the church had taken in wounded Guatemalan rebel fighters. A few were present. We needed to go to Puerto Rico to find the refugees, she said. On a map, of the Usumacinta the nun located what she was sure was Puerto Rico.

Getting there would be difficult. It was most easily accessible by small plane and a river ride of several hours. We left for Las Margaritas, some 350 miles distant, on the eastern side of Chiapas. There we could find bush pilots who would fly us into the thick Lacandon rainforest. After an all-night drive through thick fog on a winding mountain road, we hired a pilot.

Flying over the one-million-acre Lacandon, I was struck by the seemingly endless expanse of lush greenery. After forty-five minutes or so, the pilot advised we would be landing. I couldn't see a landing strip until we went into a sharp descent. Just a few feet over the jungle cover, we made a bumpy landing on a dirt strip.

We deplaned and confirmed the date for the pilot's return. Within a few minutes, some ten Mexican soldiers approached us. The leader told us we could not remain in the area. Ian cleverly offered a pack of cigarettes, which the soldiers eagerly accepted. I explained that we simply wanted to visit the refugees. The soldiers nodded knowingly. They agreed to let us continue but advised us we would need to find someone to take us down the river to Puerto Rico, which lay several hours away.

I saw smoke not far away, and so we headed toward it. There, we found several men engaged in slash and burn cultivation. After exchanging greetings, I asked if anyone they knew could take us to Puerto Rico. A young man named José offered to do so for a reasonable fee, and soon we boarded his dugout canoe. It was about noon as we set off drifting, José using a long pole to push as along. We didn't see another human for hours.

As dusk approached, José announced that we had arrived in Puerto Rico. A few minutes later, a tall man wearing rubber boots came to the river's edge to greet us. José knew him, and we introduced ourselves to Emilio. He owned the farm where we found ourselves, and I would soon learn he was the unofficial leader of the farming settlement that stretched several kilometers in every direction.

I explained who we were and why we had come to Puerto Rico. Emilio confirmed that there were about four hundred Guatemalan Mayans living in the jungle nearby. They had begun arriving a few weeks earlier, terrified, thirsty, hungry and often sick. All told of escaping Guatemalan army massacres in Quiché and Huehuetenango departments.

Emilio offered us hammocks, and so, having not slept for some thirty-six hours, Ian and I were soon asleep. Before José left the next morning, we arranged for him to fetch us in a few days.

Ian and I set off to interview the refugees. We came upon the first settlement. Perhaps two hundred Mayans, clad in colorful traditional clothes, had stretched plastic sheeting between poles, forming flimsy shelters. During the next few hours, I would hear stories of unbelievable horror. The Mayans recounted that the military had been combating the EGP, or Guerrilla Army of the Poor, near their villages for years. Most claimed to support the government or said they were neutral. A few said they backed the rebels.

The stories fit a pattern. Without warning, government troops attacked villages, raping women and slaughtering residents with gunfire or machetes. Men and women, old and young, even newly born infants were murdered. Many of the dead were piled together, soaked with gasoline and burned. Out in the jungle, the survivors endured hunger, thirst and disease. During our time there, an infant died of an unknown sickness.

Playa Grande Ixcán, Pueblo Nuevo and Cuarto Pueblo in Quiché Province were some of the villages attacked, residents told me. Several of the villages were part of the Ixil Triangle, an area of southwest Quiché Department. Others were from northern Quiché.

Here, I recount a portion of the story I wrote:

Puerto Rico, Mexico—Felipe Rodríguez squatted in the shade of a ceiba tree, idly poking at an anthill.

Only hours before, he told a visitor, he had returned from his native village, Santa María Tzeja, a two-hour walk along jungle trails in Guatemala. "I had been afraid to go back there," the tiny, wiry Rodríguez said in a monotone voice. "But I needed to bury my family, so I made myself strong."

Inexorably, the talk focused on his family's recent murders. It is the same with many of the hundreds of Guatemalan war refugees in this jungle settlement.

Even a casual conversation with the refugees, Mayans from the northern departments of Quiché and Huehuetenango, elicits talk of a horrifying, unexpected death at the hands of Guatemalan troops. Refugees from places near Mexico, such as La Unión, Santo Tomás, Pueblo Nuevo, Ixtauhacan, Los Ángeles, Mayarán and Kaibil tell of a military campaign started last year and continuing today aimed at wiping them out.

"I guess the government doesn't want any more Indian race," said one refugee.

Rodríguez carefully pulled a color photo from a nylon bag. In the photo, he stands smiling, wearing an orange T-shirt, his arms folded across his chest. Children of all ages—his children—and his wife crowd around him.

When the soldiers came to Santa María two months ago, Rodríguez and most of his children were away working on a farm. But the soldiers found his wife and several of the children.

"My wife here, they shot her in the back twice when she tried to run away," he said, pointing to a plump, dark woman. Two of his daughters, one seven, the other five, wear green dresses in the photo.

"The little one," he said, pointing to the smaller girl, "they shot her right here," said Rodríguez, his finger resting just below his left eye. "All of this," he continued, his right palm cupping the back of his skull, "got blown away. My other little one, they beheaded her."

Rodríguez and two other men offered to guide us to one of villages that had been attacked. They assured us we would find human remains, proof of the army's savagery. Ian and I agreed that venturing into Guatemala with killer soldiers on the loose was far too risky. We declined the offer.

Some forty percent of Guatemalans are Mayans, and the other sixty percent are mestizos. As a mestizo, I am more than one-third of indigenous stock. That one-third is comprised of Mayan, Mixe of Oaxaca and Pima of Chihuahua and Arizona. For most of my life, I have felt a bond with native people. It's literally in my DNA. I felt a powerful connection with the refugees. The horrific nature of the stories overwhelmed me. How could such a widespread genocide continue without the outside world's knowledge?

The guerrillas could not aid the Mayan Indians; there were too few. There were certainly too few to be a threat to the government, whose massive and brutal campaign was driven by traditional racist prejudice against the Mayas.

Throughout much of the genocide, the US provided military arms and equipment to the Guatemalan government. The CIA worked with Guatemalan intelligence officers, some of whom were on the CIA payroll despite known human rights violations.

Near the end of our first day, Ian and I set about finding a place to stay. We came upon a group of men and women who appeared to be Americans or Europeans. The locals earlier told us some foreigners were in the area collecting butterflies. We greeted them near some huts. They appeared uneasy. When I asked if they had room to spare, one of the men tersely said no. They quickly packed up and set off. I could tell from their accents they were Americans, so their wariness made me suspect they weren't simple butterfly collectors. Rather, I concluded, they were CIA operatives. I still believe this, given that the CIA and US military were backing the Guatemalan government.

A farmer and his family agreed to rent us space in their earthen-floor hut. They and perhaps another thirty families grew cacao, living without running water or electricity. The nearest road was some 70 miles away. Getting to it would require a grueling trip on foot.

The farmers had formed their own society, complete with rules. For instance, the men told me that a few years earlier they had run off other men who were growing marijuana. They had a hut used to jail wrongdoers. These included men who stole or physically attacked others.

One morning, we awoke to find several Mexican immigration agents interviewing the refugees. The agents said they were not going to deport the Guatemalans but simply wished to compile a census.

On our return trip, we stopped in Mexico City, where I interviewed the Interior Secretariat's spokesman. To my amazement, he was fully informed of our travels during the past ten days. He would not disclose how he knew, but it was apparent someone had monitored our movements the whole time.

In the coming months, thousands of Guatemalan refugees would find shelter in Chiapas. Camps would be established, and the genocide exposed. Years later, the full extent of the murderous campaign would be made public, but most of the perpetrators would not be punished.

I was haunted by my few days in Chiapas. Back home in San Diego, my mind often returned to the Mayans, the terror they had escaped and the perilous future they faced. I returned a few months later to find thousands more refugees living in still more wretched conditions than before.

⊱⊰

In October 1983, *Time* magazine offered me a job as a correspondent in its Mexico City bureau. At that time, the magazine was at its zenith with a weekly circulation of an estimated four million. It employed fewer than 120 correspondents, so it was a feat to join that elite group. For most of my nine-year career at *Time*, I was the sole Latino correspondent.

I accepted the job and in January 1984 arrived in Mexico City, where I was assigned to do a story on El Salvador. That tiny nation was engulfed in a civil war. Chiapas had convinced me that significant and terrible events were occurring at our doorstep. I was troubled that, like Guatemala's Mayas, the people locked in wars, those uprooted, weren't being heard. Too much reporting ignored them in favor of what Washington officials had to say.

I was increasingly passionate about journalism because it offered me the chance to report about the lives of Latinos, people mainstream American media either studiously ignored or misrepresented. It was important that unheard voices be heard. Also, my bicultural upbringing and deep study of Latino life in the United States and Mexico had prepared me to make a special contribution to mainstream American journalism. I would chronicle the endless, rich and fascinating stories of those who were largely invisible in English-language media. I was convinced that by accurately and fully reporting the untold stories of the poor and powerless, I would enrich the telling of contemporary events.

I loved my work, though it was grueling, sometimes dangerous and required me to be away from my family for long periods. My Latino physical appearance allowed me to blend in with the people in Latin American nations.

CHAPTER TWO
On Becoming a Mexican

"GO BACK TO MEXICO!" the enraged white woman bellowed at my mother as I stood next to her. The epithet erupted during a front yard verbal altercation after the woman's sons had beaten my younger brother with sticks. The attack had been unprovoked, and so my mother approached the woman to discuss the incident. Tall, obese and imposing, the woman gruffly denied her sons had done anything. My mom heatedly replied that the woman ought to reprimand her kids.

Hours after the argument ended without any resolution, I thought about the demand that my mother "go back to Mexico." It struck me as bizarre and ugly. What did it have to do with kids fighting? Why should my mother go to a foreign country?

"You go back to Germany or wherever the hell you're from!" my mother had shot back, leaving the woman sputtering.

We had moved to Pacoima in 1958, two years before the incident and just as I prepared to enter the third grade. Up until that time we had lived in Lincoln Heights, a largely Mexican neighborhood of Los Angeles. "The Heights" is the oldest of the city's neighborhoods, populated since the 1830s, when it was part of Mexico.

We had taken possession of a brand new home in Pacoima, in the far-flung San Fernando Valley. It was our first time living among white people. Years later I would learn that real estate agents had tried to steer my parents away from the new subdivision, suggesting we might find other Mexican or African American neighborhoods more to our liking.

My father, David Chavira, born in Sierra Blanca, Texas, was a World War II veteran who immediately understood that the agents did not want to admit us into the lily-white subdivision. It was an act of blatant racism. After he angrily complained to VA Home Loan officials, my parents bought the house they wanted.

A few days after we moved in, relatives on my mother's side visited from El Paso. Among them were three of our cousins and my aunt, who had deep brown skin. Soon, one of the real estate agents came calling to gently inquire if black people were visiting. It seemed almost incredible that our house guests would be anyone's concern. But this was 1958, and blacks near whites were cause for alarm. My parents replied that they were Mexicans, just duskier than most. That satisfied the agent.

"Never forget, this is Mexico," my father often said. "The Gringos stole California and about half of Mexico. We were always here. We were never foreigners; the Gringos were. Don't let anyone make you feel that you don't belong here. Always be proud of being Mexican, and never say you're Spanish." (Mexicans were so stigmatized that some pathetically claimed to be Spaniards. Evidently, Spaniards were viewed as cultured and racially palatable.)

My father's emphatic claims of US land theft were historically sound. His focus was the Texas Rebellion, followed a few years later by the Mexican-American War. Both were conflicts that left Mexico vanquished and forced to relinquish more than half its territory, what is today Texas and the Southwest.

My dad also frequently hammered home the message that we were American citizens—with all the rights and responsibilities that conferred. In fact, my parents and three of my grandparents were also citizens. Our US roots dated to 1870, when my great-grandfather settled in West Texas.

No question, though, I was a special sort of American, one with long and deep roots just a few hundred miles away in Chihuahua, Mexico—but a full American, all the same. In time, I would learn that balancing and blending my US and Mexican identities would be a lifelong challenge. It was one that would at times frustrate me and at other times make me proud and fully grounded in the United States, where so many have only vague, uncertain or fragmented knowledge of their roots. This duality would also aid me greatly in immersing myself in the US and Mexican history and culture.

Like millions of others who live in the United States, I was marked as a hyphenated American. I was outside of what the 1950s mainstream considered "regular Americans." And so I would remain to this day. My first inkling that I did not fit the mainstream mold came during second-grade history lessons at Griffin Avenue Elementary. Our teacher, addressing a room full of seven-year-old Mexicans, described the travails of the Pilgrims at Plymouth Rock and the story of how English refugees fleeing political and religious oppression sailed to America. We learned the tale of the first Thanksgiving, with "Indians" playing the generous hosts. And then came the struggle against English oppression and the heroic struggles of our Founding Fathers. George Washington, of course, was the Supreme Founding Father.

Slowly a doubt began to sprout. These illustrious men and the humble pilgrims were pale-skinned and hailed exclusively from Northern Europe. Not surprisingly, there was no mention of the African slaves helping build the nascent nation.

Those Europeans were alien to me, a mestizo, a racial hybrid. Most Mexicans are mestizos. There was not a single Spanish-surnamed person ever mentioned. Every member of my family and every person I knew had last names like López, Ramírez, Gómez and so on. The teacher, herself a Euro-American, must have sensed the disconnect. So, she told us we were Americans, plain and simple. As Americans, she went on, we needn't speak any language but English.

Without forgetting my Mexican identity, I quietly resolved to become "a regular American." What did it matter, I asked myself, if I had brown skin and a Spanish surname? I could and would be just as American as Dick and Jane in my first-grade reader.

Television also came into play. Almost every actor was "a regular American," living classically middle-class American lifestyles. We watched "Leave It to Beaver," "Father Knows Best" and "The Adventures of Ozzie and Harriet." The neighborhoods where those families lived were nothing like my gritty, Mexican-filled barrio. Like so many kids, I was an avid viewer of the Disney mini-series "Davy Crockett." Fess Parker played the legendary frontiersman, who ultimately settled in Mexican-ruled Texas. I even wore a coonskin cap, just like Davy's. In an early 1955 episode, Crockett joins the rebel forces at the Alamo. He holed up with 100 or so other Anglo-American rebels to await the Mexican army assault.

I admired Crockett's epic adventures in the untamed frontier. Now, watching the Alamo episode, I was troubled. Depicted as the last of the surviving defenders, Crockett was shown swinging his rifle at the Mexican soldiers coming over the walls. Mexicans fell at Davy's feet, and the scene faded leaving no doubt that the Texas hero perished at the hands of cruel Mexicans. I was left unsure if the hero really was one, and if the Mexicans truly were the bad guys.

There were just a few Latino characters on TV. Desi Arnaz, co-star of the iconic "I Love Lucy" series, was popular, but largely for his comically accented English and his staccato, Cuban-flavored Spanish. Puerto Rican actor and bandleader Tony Martínez played in Walter Brennan's "The Real McCoys" series. He was Pepino, the Mexican farmhand so devoted to the McCoy family that in one of the last episodes he became a US citizen and took McCoy as his new surname. Symbolically, at least, Pepino had become "a regular American!"

Not surprisingly, then, I rebelled against my parents' dogged efforts to make me learn Spanish. They spoke to each other in Spanish and English, while my paternal grandparents could only put together a few basic English-language phrases. With no conscious effort, I learned to understand spoken Spanish. To my parents' argument that becoming fluent in Spanish was part of my Mexican heritage, I replied that I was a native of the United States, where English was the official language. Mexican immigrants would address me in Spanish, my father pointed out, and should I not be able to reply, I would suffer embarrassment. No, the immigrants would be ashamed they couldn't speak the language of their new country, I answered. And so it went, with me resisting all attempts to make me learn Spanish, until the summer of 1960.

One day in the spring of that year, my father announced that it was time for us to explore our roots. We would be taking an open-ended vacation deep into Mexico. There was no discussion, just a firm reiteration that the Chaviras would become intimately acquainted with the country.

In time, I would learn that Mexican Americans like us, with no relatives in Mexico, did not travel deep into Mexico.

Generally, Mexican Americans that were so disconnected from Mexico that they did not speak Spanish. Mexicans often disparaged them as *pochos,* Mexicans who sought to emulate Gringos and were ashamed to be associated with Mexico. Many Mexicans from the United States felt unwelcome in Mexico, and so it was common for them to avoid travel beyond the tourist-friendly border cities, just as we had.

I received the trip news with dread and curiosity. Our visits to Tijuana and Ciudad Juárez, ragged, raucous and dusty places, combined with cowboy movies that depicted Mexico in the guise of tumbledown villages convinced me the trip would be a dreary haul. At the same time, I had a natural wanderlust that would fully develop in the future. What could be out there past Mexico's northern frontier? I studied maps that showed the cities of Hermosillo, Culiacán, Mazatlán, Guadalajara and all the way south La Sierra Madre Occidental, a mountain range nearly 1,000 miles long.

My paternal grandparents, José and María Chavira, would travel with us, making it seven of us who would cram into our sky blue 1959 Chevrolet Impala. It was a sedan with broad, sweeping fins that gave it the appearance of a manta ray on wheels.

With only a general itinerary, we departed one June afternoon. Some six weeks later, we returned to the United States at El Paso.

Often, we say that experiences are "life-changing" because they are intensely enjoyable, tragic or in some way dramatic. How many, in fact, while profoundly memorable, change the course of our lives? My sense is such experiences are rare. But the Mexico trip profoundly changed me.

Motoring across the vast and searing Sonoran Desert hour after hour in our non-air-conditioned car, Mexico's vastness amazed me. Snaking up the Sierra Madre and into the tropics, the lush and towering mountains mesmerized me.

We never drove on highways wider than two lanes. Some stretches were even unpaved. We stayed in budget motels and hotels. One night in Culiacán my grandfather and I slept in hammocks outdoors because the motel lacked beds.

One incident during our trip stands out. We stopped at a roadside fruit stand in Nayarit state, where indigenous girls in traditional Huichol dresses and blouses ran to us. They offered tropical fruits—mangoes, papayas, pineapples and bananas—and spoke broken Spanish. My father explained that they were fluent in a native language other than Spanish. I was puzzled. Why wouldn't they have a firm command of Spanish? We would encounter many more indigenous people for whom Spanish was their second language.

Suddenly, a flock of wild, brightly colored parrots descended on a tree near us. They squawked and flew from branch to branch. I felt I had been transported to some exotic place, on the other side of the world from Los Angeles. Yet, I was just a few hundred miles from where my ancestors had lived for generations and maybe a thousand miles from my hometown. Both were far closer to LA than is Dallas, Texas.

In the next couple of weeks, we would tour Guadalajara, the cradle of mariachis and tequila. The magnificent colonial buildings, bustling downtown and Mexican food more exquisitely prepared than anything I'd eaten left me in awe. I was starting to see Mexico's beauty and grandeur.

We would spend leisurely days in Michoacán state, a place of forested mountains and tropical coastline. Our visit to Lake Pátzcuaro seemed to transport us to an earlier era. Indigenous Tarasco fishermen plied the lake in canoes, carrying nets that, when folded, looked like butterfly wings.

Then there was Mexico City. We rolled into what was even then among the world's largest cities. It had to be among the noisiest, too. I was taken aback by the non-stop honking of car horns, buses and trucks crowding the streets, spewing diesel fumes. The city sprawled, seemingly endless. The sidewalks were perpetually jammed with people, Mexicans of every social class bustling along.

We settled into the modest Hotel Compostela, right off Paseo de la Reforma, Mexico City's main thoroughfare. We explored the famous and obscure attractions. Without question, the ancient Pre-Columbian city of Teotihuacan was the most astounding place we toured. Much of its history is unknown, but it was likely established around 400 BC. The Pyramid of the Sun, 720 by 760 feet at its base and nearly 216 feet high is the largest structure of its type in the Western Hemisphere. The older Pyramid of the Moon was constructed before 200 CE. At its peak in 400 CE, Teotihuacan had a population of between 125,00 and 200,000, dwarfing every European city except Rome.

Not long after we arrived in the Mexican capital, the city's disorderly traffic got the best of us. As we rounded a traffic circle, a bus struck us broadside. We were shaken, but unhurt. The car, however, suffered considerable damage. Our stay in Mexico City was extended by many days while the Chevy was repaired. My parents decided to use the time to visit Acapulco. We traveled aboard a large bus, owned by a company called "The Red Arrow." True to its name, the packed bus streaked through mountain passes and around harrowing curves. The drivers spelled each other without pulling over—an impressive but frightening maneuver for passengers.

We arrived at dawn and checked into a modest hotel without air conditioning. The rooms had windows, but neither glass nor screens. Not only did the tropical heat flow in, so did tiny lizards that darted all over the room.

Acapulco was already a world-renown resort, a favorite destination for Mexican and American celebrities. But we were staying in the two-star section of the city. That afforded us a chance to interact with the working class. My barely existent Spanish had been tested since we had crossed the border. Based on my appearance, everyone addressed me in Spanish. I struggled to reply, nodded or let my parents do the talking.

In our walking trips to the beach, we came upon black people. Although my dad had told us that African slaves had been brought to Mexico, I was nonetheless surprised to see black Mexicans. The experience brought to life my father's history lesson. At the time, the presence of Afro-Mexicans was scarcely known, even in Mexico.

My older brother David and I frolicked in the ocean. We rented long paddleboards and drifted for hours. One night, we went to see the famous La Quebrada cliff divers. They timed their dives to coincide with waves rushing into the rocky crevice far below. A poorly timed dive would mean death.

Late one afternoon, back in Mexico City, I suddenly realized an important fact. This megacity, and all the other cities and towns we had visited up to then, were built, administered and populated by Mexicans. In my hometown, Mexicans were mainly relegated to the lower rungs of society. They typically worked as poorly paid laborers. Indeed, my maternal grandfather, Juan Muñoz Parra, who owned a neighborhood grocery store, was the only Mexican I knew who wasn't a common laborer. I had not heard of any Mexicans who held elective office, nor had I even seen a Mexican police officer. I had concluded that Mexicans must be incapable of performing jobs that required skill or intelligence. Yet, here I was in a city of nearly five million, larger than any US city except for New York, and it was run by Mexicans! The mayor, city council, bank tellers, merchants, even the president of the country were all Mexicans. Mexicans, just like me but for the fact that I had lived my life 1,200 miles to the north.

I was not "a regular American," nor would I ever be one because I was of a different breed—a mestizo. An unsettling and surreal sense took hold of me: I had come home. Never mind that I had never lived there; the connection to the city was unshakable.

That feeling never left me as we made our way north through central Mexico. Guanajuato and Zacatecas, cities first settled by indigenous people thousands of years ago and founded in the mid-1500s by Spanish explorers, left me awestruck by their colonial splendor. When we pulled back into LA, I was no longer a boy longing to be "a regular American." Instead, I was an American intimately knowledgeable of his roots and intensely proud to claim his Mexican ethnicity. I was forever changed.

CHAPTER THREE
The Exodus

FOR A FEW YEARS, Jesús Chavira, my great grandfather, had anticipated his uncertain journey. Orphaned in his native Ciudad Camargo, Jesús found a home with his grandfather, Gregorio. The old man lived alone on his ranch, and so young Jesús provided much-needed help and companionship to him. The year was about 1865.

Jesús, a tall, thin pre-teen, provided labor on the cattle ranch near San Francisco de Javier Satevó in Mexico's sprawling Chihuahua state. The Jesuit José Pascual had founded Satevó as a mission in 1640. Rarámuri native people destroyed the mission in 1652. Twenty-two years later, it was founded again but as a village, which Pancho Villa's troops sacked in 1918. Today, Satevó is home to some 500 inhabitants.

During Jesús' time there, Satevó was surrounded by pastures where cowboys still plied their craft. While dedicated to caring for his grandson and the ranch, old man Gregorio felt death closing in. He periodically told his grandson that upon his death, Jesús should abandon the ranch and secure his future at Fort Davis, Texas, the site of a US Calvary post.

With no family members left, young Jesús alone would have to operate the ranch and defend it from envious neighbors and marauders who would kill him to steal it. In those days, some one-hundred sixty years ago, law and order were scarcely present.

One day in 1870, Gregorio died. Jesús, born in 1853, was just shy of his seventeenth birthday. He took no time to grieve and instead saddled his white mare, Pabellón, and began his odyssey northward. His trip was perilous, as it took him across a lawless stretch of desert. Several days after he set out, he arrived at the US Army fort and solicited work. The soldiers hired him as a stable boy.

Soon, Jesús was tending to dozens of horses. Some belonged to the Army, others to a stagecoach service. Fort Davis was a key base in what had become an all-out war to exterminate all the Native Americans they could and imprison the rest on reservations. After years of fighting a defensive war, the Amerindian nations took the offensive, intent on expelling from southwest Texas the soldiers and all other whites and Mexicans. In the tit-for-tat violence, thousands were murdered or killed in combat.

The soldiers discovered that Jesús was an accomplished tracker, a skill he had developed in the Mexican wilderness. Like many Mexicans, Jesús was a mestizo, largely of indigenous stock. Given his origins, he more than likely was partially descended from the Pima, the Rarámuri or Tarahumara, a hearty people making up one of the largest indigenous groups in modern Mexico. In short order, he was accompanying soldiers on patrols.

It is almost certain that he would have patrolled with African American soldiers of the 9th or 10th US Cavalry based at Fort Davis or with the Buffalo Soldiers of the 25th Infantry that arrived in 1870, the same year Jesús began working at the fort.

Between 1867 and 1885, the soldiers engaged in several military campaigns against the Apache and Comanche peoples. Young Jesús was in the thick of combat, but my grandfather told me Jesús had little to say about his years at Fort Davis. He did, however, remember that some of his encounters with Native Americans were quite amicable. It was his custom to offer them tobacco, which he said they greatly prized, and exchange pleasantries with them in either Spanish or their native languages.

As the war subsided and these nations were decimated and/or forced onto reservations, Jesús found work on a cattle ranch owned by a German immigrant, recalled only as Mueller, who came as part of a wave of settlers intent on making a living in the foreboding desert.

At the ranch, Jesús was paid with room and board and a certain number of cattle each year. After he had amassed what he considered a decent herd, Jesús decided to make a go of it raising cattle. He took possession of a parcel of land he concluded belonged to no one. It is unclear if Jesús ever owned his ranch, but for practical purposes, it was his. He was one of many homesteaders who settled on land that seemed to have no owners.

After several years of laboring alone, Jesús met a young woman, Estefana Molina. Also orphaned in Chihuahua, she was living with a nearby family. It's not known if there was a proper courtship or just an agreement. Whatever the case, they married and promptly began producing children: eight in all. José, the eldest and my grandfather, was born on October 26, 1896, near Shafter, Texas, a town of a few hundred between Marfa and Presidio.

The land there is arid and unforgiving; summertime temperatures generally range above 100 degrees, and there is little natural shade. As might be expected, the Chaviras' life was hardscrabble. It is such an inhospitable region that even today it is among the most sparsely populated in the United States.

Fortunately, Jesús was an exceptionally adept farmer and rancher.

"I remember when I was not yet five, my father found a cave for us to live in," my grandfather José recounted to me. "What he told me later was that he had not been able to find everything he needed to build a house. Well, he made that cave pretty comfortable; he carved out shelves for our things and a place to store food."

Jesús devised an irrigation system of rudimentary canals that drew water from a small creek. He grew corn, beans, tomatoes, chile peppers and many other crops. He also had a variety of livestock, including goats, sheep, pigs, chickens and ducks. He even had beehives. Most important, Jesús had a sizeable herd of beef cattle that he often took to the nearby Davis Mountains for grazing. The cattle would be sold, sometimes across the border in Chihuahua, providing the family with income.

"We had everything else, thanks to my father," said my grandfather. "My mother made our clothes and shoes out of leather, and we bought very few things: salt and coffee, for instance."

The Chavira children did not attend school at first because the nearest one was several miles away. But their parents decided to have the oldest of the children board with a family in Shafter so they could get an education. The mining town had a one-room school; its ruins remain today.

"Dad gave me some money and told me to use it to buy food," Granddad José recalled. "Well, I ended up spending a lot of it on candy and invited some kids to a little party."

After the children had been at school for a week, Jesús came to visit them. When he learned how the money had been spent, he decided there would be no further schooling and returned to the ranch with his kids.

Asked what he had learned during his brief educational stint, José thought for a minute, and told me, "The clock on the wall goes tick-tock." He would remain illiterate and a monolingual Spanish-speaker all his life. He and his siblings spent their childhood working on the ranch. José's job was to rise well before dawn, milk the cows and take the milk and cheese his mother made into Shafter, where he sold it. "I carried the milk in clay jugs, and the cheese was wrapped in cloth," my grandfather recounted. "We were many miles away, so I rode a mule. I had my regular customers and other people who would look for me." He was about eight when he began working as a milkman.

As he grew into manhood, José learned all the skills required to coax sustenance from the unforgiving land. He also became his father's right hand. My grandfather recalled his father, Jesús Chavira, as a tall, bronze-skinned man with indigenous facial features. He was also taciturn and reserved. His mother Estefana, by contrast, was loquacious and strong-willed. I remember my grandfather, José, as squat, muscular and stoic.

When the war on the indigenous peoples was over, new conflicts loomed. The Mexican Revolution of 1910 broke out just a few miles to the south, in Chihuahua, with Pancho Villa at the head of an army. From the start, it was an exceptionally bloody and disruptive war, one in which a million Mexicans would perish. In the borderlands where the Chaviras lived, US authorities and settlers feared the war would spread north. For white people, Mexican males were potentially violent criminals. It made no difference to them that the revolution was, of course, politically motivated. Compounding the hysteria was the fact that the border was not clearly demarcated, let alone patrolled. Texas Rangers, notorious for their violence against Mexicans, began shooting any Mexican they considered suspicious.

Hostility was greatly heightened after the governor of Texas, Oscar Colquitt, said he had uncovered a plot by Mexican revolutionaries to target and kill whites north of the border. The governor, according to historians, responded by ordering the Rangers to crack down on Mexicans. Some three-hundred Mexicans were killed without ever being arrested or tried.

A few years before the revolution, Jesús had his own brush with racist violence. He had been raising cattle some distance from Marfa, when white men took potshots at him. They were strangers and plainly not trying to wound or kill Jesús, just scare him. After taking fire a few times, he ceased working the land and moved closer to Shafter.

"Dad wasn't able to fight back," said my grandfather. "He was alone. . . . We kids were too small to be of any help. . . . So it's likely those men would have killed him. And if he had shot back, it was also possible they would have brought in the law, and my father would be dead. That's how it was for Mexicans in those days. He hadn't done anything to them, and there was no clear reason why they wanted him gone. Most likely they wanted the land."

When the United States entered World War I, even in remote southwest Texas, the draft pulled in young men. My grandfather José decided to avoid being drafted. "I heard about the war, but I didn't know why they were fighting," he said. "Some of us started hearing stories about soldiers getting poisoned by gas. It burned your lungs, and you were never the same again. Well, I decided to go to Mexico for a while." He remained there until the war ended.

After the war, my grandfather and great-grandfather went into the freight hauling business. They transported agricultural goods, building materials and consumer items. They used a large, flatbed wagon, drawn by a mule team. Their route covered the dirt road that connected Presidio on the

Mexican border with Marfa. The entire route was about sixty miles long. Business was brisk, and in time the Chaviras were hauling freight as far north and west as Quitman, Alpine and Sierra Blanca. Their prosperity made the Anglo-American competitors envious. Once again, white strangers started shooting at them as an ominous warning of greater violence.

"My father and I were going to stay with the business, no matter what, but my mother was very much against it," said José. "She told my father that she wouldn't be able to care for so many children if anything happened to us, and so we quit."

During one of their runs to Sierra Blanca, my grandfather met and fell in love with María Ramírez, a petite young woman. She was the daughter of Timotea Sosa and Félix Ramírez, refugees from the revolution. They were married on October 13, 1877, in Ojinaga, Chihuahua, just over the border from Presidio, Texas.

Félix Ramírez owned a cattle ranch near Coyame, Chihuahua, when the revolution flared. Pancho Villa's troops descended on the Ramírez ranch one day and announced they were taking all the cattle to feed the soldiers. They promised to pay for the cattle at some point. Somehow, Félix and his sons managed to restock the ranch, only to have *villistas* again appropriate the entire herd. The insurgents had not paid for the first herd they had taken and once more promised to pay for what they stole.

"Papá got angry and told the *villistas* they were thieves," my grandmother recounted to me. "After he complained about them taking our cattle, they said they had better not find him at the ranch when they came back. It was a serious threat. Leaving made my father cry," she said. "We left at night, riding mules."

They made it to Sierra Blanca. A local rancher named Dick Love, who had bought cattle from Félix in the past, offered to help the family get settled. He also lined up a mining job for Félix.

"We lived in a tent while my father scrounged around for wood scraps to make our house. After a long time, we had a little shack. My mother found work cleaning passenger trains that stopped in town and the homes of the rich Gringos," said my grandmother María. "We would be very happy when she brought home leftover food."

Her parents' jobs left them exhausted, she recalled. "They were sad sometimes when they thought of all we had left behind in Chihuahua." One of her older brothers made an ill-advised trip back to the ranch to reclaim it. Followers of revolutionary leader Venustiano Carranza captured him, accused him of spying and then executed him.

In Sierra Blanca, María and her siblings got one year of Spanish-language education. They stopped attending the school set aside for Mexicans after white youths amused themselves by beating and teasing them. "They called us dirty Mexicans, threw rocks at us and tried to run us down with the horses they rode. We would come home with bruises and torn clothes. One day, Dad just said we were not to continue our schooling."

Granddad José set his eye on María just as she blossomed into a lovely young woman. He confided to a friend that he dreamed of marrying her, and his friend relayed word back to her. "The fellow came back with a message from her," José would tell me some sixty years later. "She said that if I was serious, then to ask for her hand. Man, I wanted to go crazy! I was the happiest I had ever been."

The Chaviras found a person to write a letter to the Ramírez family to formally request permission for José to marry María. The request was granted, and they married in 1919. It was a marriage and love affair that would last more than sixty years and see the couple persevere through the most arduous times imaginable.

The newlyweds settled in Sierra Blanca, but the isolated town offered little economic opportunity. They joined an army of Mexican cotton-pickers in Texas and Oklahoma who were replacing African Americans. It represented a major shift, as blacks had toiled in cotton fields throughout decades of slavery. They would remain the dominant force in the Deep South, but in Texas cotton growers found Mexicans willing to work for less than the African Americans.

Elena, José and Maria's first child, was born in 1920. Their son, David, was born the following year; he would be my father. The small family followed the cotton crop across Texas and into Oklahoma, returning to their home in Sierra Blanca from time to time. "We were like a bunch of gypsies," recalled my dad in the twilight of his life. "All of our relatives would travel with us in Model As, hitting farms all over. We cooked and slept outdoors, or if we got lucky, in barns."

My grandfather would reflect on those times as bleak and filled with humiliation. "You have to understand that Gringos were free to treat us like dogs, and they did. When we got to a town we didn't know, sometimes I would make the mistake of going into a store where Mexicans weren't allowed. 'Get out of here, you goddamned Mexican!' a clerk or customer would yell. All you could do was run out and not say a word," he continued. "If you even looked like you might cause trouble, then the cops would come, beat you and lock you up."

He had a brush with Texas justice after his brother Cecilio had exchanged gunfire with Sierra Blanca's sheriff. Cecilio was a bootlegger who smuggled *sotol*, a potent local brew, across the border into Texas. The sheriff and a few deputies had attempted to nab Cecilio along with his cargo, and then a gunfight followed. Reportedly, Cecilio, a marksman, shot the sheriff's hat off his head, leaving a welt on his scalp. Cecilio managed to get away, and the sheriff was determined to find him. Instead, he came across José.

"He and his deputies grabbed me and told me to take them to Cecilio," he said. "I really didn't know anything about what had happened and had no idea where he was. They started yelling and punching me, then they tied me to a post. The sheriff pistol-whipped me until blood was running down my face and onto my chest. I wouldn't beat an animal the way they beat me."

They went away, leaving José to broil in the desert sun. "Everyone could see me all bloody and thirsty, but they were afraid to help me because of what the sheriff might do."

By chance, the sheriff's mother happened onto the scene. She asked José what had happened, and when he told her, she became angry with her son. The woman untied José and gave him some water. When her son returned, she berated him. Still, the sheriff took José to jail for more questioning.

Apparently realizing that further grilling was useless, the sheriff freed him. "My brother Gustavo came for me, and he had a clean shirt. He had heard I was all covered in blood. You know, not long after that, the sheriff was diagnosed with fatal cancer. He committed suicide by cutting his own throat. I have always believed that God punished him for his cruelty."

Jesús, meanwhile, was feeling economic pressure and nostalgia for his native Chihuahua. After being run out of the freight business, my great-grandfather moved his ranching operations closer to Sierra Blanca. There, however, he was unable to find enough suitable land for his cattle, and so he went back and settled in Chihuahua, some 100 miles southeast of Ciudad Juárez. He prospered for a time, but then a horrifying catastrophe swept in. David, one of his brothers, contracted tuberculosis. But he was not isolated from the five siblings who lived at home with him and his parents. Jesús was convinced that his brothers and sisters could not infect each other; of course, he was tragically wrong. Within a few months, David, Cecilio and Beatriz were dead.

"We paid a big price for being ignorant peasants," José would recount.

María and José, meanwhile, continued to scrape by on their meager earnings from picking cotton. David, my father, recalled the work as awful. The heat and dust were ever-present, and the hours stretched from pre-dawn to late afternoon. More than once, the family was cheated out of earnings. In one terrifying incident, they narrowly survived a deadly tornado in Oklahoma. They sheltered in a storm cellar. Others were not so fortunate.

"I went into shock when I saw what the storm did," María said. "All around were dead people, some of them torn into pieces. It was like a nightmare, and I felt I was going to lose my mind."

During their infrequent stays in Sierra Blanca, young David and Elena attended the same Mexican school as had their mother. "I would go there to see how they were doing," said my grandfather José, "and they would be just singing songs. Sometimes the teacher was off with a boyfriend, and the kids were alone. They weren't getting any kind of education."

Having struggled with the burden of illiteracy, José was determined that his children would receive an education. That, however, would require that the family move to a town or city with proper schools. And so, the Chaviras headed for El Paso, eighty miles to the west, where they used their small savings to rent a tiny, brick tenement apartment, popularly known as a *presidio*. They had no electricity, and the only running water came through an outdoor communal tap. During the summer, the apartments became ovens; many residents slept outdoors for the relatively cooler temperature.

My grandfather had to find work, no easy task in a border town with perennially high unemployment. The year was 1929, and times would get dramatically harder with the onset of the Great Depression. Like many unemployed Mexicans, José went to a street corner, where day laborers were hired.

"I remember my first day out there," my granddad said. "This mean-looking Gringo came by in a truck. He looked us over and picked a few, including me. He put us to work at a construction site, and I did my best to show I was a hard worker. If you looked weak or slow, the Gringo would tell you not to come back. He told me to return."

My father once visited his father at his job: the Plaza Theater under construction. "I couldn't believe what I was seeing," he said. "My father was a hod carrier, and he had all these bricks stacked on his shoulder. He had to carry them up ramps to the upper stories. My father was drenched in sweat and dirt, and he was running—running!—up those ramps. It was worse than how an animal would work. I felt horrible. I was sorry to see what my dad went through. Seeing that also scared me. More than anything, I knew I had to avoid ever working like that. I was afraid that was the only work Mexicans could find, but I decided I would find a way to escape it."

My father David and my aunt Elena attended Alamo Elementary, a Mexican-only school. Residential and educational segregation prevailed at the time and for years to come. The children who attended the school spoke only Spanish and were years behind their grade level. My dad was not a diligent student. While Elena kept to the straight and narrow, Dad fell in with a crowd of rowdy boys. There was nothing unusual in that. The place and times pretty much dictated it. By thirteen, my father was stealing firewood and whatever else he could. He also took up drinking alcohol in neighboring Ciudad Juárez and El Paso's sole black pool hall.

One day, he and two other boys stole a physician's handbag when the doctor was making a house call and had left his bag in his car.

"We saw that damn thing, and we just had to take it," he confessed.

They played with the doctor's instruments, especially the stethoscope. Older, savvier boys focused on the drugs the doctor was carrying. David and his pals sold them to local drug addicts.

Word of the incident spread through the neighborhood, and it wasn't long before the police arrested my father and his companions. Jailed with adult prisoners, as an adolescent he was facing a few years in juvenile prison. It didn't matter that it was his first offense.

"When it came to Mexicans, the law was really tough," he told me. "Luckily, my dad knew a Mexican lawyer. See, my father, because he was a citizen, was involved with LULAC, the League of United Latin American Citizens. Well, the lawyer knew the judge, and so I got out of that scrape."

Even when they had not done anything wrong, young Mexican males in El Paso often fell afoul of the law. Patrolmen who found young Mexicans in white areas of town beat them and warned them of even more severe thrashings if they were caught again. Fortunately, my father found work caddying at a local golf course on the "good" side of town and developed a lifelong love of the sport, although he never played it.

School segregation meant that most Mexican teens attended Bowie High School. My aunt Elena, however, fiercely ambitious and a future millionaire, was determined to get admitted to a school that taught office skills, and the only option was a school for whites. She hoped those skills would land her a job as a secretary or office assistant. Years later, my grandfather recalled her pleading with him to see if the school would admit her.

"I told her, *'M'ija*, they won't let you in there.' But she kept asking, so we went to the office. An old Gringo at the desk didn't let me finish asking. He got mad and told me in Spanish, 'You have no business here. Get out and don't come back.' I was so humiliated because I could do nothing to help my daughter. Her dream ended there."

Showing a restlessness that would keep him on the road for most of the next forty years, my father and a high school chum nicknamed "Red" decided to hop a California-bound freight train. They were just sixteen. The boys were sure they would find farm work. El Paso in 1937 was as economically depressed as ever, and jobs for Mexican teens scarcely existed. Somehow, they convinced their parents to let them make what was a perilous journey. The biggest danger was tumbling off the cars or falling into the hands of the railroad security guards known as "bulls." Those goons were notorious for meting out cruel beatings to anyone they caught taking a free ride. But the times were so desperate that entire "Okie" families, refugees from the Oklahoma Dust Bowl, rode the train with my father and Red.

They made it to the Sacramento area and found enough farm work to put together some modest savings. The trip convinced David that California offered relatively good economic opportunities, and my dad resolved to go back to stay one day. The following year, he made the trip again, but this time with his father. Their first night in California was spent near the desert town of Indio. There, they landed jobs picking melons, backbreaking work under a searing sun. To save on costs, they camped outdoors. During that summer, they would work their way up into the fertile San Joaquin Valley, harvesting a variety of crops. With summer's end, my father and grandfather returned to El Paso.

Once back, my father decided to join the Civilian Conservation Corps (CCC), one of President Roosevelt's so-called alphabet work programs. This one sent young men into rural areas to work on construction and conservation programs, part of a Herculean effort to revitalize the heartland. Unfortunately, my father would have to drop out of high school in order to participate.

My grandfather was convinced that his son David would never return to high school, dashing his dream to see his two children receive a solid education. My father promised he would not only go back but would graduate no matter how long it took him. And so, off he went to the mountains of New Mexico. My father and many other Mexicans planted trees and built dirt roads to connect farming communities. During his stint, he came up hard against the virulent racism of the time.

"We were mixed in with a bunch of Gringo kids," he recounted to me. "Because we didn't like each other, we kept to ourselves. But they started making comments about fucking greasers until things had to be settled. So, one day we were out planting trees, and someone said the wrong thing." A melee broke out, with combatants swinging shovels, picks and fists. "A whole lot of guys got pretty banged up. We made our point that we weren't going to take shit." The brawl seemed to soothe tensions for the remainder of the stint.

As promised, my dad re-enrolled in Bowie High School and graduated with the class of 1941 at the age of twenty. He promptly enlisted in the US Army. Although the Second World War was already raging in much of the world and there was talk that the United States would be dragged in before long, my father told me he joined for the money.

In 1941 most adults did not have a high school diploma. But his education gave David no advantage. Racism trumped all. And a Mexican in El Paso without a job was looking at a lengthy period of unemployment. So, David began his basic training and was posted to Fort Bliss in El Paso, and the suddenness of the United States joining the war effort came as a shock.

"I had been out drinking in Juárez on Saturday, and when I got back to base the next morning, we had news that the Japanese had attacked Pearl Harbor."

Eager to join the fighting, he volunteered and was selected to train as a bomber tail gunner. Standing just five feet-five inches and weighing under 130 pounds, he seemed physically suited to fit into the cramped rear gunner's station. Unfortunately, the gunshot reparts he endured during training left him deaf in one ear, and he was not allowed to serve as a gunner.

Back to training as a foot soldier, David proved poorly suited to military discipline. While based at McCook Army Air Base, Nebraska, he and another soldier got drunk and stole a car. They had a terrible wreck, leaving my father hospitalized for several months. Somehow, he escaped punishment. Over the years, I would ask how that was possible, but he never offered a clear answer.

My father spent the last year of the war overseeing a German POW work detail. The Germans were officers and fluent in English. In a macabre twist, their job was to pack the personal belongings of American soldiers killed in action and send them to family members.

Once, one of the prisoners asked my father how he reconciled serving in the US Army with the severe racial prejudice Mexicans faced. "He said something like, 'Mr. David, the United States stole half your country and discriminates against you, and yet you volunteered to fight for the Americans. Why?' I couldn't think of a satisfactory answer, so I just told him to shut up."

During his service, my father married his high school sweetheart, Helen. She moved in with my grandparents in Los Angeles and gave birth to their first child, David Jr. Like many Mexican El Pasoans, the Chaviras were drawn by plentiful and relatively good jobs. But after being discharged, my father balked at taking a manual labor job, the only type available to Mexicans in El Paso. He believed his time as a soldier entitled him to something higher than work at the bottom rung. They settled permanently in Los Angeles.

There by chance, a father and son whose surname was Tonkin decided to hire my father on a trial basis as a salesman of paintings and statues of Catholic saints. The younger Tonkin happened to drive by the Chavira home and saw my father's car parked in front. Civilian car production had been halted during the war, and so the Chevrolet prompted Tonkin to see if my father was interested in sales. Having a car was a necessity for what would be a traveling sales gig of driving to an area and then walking door-to-door.

"I didn't have any sales experience, but they gave me a little training and sent me to East LA to peddle statues and portraits of the Virgin and saints," he told me. "Old man Tonkin said that Mexican women would want one or more because they probably had lost someone in the war, or they were grateful that a son, husband or boyfriend made it back okay."

That job set David off on a career in sales, which eventually involved extensive road travel, selling watches, costume jewelry, transistor radios and other inexpensive electronics. During the war and for twenty more years, Mexican temporary agricultural workers, called *braceros*, labored on American farms, mostly in the West. They usually worked for several months under contract and then went back to Mexico. These men became my father's prime customers.

In about 1952, he and a cousin impulsively got into the people-smuggling business. As *coyotes*, as such smugglers are known in Mexican slang, they transported farmworkers from Mexicali on the US-Mexico border to as far north as Sacramento. My father recalled getting into the business when a man approached him in a Mexicali bar with a proposition. Would my father take him across the border for $200? He and our cousin, Armando, agreed. The man rode in the trunk right under the noses of border guards.

After that crossing, the pair quickly organized a small but busy operation smuggling job-seeking Mexicans into California. My father estimated they soon were clearing about $500 per week, a huge sum in those days. But they spent their earnings partying. Two years after their illicit business began, it ended when one of the undocumented immigrants informed on my father and Armando. I have a dim memory of visiting him in Arizona at the minimum-security prison where he was serving six months. His prisoner status was apparent, but I did not consider him a criminal. Yet, I concluded that he had done something wrong. It was a strange and disorienting experience.

Tragically, my father was an alcoholic. When drunk, he became mean and violent, and beat my mother several times over the years. His binge-drinking away from home left us perennially short of household money. He had several drunk driving arrests, some involving car wrecks.

Ironically, he became a car salesman. But he earned so little that my grandparents had to financially prop up their son and his family. As happens to so many families, alcoholism rendered us dysfunctional.

Beginning at age four, I suffered greatly from asthma. The attacks struck every few months with frightening ferocity. When I felt the onset of an attack, I would be consumed by panic and terror. An asthma inhaler only offered minutes of relief. More than once I felt I was dying as I thrashed about struggling to breathe. My mother would assure me I was not dying. Years later, I would realize that I should have been taken to an emergency room for treatment. From time to time, my mother would take me to see our family physician, who would simply prescribe medicine to be used in my glass inhaler.

Worry and insecurity haunted me. Our home offered scant security. Either we would run out of money, or my father would end up in jail, or he would come home and engage in altercations with my mother.

Although I was never diagnosed, I am certain I was depressed for much of my childhood. The bouts of asthma, insecurity and looming violence overwhelmed me. I was consumed by a sense of dread. How could I grow up to be a normal man? I wondered. Yet, somehow I thought I would be able to repair our broken family by simply reasoning with my father. Many times before I had reached adolescence, I asked my father to stop drinking. No one else was part of these conversations. Dad would listen patiently and agree that his drinking had gotten out of hand, and he vowed to me that he would give up alcohol. The first few times we had these talks, I was overjoyed that I had persuaded him to cast aside his vice. But Dad never meant what he promised, and his drinking continued unabated. I clung to the hope that one day he would heed my pleas.

In 1966 my mother left, fully intending to divorce my father. My older brother David was in the Air Force, and my younger brother Steven went with my mother. I chose to stay with my father to look after him. This was a difficult decision. My father was not working and continued to drink heavily. He always appeared depressed. As I had for many years, I took it upon myself to get him off alcohol and eventually have my parents reconcile. But with the family split, Dad plunged into daily alcoholic binges. I prepared meals, cleaned up around the house and sometimes talked my father out of going drinking. A few times, I disconnected one or two spark plug wires on his car without his knowledge. He never determined why his car would not start, and so my sabotage kept him from driving while drunk. I kept attending school and would return home dreading what I would find. Usually, it was my dad passed out or reeling around the house drunkenly.

Although I was stressed and saddened, I believed that I could help rehabilitate my dad and have our family reunited. At the age of fifteen, obviously, I lacked the maturity and wisdom required for a task of that magnitude. It was a responsibility I should not have been allowed to take on. Still, I persevered.

Eventually, Dad joined Alcoholics Anonymous and stopped drinking. My mom returned to what turned out to be an improved but still flawed marriage. As for me, I matured greatly. I had taken on adult responsibilities and carried them out like a man and not the boy I was.

CHAPTER FOUR
Ghetto Life, Survival and Transformation

OUR MOVE TO PACOIMA brought us into contact with not only Anglo-Saxons but African Americans too. While the outer edge of Pacoima where we lived was almost exclusively white, the rest of the community was overwhelmingly African American. After two years there, an African American family moved into our subdivision. That prompted panicked "white flight." So many FOR SALE signs cropped up in the following weeks that we made local TV news. Just like that our neighborhood went from white to black.

My new school was Pacoima Elementary, where some seventy-five percent of the students were African-American. Another twenty percent were Mexicans, with the remainder comprised of poor whites.

Located across the street from the San Fernando Gardens housing projects, the school was right in the middle of a rarity for its time: a suburban ghetto. I sensed that attending a school heavily populated by blacks would be a challenge. I had never even spoken to an African-American until my first day of third grade at Pacoima Elementary. That day and the next few weeks saw me confronted by African-American boys who threatened to beat me unless I gave them money.

I refused the demand, countering with my own threat. I told the bullies that if they beat me, I would retaliate the next day. My brother David was five years my senior and a fierce and fearless brawler. "You might kick my ass today, but my brother will kick yours tomorrow," became my standard rejoinder to threats of bodily harm. It did the trick.

We Mexicans were called "chile chokers" and "taco benders," racial insults so weird I almost found them funny. The Mexicans responded by calling the blacks "spear chuckers" or "jungle bunnies." In the event of extreme conflict, some Mexicans would resort to the "N-word."

My teacher, Mrs. Hunter, was a tall and stately African-American. Four other teachers were also black. I recall her as a no-nonsense and effective teacher. She could be amusing, too, like the time she shared with us the ongoing story of her daughter becoming a vegetarian. Like us, she found the diet incomprehensible. Who would want to forego meat? It was, after all, the 1950s!

Over the next several years as I progressed through elementary and middle school, I learned to coexist peacefully with my African-American classmates and got comfortable with black urban culture. Developing cultural comfort meant acquiring a deep appreciation for soul music, African-American slang and street smarts that would stay with me for life.

My family and I had no idea that Pacoima Elementary was academically feeble. In fact, it ranked near the bottom among California's public schools. I had a sense that something was amiss when we received used textbooks. They were hand-me-downs from public schools serving the white middle class. The names of the schools had been blotted out with markers. But sometimes the complete name was not deleted, and we could tell where they had been used. We never said anything, but I thought to myself we were not deserving of new books.

Today, Pacoima Elementary is a charter school and nearly one hundred percent Latino. Academic scores overall have improved since my time there, but in some areas, they fall below the state averages.

Fortunately, I was an avid reader of non-fiction. Histories and biographies intrigued me the most. I always had one or two books in progress. During my hours of reading, I kept a dictionary and a thesaurus by my side. That's how I unwittingly bolstered my knowledge of the world and built a rich vocabulary.

Pacoima, while part of the City of Los Angeles, was twenty-five miles from the city's center, so practically disconnected. The main drag, Van Nuys Boulevard, was lined with mom-and-pop stores, liquor stores, bars and a notorious pool hall, the Satellite Club frequented exclusively by African-Americans. It was the scene of deadly brawls. On the sidewalks, winos passed the days seated on wooden crates, in empty lots, high on cheap wine and panhandling to buy more.

We had no supermarkets, just a few small, poorly stocked grocery stores and one barely maintained park that served as a haunt for drunks and drug addicts. The park had few after-school activities. There were some Little League teams, and I joined one. My teammate, Gary Matthews, went on to become the 1973 National League Rookie of the Year while playing for the San Francisco Giants.

For kids, it was hard to find something fun to do after school or during the sweltering summers. Paxton Park, some two miles from my home, had a public pool that was always crowded. Still, I often made the trek.

The presidential election of 1960 unexpectedly awoke in me an interest in who would lead our country. Until the night I watched the Democratic Convention TV broadcasts, I had never paid attention to politics. From the start, I was for John

Fitzgerald Kennedy. My father, too, was a Kennedy man. The JFK campaign organized a Latino voter outreach effort through "Viva Kennedy" clubs. Even in 1960, Latinos were predisposed to vote Democratic, thanks to FDR's legacy. My grandfather José was also keenly interested in politics. Kennedy was especially appealing because he was Catholic and a war vet, like so many Mexican men.

My dad got a few buttons that displayed a Mexican sombrero with Viva Kennedy written on it. Of course, today the sombrero rightly would have been criticized as painfully stereotypical.

When my father learned that Kennedy would make a campaign appearance at Olvera Street, the site where Los Angeles had been founded, my parents offered my brothers and me the chance to see him. We eagerly accepted and were on hand hours before the scheduled speech.

My father, dressed in a business suit for the occasion, was approached by a man who appeared to be a Secret Service agent. He ushered him to a small group of other Mexican men, also in suits. It turned out they were special invitees who would greet JFK one-on-one. Dad was mistaken for a VIP! He shook Kennedy's hand, introduced himself and that was that. We laughed about the incident years later.

Meanwhile, I maneuvered my way to the front of the crowd gathered in front of the Avila Adobe, built in 1818, making it the oldest building still standing in LA. Kennedy delivered a standard stump speech on its front porch. Standing some thirty feet from him, I was mesmerized. He was the first renowned person I'd seen in person. Even at an early age, I was sure I was witnessing a historic moment. I became an enthusiastic Kennedy supporter and even wrote him a letter wishing him victory. To my delight, I received back from his campaign an 8 by 10 glossy photo of a smiling JFK. For years, I thought Kennedy's autograph was hand-signed, and I was a bit disappointed to learn later that it was written by a machine.

A few years later, my classmates and I were stunned by news of his assassination. Several of our teachers cried. That horrendous event followed in short order by the Oswald murder, which I saw live on TV, caused me to realize that we lived in a country capable of such violence and turmoil. The rest of the 1960s forever shattered for me the myth that the United States was the world's model for a pristine and stable democracy.

In the sixth grade, I made friends with two boys. Throughout high school, we would share the usual coming-of-age escapades, adventures, acts of mischief and many unpleasant encounters with cops, all too common in poor America, then as now.

Buster Leroy Scott, the son of Oklahoma Dust Bowl refugees, and Tony Castellanos, whose parents hailed from Jalisco, Mexico, were my main running mates. We were practically inseparable. Exceptionally resourceful thieves and hard workers, Buster and Tony never lacked cash. Their thievery consisted of shoplifting and pilfering cash from their employers. In high school, grand theft auto—not the video game—became their favored illicit source of income. They stole cars at night and within the hour had sold them for several hundred dollars to junkyard owners. It was never clear what became of the vehicles after that, but I suppose they were dismantled and sold as parts.

I steadfastly declined their periodic invitations to join them in theft. I was too afraid of getting caught and going to jail. It was, of course, a wise decision to not commit criminal acts. Buster and Tony were not the least bit afraid of getting nabbed and remained prodigious thieves for years.

Early on living in Pacoima, I became acquainted first-hand with the Los Angeles Police Department Foothill Division, responsible for Pacoima and much of the eastern San Fernando Valley. It was staffed by mean-spirited and violent cops. I was arrested a few times before I was twenty. But some years before those arrests, I saw what law enforcement could look like if you were black or brown.

One day as school let out at Pacoima Elementary, several of the kids reported the cops were making a major bust in the housing projects right across the street. A large group of us dashed over to find several policemen struggling with a fat, middle-aged, hysterical African-American woman. Screaming, she struggled to pull free from three officers while a crowd of black men and women gathered to watch. Suddenly, two of the cops struck the woman with their batons repeatedly on her arms and legs. She yelled louder than ever, and the officers wrangled her to a rear door of the police car.

"Hey, man, stop hitting her!" shouted one man. Others also protested. The crowd of maybe twenty soon pressed toward the cops and the woman, who by now was in the car. At least one of the officers kept hitting the woman, evidently hoping to subdue her. A cop ordered the crowd to back off, and finally the car sped away.

I was left shaken. I had not imagined police capable of such needless violence. Plainly, the cops could have outmuscled their suspect, cuffed her and left without much notice.

❧

A large, undeveloped hill sat behind our house. It offered minor entertainment. We climbed it, pretending to be explorers or we scouted for jackrabbits. One day when I had just turned thirteen, Buster and another school mate and I devised a new source of amusement. Standing at the top of the hill, we could look down a busy street. We decided to see who could throw a rock the furthest.

This required that we toss the rock across the busy street below, Foothill Boulevard, and onto a broad shoulder. While two of us made sure no cars were coming, the other threw a rock as hard as he could. Lost in the heat of competition, we were unaware that two policemen were creeping up the hill. Approaching in a half-squat to avoid detection, they were about 75 yards away when one of my buddies spotted them.

Without saying a word, we bolted. We probably had broken some law unknown to us. We had no interest in finding out what law it could be. Instead, we wanted to elude detention. We made for my house, where my older brother David met us. We told him the cops were in pursuit, and he told us to hide in a bathroom. As I peered out a window, I saw the cops reach the bottom of the hill. A black neighbor pointed to my house. We were had.

In a minute or so, the cops were pounding on the front door.

David answered and somewhat sheepishly called us to come out of hiding. At the front door, the cops grabbed us and slapped cuffs onto our small wrists. David protested that our parents weren't home and that the officers should wait for them to return. When they ignored him, he moved closer to them. One of the cops put his hand on his holstered pistol and warned him to stay where he was.

On the way to Foothill Division substation, one of the cops said David was lucky they had not shot him. His sudden movement warranted an armed response, the officer said. I was shocked to hear such talk.

We were fingerprinted, had our mug shots taken and then two cops grilled us individually. Officer Moody, rangy and grim-faced, angrily asked why we had run. I replied we'd done so to avoid being exactly where we now found ourselves. We had not knowingly broken any laws, but maybe we had inadvertently trespassed. So, we ran to avoid trouble.

Well, that was "fucking bullshit," Moody said. We had thrown rocks at cars, according to several witnesses, and shattered the windshield of one man's car.

"That's a lie," I said, indignant that we had been accused of such an outrageous act. "Bring that man here, and I'll tell him we didn't throw rocks at him."

Moody shoved me all the way across the room, sending me crashing into a wall. "Don't get smart with me, you little motherfucker!" the irate cop bellowed.

In a flash, fear, anger and self-preservation took hold, and I refused to say another word. We were locked up in holding cells, and a few cops wandered by to curse and tease us.

My dad came to the station a few hours after my arrest, seething that the cops had taken me from our home without his or my mom's knowledge. Several days later, we had to attend some sort of judicial proceeding and were warned that any future misdeeds would be dealt with severely. That we had done nothing wrong, except run, had no bearing on the outcome. The official in charge—I don't know if he was a cop or juvenile judge—decided we were guilty of throwing stones at vehicles. We had criminal records.

Years later as a teenager with a car, LAPD cops pulled me over countless times to conduct unwarranted searches. Frequently, officers sought to bait me by calling me asshole, pussy or some other obscene word. We Pacoima youth knew never to take the bait, to just absorb the abuse and avoid a beat down and jail.

When we were about sixteen, Buster, Tony and I went shopping at a fancy department store in Panorama City, then a clean, middle-class community. My friends decided they would shoplift clothes. As usual, when they prepared to steal, I distanced myself from them. Instead, I just browsed through the pants section. Finding nothing to my liking, I told Buster and Tony I would wait for them in my car, a 1962

VW Beatle. In a whispered conversation, they said they would not be far behind. They had "made" two undercover cops, and so they would make a leisurely exit so as not to draw even more suspicion.

Seated in my car, I stared at the store exit expecting my friends to join me. I heard two metallic taps, turned toward the sound and saw an angry young man pointing a pistol at my head, just inches from the driver's side window.

"Get out now!" he commanded.

Instinctively, I scooted toward the passenger side to exit away from the pistol.

"Get out on this side!" he yelled, now in mad-dog mode.

I complied, and he ordered me to spread my arms and legs and place my hands on the car. He kept the pistol pointed at me. In a few seconds, I saw another young Gringo holding Buster and Tony by one arm and walking quickly toward me.

None of what was happening made sense. I had immediately surmised the gunman was a cop, but what caused him to draw down on me? Now, with friends in custody, it all made sense. They'd probably been busted shoplifting.

The three of us were now spread eagle, hands on the VW, the pistol trained on us. I could see spectators gathering. I imagined the onlookers thinking some dangerous criminals had been captured.

One of the cops read us our rights.

Through my teeth, I hissed to Tony in Spanish: "Did you guys take anything?"

"No," he answered.

I was relieved.

The officers searched the car, and then one of them asked, "What did you do with the stuff?"

Buster feigned innocence. "We don't know what you're talking about."

"We know you punks lifted clothes in that store. . . . Where'd you stash them . . . ? Somewhere in the store?"

"We didn't stash anything," I said. "And even if we did, it wouldn't be a crime."

Frustrated, the cops heatedly ordered us to leave the shopping center. Their order was, of course, illegal. But we opted to comply.

"So, we're no longer under arrest?" Buster asked in a distinctly mocking tone.

The cops glowered. An apology for their misbehavior was out of the question.

In the years to come, I would experience and witness many instances of police verbal and physical abuse. I became convinced that too many cops were dangerous psychopaths. The line that cops are general do-gooders defending the public simply never squared with what I lived through. The good cops were in the minority. Policing, I came to believe, was a magnet for particularly violent bullies and racists.

We three so distrusted the police that when Buster's family suffered a crime, no one thought to call the cops. It was about Buster's older sister Sandra, who had left to live with her boyfriend. After a few days, she changed her mind and wanted to return home. The boyfriend, though, refused to let her leave. We decided to rescue her by going to the boyfriend's house and demanding the girl be set free. We took things into our own hands. We thought the police would take the boy's side. Looking back, that was a crazy thought, but it made lots of sense to us at the time.

We headed for Huntington Beach, some sixty miles away, where Sandra was being kept. Our knock on the door was answered by a large, middle-aged man, the boy's father it turned out. Buster explained why we had come. The man gruffly invited us to step into the entryway. His sister and the now ex-boyfriend stood a few feet behind the man.

"She's not going anywhere," the boy announced menacingly.

"I'm going home with Buster," Sandra insisted with fear written on her face.

"Look, Mack, one way or another, I'm taking Sandra home, where she belongs," Buster promised heatedly.

It was a tense stand-off. I expected we would come to blows with the boy and his father.

"Fine, the bitch can leave," Mack relented.

"Fuck you, asshole," Buster shot back.

"Okay, okay, stand down, the both of you," Mack's father said.

Just like that, Buster's sister was free to leave, and she quickly gathered her belongings.

We did not want to fight, but the tension remained thick as we helped load Tony's car. After the trunk was packed, Tony began to tie it closed while the rest of us sat in the car. Suddenly, Tony squatted, the man dashed out with a two-by-four. He crashed it down on Tony's head and then ran back inside his house. Tony was stunned for a moment, and blood began to gush from a deep laceration on top of his head.

He got up, nevertheless, and we three guys rushed to the front door and banged hard on it.

"Come out, motherfucker!" Buster yelled.

"Just get the hell outa here, and be thankful I didn't plug you with my .45," the man shouted through the door.

"They're just chicken shit," Buster blurted out. "Let's break their windows!"

So we started picking up rocks. We shattered every damn pane in the house.

From inside we heard them yelling, "We called the cops! They're on their way," over and over.

It was too late. We finished our assault on the house and got out of there. We felt like heroes who had rescued a female in distress.

உஓஇௐ

Buster, Tony and I were all enrolled in the public high school in San Fernando. The school was notorious for the violence of gang members and non-gang members alike. It had gotten so bad that for two years the school board did not allow San Fernando to host football games because its students would physically assault students from rival schools.

Teachers had their own notoriety: they didn't teach. It was hard enough for them just trying to impose order in classrooms.

In my freshmen year at San Fernando High School, I realized that all of my education had been abhorrently inadequate, and the outlook was for more of the same. In grammar school, I wanted to be an archaeologist. In middle school, I imagined I would get a college degree, although I had no clue what it would cost, or the academic performance needed to get into a four-year university. Now, in the tenth grade, it hit me that I was not college material. How could I be when I was learning almost nothing?

The classes at San Fernando were rehashes of what I'd taken at McClay Junior High. The teachers were obviously burned-out, disinterested in the curriculum and only concerned with maintaining a semblance of order. Typical was an English teacher, a middle-aged woman with bleached blond hair and heavy makeup. She would start each class quickly writing exercises on the blackboard we had to complete in the next 30 minutes. Next, she would warn us to turn our papers in by the end of class. Then, right on cue, she would march out the door and return when class was about to end. Most days, few students even bothered to complete the exercises.

What a joke, I thought. We were doing what should have been our homework during class time. One day, I snuck out and followed her to the teachers' lounge, where she sat on a sofa and started puffing on a cigarette.

⁓⊚⊚⁓

Buster, Tony and I found part-time work here and there. By the time we were sixteen, we had enough money to buy proper cars, as opposed to cheap clunkers. Buster and I had 1956 Chevy Bel Airs and Tony owned a 1955 Bel Air. We had them painted, reupholstered, their wheels chromed and high-quality stereo systems installed. Buster and Tony were accomplished mechanics, and so they modified their engines to give them added horsepower. Tony converted his automatic transmission to four-speed manual.

Few youths in Pacoima had cars that could match ours. Behind the wheel of our vintage Chevys, we set out to explore the San Fernando Valley and eventually beyond. Our travels filled in details of what I already knew: we lived in a poverty-stricken enclave surrounded by white middle and upper-class communities. While public schools in Reseda, Encino and Woodland Hills were part of the LA Unified School District, their high schools enjoyed every sort of educational amenity that San Fernando High did not. Buildings were new and air-conditioned, lawns and gardens were maintained and they had open campuses.

San Fernando High, with its industrial architecture, looked more like a factory than a school. There was no air conditioning, and lawns were dry and trampled. Even the windows lacked screens. They were opened wide when the temperature from May until June hit the high 90s. Ours was a closed campus, which meant we were locked in until dismissal time. Plainly, we could not be trusted to go off campus, eat lunch and return. A security guard, known only as Harvey, patrolled the school to keep order and prevent us from jumping the fence when lunchtime rolled around and jumping back in when the break ended.

Violence and class disruptions were common. In one incident, a math teacher, Mr. Roppo, accosted a drugged Mexican gang member who was wandering the halls during class time. The boy stabbed Roppo in the stomach, nearly killing him. After school, several of us rushed to the crime scene and saw a huge pool of blood where Roppo had fallen and nearly bled out. There were other various assaults of teachers, and drugs were sold in class behind teachers' backs.

A young science teacher, Mr. Avalone, once ordered a *cholo* named Paz to quiet down. Paz slowly rose from his desk and walked slowly and menacingly toward Avalone, who went white with fright.

Standing just inches from the science teacher, Paz grunted, "Never fuckin' tell me to be quiet."

In a quavering voice, and with all the class as witness, Avalone said, "Look, Paz, if you just behave, I'll pass you. You don't have to do any work."

Paz nodded in agreement and sauntered back to his seat.

In another incident, an elderly teacher, Mr. Crump, was assaulted by some male students in his class. They held him by his ankles and dangled him from the edge of a second-story window. They eventually then pulled him back in.

❧

Defying the lunchtime lockdown, Tony, Buster and I frequently jumped the fence to eat burgers at Bob's Big Boy. We often cut class, too. Sometimes we headed out of the Valley, either to Santa Monica or downtown LA.

I toyed with the idea of dropping out because I wasn't learning much. But I anticipated my parents' angry reaction if I ever raised the subject. Also, I knew that high school dropouts were stigmatized as losers. So, I trudged on.

In my sophomore year, the drug revolution hit San Fernando High. The favorite drugs were barbiturate capsules, including Tuinal and Seconal, as well as amphetamines. A lot of us took barbiturates during the morning and walked around in a daze, our speech slurred. Pills and marijuana were peddled all over school. Lots of students were stoned every day.

On the weekends, we added malt liquor to the mix. I never tried LSD but I knew kids who did; some of them even sniffed glue or shot heroin. That shot was too risky for me. I saw what young heroin addicts looked like. They were thin and fidgety, with a yellowish pallor.

I started to reflect on my surroundings and how they contrasted with nearby white middle America.

Whoever it was that ran the country—the President, Congress, the police, the wealthy—had arranged things so that we would not partake of the American Dream. We lived within a profoundly bleak few miles of an otherwise upscale swath of suburban LA and would never land a well-paying job nor live in fancy neighborhoods. I was fully convinced that it had all been arranged just so.

Unavoidably, I felt largely removed from mainstream society, physically, culturally and psychologically. I believed I understood mainstream America quite well, yet I knew I was not part of it and almost certainly never would be. How and where would I fit in, in my native land? I apathetically accepted my uncertain fate, convinced this was the way things had to be for a young Mexican in America.

High school was supposed to prepare us for college. We should have had a wide array of wholesome extracurricular activities. A sizable percentage of San Fernando students were "vocational education majors." They did not attend classes with books. Instead, they spent their days in auto shop, carpentry and electronics classes. Visits by two recruiters, one from the Army and the other from the Marines confirmed for me that none of us was college material. Our PE teachers required us to attend the military pitch sessions in the school gym. The Vietnam War was at its height, and so young Mexicans and African-Americans, who made up about 70 percent of the student body, were particular targets. Unsurprisingly, the recruiters depicted a military stint as the first step toward the American Dream. Serving our nation would make us noble and respected citizens and provide money for college. The word Vietnam was never mentioned.

No college recruiters came to San Fernando. I took that as further confirmation that we had no place on university campuses. The military recruiters sold me and Buster on enlisting. The only question was if we would enlist in the Army or the Marines.

༼ঔৣ༽

As is true of most teens, having money became important to me. My parents required my brothers and me to complete unpaid chores. Usually, I was tasked with cutting the lawn using a push mower and watering the grass, trees and plants with a garden hose. One summer, I painted the interior and exterior of the house. It was an unspoken rule that chores did not earn us compensation. In fact, my parents simply refrained from giving us spending money for any reason. I never questioned the lack of generosity. Instead, soon after I turned sixteen, I resolved to find a job.

In the summer of 1966, I began a full-time job at Price-Pfister, a plumbing hardware plant, one of the largest factories in Southern California at the time. For the next year and a half, I worked as an "expediter," and my function was to keep assembly lines supplied with parts: faucet bodies, stems, valves and the like.

It was far more demanding than I could have imagined. Hoisting boxes of brass fixtures, packing assembled faucets, all the while scrambling is what I most remember about the job. The pace was unrelenting. Bathroom breaks were grudgingly granted because someone had to cover for you during the few minutes you dashed off to relieve yourself. The assembly line just kept rushing along.

Price-Pfister gave me a brutal introduction to blue-collar labor. It also introduced me to the reality of undocumented labor. The plant sat adjacent to a heavily populated section of Pacoima on Paxton Avenue. Yet, only about five percent of the workers were African-Americans. The rest were Mexicans, many of them undocumented and eager for work, no matter the level of exploitation.

Working a forty-hour week made high school a total afterthought. I did not have much homework assigned, and the classes were devoid of any useful educational content. My focus was on making money.

By early 1968, along with every other American youth, I was in a state of turmoil. Now eighteen, I had to find a grown-up pursuit of some sort. Nearing high school graduation, Buster and I agreed we would join the Army. A two-year stint would give us the chance to learn a job skill and get a better fix on what to do with the rest of our lives. We knew we would be deployed to Vietnam. We were unafraid of going off to war. Stupidly, we were sure that our rough and tumble Pacoima upbringing would allow us to dodge death, injury or psychological trauma. We would outfox the perils of war.

At some point, my dad asked about my post-high school plans. He was aghast, a rare emotion for him.

"The Army will send you to Vietnam, and you'll come back dead, or all messed up," he said. "Go to college. The Army already has plenty of Mexicans."

When I pointed out that he'd enlisted, he replied, "There was no opportunity for me to go to college. Only rich people could afford to go. It was a different time. Young Mexicans in El Paso couldn't get good jobs even with a high school education. And this is a stupid war. The US isn't threatened like in World War II. "

Seeing I would not take his advice, my dad offered a compromise. Go to community college for one semester. If I decided higher education wasn't really for me, I could drop out and enlist.

"That way you could go with my blessing."

Getting his blessing struck me as out of character for him. He had never offered to bless anything I did. I ended up deciding there would be no harm in humoring him.

With reservations, I enrolled in Los Angeles Valley College, a two-year school, just weeks before the fall 1968 semester began. My abysmal high school education, I feared, left me scarcely prepared for what lay ahead.

Dr. Beebe, my freshman composition instructor, very nearly ended my college career three weeks into the semester. We were to write several essays during the course, and our final was to be a lengthy research paper, complete with footnotes and a bibliography. I had never produced anything like the paper Beebe described, with multiple sources and a meticulously detailed format. The only good news was that the topic was Mexico, which that year was hosting the Olympic Games.

The unwelcome news came when I received my first two essays, both with grades of F. Stunned and baffled, I struggled to understand how my essays could be worth nothing—the same as not turning in the papers. I had to find out what I'd done wrong, so I worked up the courage to speak with Beebe, an imposing redhead. Never had I taken the initiative to talk to a teacher about my classwork. Right after class one day, I nervously approached her.

"Dr. Beebe, do you have time to talk?" I asked in a quiet voice.

She nodded.

"Dr. Beebe, I got F's on my essays."

"Yes, I know," she replied icily.

"Well, I'd like to know what's my problem," I said.

Looking irritated, she replied, "It's obvious, you can't write."

I don't recall saying anything. All I remember is walking out of the room, my face hot with embarrassment. Soon, I was overcome with anger at myself for having set foot on a college campus. I knew I was not college material, and so now that had been confirmed in humiliating fashion. No wonder there were so few minorities on campus, I thought. We're too stupid to make it through college. I was on the brink of quitting college right after I had started.

Army or Marines, here I come, I thought.

CHAPTER FIVE
The Making of a Journalist

DR. BEEBE'S DEVASTING DIAGNOSIS of my writing left me feeling like a moron. I couldn't write! As I walked across campus, intense anger took hold. I was incensed that Dr. Beebe would indirectly tell me I had no business being on campus. How could she know that based on two essays? I had the raw intelligence, I told myself, but I lacked the necessary skills to navigate the many courses ahead.

That was a pivotal moment. I was questioning a teacher's wisdom and knowledge, something I had never done before. I also had the gnawing sense that Beebe was a racist. She did not want Mexicans in her class, I suspected, and probably not even on campus

From that day on, doubt about my ability to make it through college would dog me. But at one point, I squeezed all doubts out of my mind and forced myself to believe I would overcome all barriers. I could not appreciate the importance of that experience, but I was deciding to brush off racist assumptions—mine and those of others—and steeling myself for a long, grueling life-struggle.

In large part, I was motivated by the examples my fellow students set. I overheard them talking excitedly about transferring to a four-year university, getting degrees and moving right into lucrative careers. As far as they were concerned, it was all laid out. Why did they exude such confidence while I did not?

I thought back to my senior high school class. As best I could tell, no more than thirty of the five-hundred or so graduates intended to continue their education. The phone company and the General Motors plant in Van Nuys held their dream jobs, the ones they hoped to keep until retirement. Why did all these college kids not even mention the military as a desirable option? The answer came into focus for me: those were the options for society's perennial losers: poor whites, African Americans and Latinos. But those headed for white-collar jobs, middle-class lives and running the country were overwhelmingly white. They would make college campuses their homes for the next few years.

Why shouldn't I do the same?

To my surprise, I was doing well in courses that included German, Spanish and Latin American history. My immediate challenge was passing the writing class. What happened next was a near-miracle.

The few Latino students—maybe a couple hundred out of more than fifteen thousand—gathered to have lunch regularly. One was a military veteran who I'd gotten to know. I told him about my Beebe troubles, and he offered a fix. His wife was a college graduate and an English major. I could hand him my rough drafts, and he would have his wife edit them.

That was a godsend. I got back my first draft heavily edited with red ink. I perused the edits and notations. Now, I had a clear picture of the task before me. I was a terrible writer, but I could see the things I needed to do to become competent.

My grades improved, and after a few assignments, I was no longer on a path to failing the class. However, there was a term paper that needed to be about ten to fifteen pages. My subject was Francisco "Pancho" Villa, the Mexican revolutionary leader. I delved into the research, taking notes on index cards. I typed a draft and handed it to my veteran friend. When he did not show up at our usual meeting place, I realized I did not have his phone number. A few days went by and still no vet. I would fail the class, I feared.

Finally, he reappeared with the edited paper in hand, and I was able to rewrite the paper in several hours. I was thrilled to receive a B and I passed the class with a B-minus. My writing class experience greatly boosted my morale and gave me an inkling about a future career. Thanks to my editor, I learned that writing was not necessarily a gift. It was above all else a skill that could be learned.

My other classes were mildly challenging, and I earned Bs in those. What I came to understand was that my years of voracious reading and vocabulary building had given me the essential tools for solid reading comprehension. Poor writing was my debilitating deficiency.

Surviving that first semester made me believe that a four-year degree was not out of the question. I would need to build academic skills and work my ass off, but the goal was achievable—one that fewer than five percent of Latinos had reached in 1968.

We few Latinos and African Americans on campus were typically shunned. The middle-class white students, faculty and staff who represented the clear majority, for the most part, were aloof. I often felt like someone who had crashed a social gathering. It was a major accomplishment when I finally was able to shake off that feeling. The experience reminded me of the woman who told my mom to go back to Mexico. I was going to stay on a college campus, no matter what.

⤳⟨◉⟩⤶

Los Angeles Valley College, like just about every US campus, was the scene of regular anti-Vietnam War protests. Speakers that came to campus and other students eventually caused me to see the war as an American tragedy. Young men were dying for no defensible reason.

Buster was one such casualty.

As happened with many enlistees, his promised non-combat assignment was simply a ruse. He was shipped to Vietnam as a member of a chopper crew. Buster manned one of the machine guns, a duty he seemed to enjoy, according to one of his brothers. He arrived in Vietnam just before Christmas 1969. In June of 1970, he was killed when his chopper was shot down in Quang Tin Province.

Just twenty years old, Buster was gone. I grieved and felt anger at the sick American policy that ended his life. His death brought the war home to me with a vengeance. Naturally, my earlier determination to become a soldier had vanished and was replaced by an even more ardent resolve to earn a college degree.

At about this time I began to feel a strong duty to demonstrate to my white classmates and teachers that a Mexican could be an outstanding student. I wanted to make a resounding statement. Later, as a journalist, I knew sometimes I was being judged based on my ethnicity. Some even complimented me on my excellent English. They could easily conclude that I lacked knowledge and skills, simply because I was Mexican and inherently inferior. My work would prove them wrong.

Tony, meanwhile, was happy with his blue-collar life. He worked at the GM plant and continued to steal cars. I tried to convince him to become a college student so he, too, could find a career more uplifting than assembling Chevys. So, I got him to tag along with me one day at LA Valley College.

Just as we parked at the college, a young woman student pulled into the lot driving a new Camaro. Tony stared, wide-eyed.

"I gotta have that car," he whispered.

At first, I thought he meant he'd like to own one someday. But, no, he meant he wanted to take possession in the next few minutes.

"You're crazy!" I told him. "It's broad daylight. Everyone will see you."

He laughed. "Go ahead to class. I'm gonna take the car. Don't worry."

My attempt to set Tony on the path to a college degree may have failed straightaway, but the theft was a success.

After school, I stopped by Tony's place. He had kept the Camaro's interior and would modify his '55 Chevy so that it could accommodate the sporty bucket seats. The rest of the car was at a Sun Valley junkyard.

⌘

My brother Steven, jovial, chubby, scrappy and seven years my junior, had become culturally African American. He had also fallen in with some rough and tumble black boys.

There were no signs that his association might land him in trouble until Martin Luther King was assassinated. That murder set off days of violence at area schools. African-American boys hunted down and beat any white youngsters they could catch. Steven and his black pals badly beat a white boy at school. Officials did not call the police but they did suspend Steven and the other assailants.

The San Fernando High disturbances left a lasting impression. I had not imagined that my African-American classmates would react violently. We Mexicans were not attacked, but tensions remained, and sometimes classes were canceled for fear violence would erupt, even with the dozens of cops on campus.

Steven continued to hang out with his black friends. They got into no further trouble, but my dad decided that it would be just a matter of time before they ended up developing police records. And so, we moved far away, to Cerritos, on the border of Orange County.

Our new neighborhood was predominantly white and middle-class. Nevertheless, Steven did not become a model youth. He befriended white kids who drank and smoked pot every day.

As for me, within a year I had transferred to Cal State Long Beach with an undeclared major. Soon I was in a financial bind. I needed to earn more money to cover higher tuition costs.

With the military draft in effect, a lottery system based on birthdates was in force. My number was 102, which meant that without a student deferment, I would be drafted. I took a thirty-hour per week job. But I was still too academically shaky to carry a full load. So, I dropped to part-time student status for a single semester and planned to save my extra job earnings and return to full-time academic status the following semester.

The plan proved disastrous. Within weeks of reducing my academic load, the Selective Service notified me I had been reclassified to 1A. I was surprised and shaken, but I did not panic. I would be back to full-time student status in a few months and regain my student deferment. But the Selective Service weeks later summoned me to report to the induction center in Los Angeles for a physical exam. I was told to bring a change of clothes, because if I was found fit for service, I would immediately be sent to basic training at Fort Ord. That's when I panicked.

Like most young Americans, I had come to realize the odds of coming back alive or in one piece physically or psychologically were very long. I'd heard of draft counselors, anti-war activists who offered guidance on how to avoid being dragooned. I found one who said my only hope was to offer a medical condition serious enough to be unfit to fight.

As a child, I had suffered from frequent and severe bouts of asthma. Thankfully, in adolescence, the illness had subsided some, though great physical effort would cause an attack. I went to see our family physician, Dr. Jorge Hoyos, and told him I wanted a letter from him affirming that my asthma made me unfit for military service. He replied that he'd not treated me for years, which was true. So I told him that I still suffered from the illness, just less than when I was a child. This was also true.

Dr. Hoyos, a Mexico City native, looked at me for a long time. I feared he was about to refuse my request. Instead, he agreed to write the letter. In it, he described my prognosis as "poor" and stated that I would not be up to the rigors of military duty.

I reported to the induction center. A couple of hundred young men and I stood in line for the medical exam and a written aptitude test. With considerable dismay, I learned that many other potential draftees also had doctors' letters deeming them unfit to serve. After the exams, those of us with letters were directed to one of several windows, behind which physicians sat. They read the letters and quickly determined if we were going to be sent to boot camp or home.

Nervously, I handed my letter to the doctor. His face remained expressionless when he said loudly that I was "unfit for service now." That meant I was no longer 1A, but 1Y, which meant I was rejected for now but subject to reclassification. In practical terms, it was highly unlikely anyone with a 1Y would be called back.

Commander Allfa (left), Ricardo Chavira (center) and combatant known as "Tortola" (front right) at the Honduras-Nicaragua border in April 1984. They had just completed a raid into Nicaragua. Photo courtesy of Robert Nickelsberg.

Contras on patrol in Nueva Segovia, Nicaragua, April 1984. Photo courtesy of Robert Nickelsberg.

FMLN fighters, Perquin, El Salvador, January 1986.

FMLN combatant and radio operator, Usulutan, El Salvador, March 1985.

Unidentified FMLN fighter (left), Ricardo Chavira (center) and FMLN commander Cirilo (right), near Santa Ana, El Salvador, March 1990.

Perquin, El Salvador, December 1985.

Ixil women in line to vote, Nebaj, Guatemala, November 1985.

Ricardo Chavira with his paternal grandfather José Chavira, Los Angeles, 1956.

CHAPTER SIX
Roots

Sixto Real y Vázquez was born in 1797 in San Bartolomé, Chihuahua, Mexico. The village, today called Valle de Allende, was populated by indigenous people for thousands of years before Spanish colonial citizens settled there in early 1569.

He was my great, great, great-grandfather, and the earliest ancestor I can trace. One of his sons, Andrés Real y Vázquez, was born in 1845 in Santa Rosalía, Camargo. On January 12, 1864, he married María del Refugio Carrasco Arrasolo. She was born on February 14, 1845 and baptized on March 10 of that year in Santa Rosalía, Camargo. She died in El Paso in 1923 and is buried in Concordia Cemetery. Her parents were Pablo Carrasco and María Arrasolo.

Attending the wedding of María del Refugio and Andrés were José Julián Arrasolo and Elogia Loya, my great, great, great-grandparents. The couple had several children, among them José Manuel Santiago Real y Vázquez Carrasco, my great-grandfather.

María Anasleto Guadalupe de Jesús González Molinar was born July 28, 1852, in Aldama, Chihuahua to Pedro González and María Sara Molina. She married Félix Gameros.

They are my great, great grandparents and parents of my great-grandmother, Belén Gameros, also born in Aldama in 1876.

I was fortunate to spend time with Belén. As early as I can remember, my mother, brothers and I would visit her at our great-aunt Felicitas' home in Tujunga, California. Also, she would spend days at our house. Already quite elderly, even in my earliest memories, I still retain a clear image of her as prim, dressed in a fine woolen skirt, elegant blouses and black, medium-height heels. She wore her hair in a bun and walked with a cane. Though she did not attend Mass, she was overtly and devoutly Catholic.

We did not have long conversations, but she recounted one story that at the time I was unsure was true. It had to do with Apaches on the warpath threatening her childhood hometown, Aldama. "I was a little girl, but I remember how the Indians in the mountains were signaling each other with mirrors," she recounted. Before long, the Apaches swept into Aldama unopposed. "Nobody was hurt or even mistreated, but the Apaches demanded food, blankets and a variety of supplies. All of it was readily handed over. The Apaches, of course, were greatly feared throughout the region."

When my family and I visited Aldama, the town's historian confirmed my great-grandmother's story. I had doubted her memory because it seemed unlikely they would still be at war during her lifetime. Of course, history tells us that the last pockets of resistance were not eliminated until the 1880s. The historian showed us a diorama depicting Aldama's history. In one panel, Apaches were shown razing the town. That occurred on October 22, 1769. The town was abandoned until 1783, when soldiers led its successful repopulation.

I don't know when or where Belén met her husband, José Manuel Santiago Real y Vásquez Carrasco. He was better known as Manuel Real y Vásquez. They were married on June

8, 1895, in El Paso's Sacred Heart Church. He was 25, and she was 19 years old.

They settled in El Paso, where US census records for the year 1900 show them living in the Second Ward. I recently visited the tiny apartment on Campbell Street where they lived at the time. Manuel's occupation was listed as "cigar maker."

He died two years later, leaving my great grandmother with five children, among them my grandmother Sara. I have not been able to learn Manuel's cause of death, though family lore attributes it to his job.

Though just 26, Belén did not remarry or have any romantic relationships. She inherited some modest rental property and used the income it generated to raise her kids. As with most of my family, in time they would move to Los Angeles where jobs were more plentiful. Only my grandmother, Sara, born in Ciudad Juárez, would stay behind until her death in 1989.

On April 27, 1919, at the age of 21, Sara married Juan Muñoz Parra. He was 22 years old. Juan was the son of Juan Muñoz Parra and Hermelinda Vázquez del Mercado. Natives of Valle de Cos, Zacatecas, they moved to Ciudad Lerdo, Durango, where they had ten children and owned a wholesale fabric business.

Juan and Hermelinda had prospered economically, but with eight sons and the 1910 Revolution's violence spreading, Mexico became dangerous. Young men were being forcibly recruited by the revolutionaries and government forces alike. To keep his sons safe, Juan uprooted and settled his family in El Paso.

Sara and Juan had two children, Ernesto and my mother, Helena. In time, she dropped the A and became Helen. My mother recalls that white kids in her neighborhood would call her "Mexican dumbbell." She laughed in recounting how she called them the same thing.

According to my mother, Juan was unusually successful for a Mexican living in the United States during the 1920s. He was a salesman for a wholesale hardware supply firm and had all of Mexico as his territory. She recalls he traveled by airplane, a rarity in those years.

The Parras lived comfortably. However, Juan's job required extensive travel. Sara at some point began a romantic relationship with a man named Rodolfo Gándara. She became pregnant with his child and filed for divorce from my grandfather. My mother recalls him pleading with her not to go through with the divorce. She was adamant, and he was devastated.

The Great Depression hit along with the divorce, and Juan was fired. At that point, he moved to Los Angeles. He had brothers there, and it seems he just wanted a fresh start. Jobs were scarce, but Juan found work as a dishwasher at a fancy hotel. He told my mother that he was quite poor and ate lots of potatoes and oatmeal. They filled him up and were cheap.

Before long, he was promoted to the food preparation crew and eventually head chef. He did well in his new position and bought a house in South Central LA. Even then, it was largely an African-American section of the city. Bit by bit, Juan set up a modest variety store in his house. He sold canned goods, thread and miscellaneous items. Eventually, he opened a neighborhood store on Hooper Street. By the early 1950s, Juan had established a large market on Main Street at the corner of Clover, about two miles from downtown. He named it "Toma y Daca," Spanish for "give-and-take."

My grandfather Juan was on his third marriage when I first met him. As a six-year-old, I would on some Sunday mornings after Mass ride my bike to Juan's store. The promise of a dollar and a bowl of *menudo*—spicy tripe and hominy soup—lured me there. For the dollar, Juan had me do a few minor chores, such as dust canned goods with a feather duster, sweep up sawdust from the floor of his walk-in meat locker, spread fresh sawdust and handle the sale of penny candies to eager kids. I was fascinated by how this modest capitalist venture worked. My grandfather explained to me that he bought wholesale, which allowed him to sell goods at a profit. He extended credit to some of his customers, a practice that struck me as novel and generous. One day, my grandfather asked me if I would like to work with him once I had grown up; I eagerly accepted what I took to be a job offer. Lung cancer took Grandpa Juan in 1959. He was just 62.

Many years earlier in El Paso, my grandmother's husband, Rodolfo, was deported to Ciudad Juárez. After years of living illegally in the United States, the immigration authorities learned of his status. My grandmother and my mother moved to Juárez along with Rodolfo; nevertheless, my mother kept attending Bowie High School. Soon, US immigration officials noticed her daily crossings and questioned her about her frequent entries. She told the officials she was enrolled in school.

Living in Mexico and being a student north of the border required payment of a monthly fee. My grandmother couldn't afford to pay, and my mother was unwilling to attend high school in Mexico. Her uncle Octavio, Sara's brother, and his wife Mercedes offered a solution. She could live with them in East Los Angeles. She accepted and enrolled in Roosevelt High. But Juan, learning of her plight, insisted she move in with him. She reluctantly agreed. Juan had remarried a Mexican woman. Like I would many years later, my mother experienced culture shock during her first few months at Jefferson High. It was predominantly African American. This was a new cultural experience for my mother.

In El Paso, she developed a romantic relationship with my father. By 1940, David was intent on joining the Army and wanted to propose marriage to my mother.

"I never really felt at ease anywhere, not at my mother's nor my father's. He had a new family (Juan's second wife was from Mexico City and had two daughters from a previous marriage), and I didn't think I fit in," she recalled.

During one of her trips to El Paso, my father confronted my mother about her allegedly dating boys in LA. She said the rumors were untrue. David brutally beat her. Looking back at the horrible incident, Helen said she should have ended the relationship immediately. Instead, at the age of seventeen, she married my father, David.

With him in the Army, Helen went to live with my grandparents, José and María, in the Bunker Hill section of downtown Los Angeles. After a miscarriage, she gave birth to my brother David Jr. on April 30, 1945. I would follow almost exactly five years later. By then, we were living in LA's Atwater neighborhood.

Our family life was dysfunctional, largely because of my father's behavior. Pampered when growing up by my grandmother, he was egocentric, an alcoholic, averse to arduous work and generally neglectful of his family's well-being. While employed as a traveling salesman, my father spent lots of time away. When he was home, he drank heavily, often with his El Paso pals.

My mother recalls that when I was born, I had only hand-me-down clothes a neighbor had donated. "The diapers were rotten, so they tore when I tried to pin them on you," She told me. My father hadn't provided any money for her to buy my clothes. Instead, he bought a new car.

"I had to tell him to go buy you some clothes so I could take you home from the hospital," she said.

My grandparents were intimately involved in my up-bringing. José's nickname was Miko. The name originated when my brother David was a toddler, and José would call him *m'ijo*, a common Spanish endearment meaning "my son." Through hard work and thrift, José and María acquired two small apartment buildings in Lincoln Heights. The rental income the apartments produced helped support our family.

María, whom we called "Nina," was the most important person in my life. Petite and with strong indigenous features, Nina was loving and usually happy, and by far the most loving person in my family. She adored my father, and always proclaimed it, even when he was at his alcoholic worst. If he totaled a car and was busted for drunk driving, she *gently* reproached him, saying, *"No hagas esas cosas, David. Pórtate bien"*—"Don't do those things, David. Behave yourself." He would appear remorseful and agree to avoid his excesses, only to repeat them weeks or months later. And Nina would offer her gentle scolding again.

She had spoiled him. My father admitted it in later years. He recalled that he had constantly gotten into trouble grow-ing up. "My father would give me some pretty rough whip-pings," my dad would say. "But if my mom was around, she wouldn't allow it."

Nina was born in Coyame, Chihuahua in 1900. Her fa-ther, Félix Ramírez, born in 1859, was a cattle rancher and a rural postman. Nina's mother was Timotea Sosa, born in Oji-naga, Chihuahua, on February 23, 1863. Her parents were Reyes Sosa and Euleteria Sosa. I don't know where my great, great-grandparents were born, but surely it was a village or town in Chihuahua.

Félix and Timotea endured a joltingly bleak life in Sierra Blanca. No longer ranch owners who lived simply, they had to get by on the meager wages of manual labor. In a photo of Grandmother and Félix taken about 1908, my great-grandfather appears robust, sitting with his chest thrust forward. In another photo taken in Sierra Blanca around 1915, Félix appears to be a withered old man. He is slumped in a chair outdoors, his family standing beside him. Félix died in Sierra Blanca in 1925. No one seemed to know his cause of death.

My grandparents lived in the apartment downstairs from ours in Lincoln Heights, so we spent time with them almost daily. By the age of five, I was spending lots of time with Nina. She worked much harder than most. Well into her 50s, she swept and scrubbed streetcars and buses in a sprawling terminal. Right up to age 65, Nina cleaned patient rooms at California Hospital in downtown Los Angeles. Nightly, after her shift at the hospital, Nina would soak her aching and gnarled feet in warm water.

My grandmother radiated so much love for my brothers and me, I craved being with her. Sometimes on Sunday afternoons when she ended her shift, I would ride the bus to meet her. She groaned from the pain in her feet, but then smiled and acted silly just to make me laugh. Then we would go to the Million Dollar Theater, where famous Mexican singers and dancers performed. Mexican movies followed the acts. Given my limited Spanish, I missed much of the dialogue. I didn't mind because I was with Nina, and she made sure we treated ourselves to a meal at Clifton's Cafeteria. Clifton's was a special dining experience. It was decorated with faux redwood trees and ferns. Customers could serve themselves limeade from a huge tank that looked like an aquarium. And Clifton's served kid's meals with a prize, á la MacDonald's, years before the advent of the Happy Meal.

I was also Nina's traveling companion on her trips to El Paso. She had two sisters, Elena and her twin Anita, who lived there. While I did not find much of interest in El Paso, I enjoyed my grandmother's company. On one of our trips, I spent a day with my maternal grandmother, Sara Real y Vásquez. She had taken the last name Gándara, although she was divorced from her second husband Rodolfo Gándara. Sara was the opposite of Nina; she offered no hugs and only sparse conversation.

In the summer of 1972, Steven, Miko, María and I drove to Shafter, Texas. For many months, Miko had talked longingly of visiting his homeland before he died. We set off early one morning and drove in my non-air-conditioned Chevy Nova across Arizona and New Mexico. The next morning, we arrived in El Paso for a short visit with my great-aunts. Finally, we headed east, stopping briefly in Sierra Blanca. A few hours later, we arrived in Marfa and then drove south 40 miles to Shafter. The landscape was extremely barren and desolate. Presidio County, which includes Marfa, Shafter and Presidio on the border with Chihuahua, covers more than 3,800 square miles, and its population is just under 7,000.

It was a brutally hot day, yet we strolled through the ghost town Shafter had become. It once was a bustling mining town. Miko showed us the ruins of the one-room school he and his brothers had attended for a week. Weathered wooden desks were piled in front of the school, and a bell still hung above the building. Miko reminisced about delivering milk and his infrequent visits to the town. He asked a few remaining residents about families he'd known, but no one remembered them. The Chavira ranch was several miles to the west. With no roads leading there, we did not attempt to visit the site.

On the drive back to Los Angeles, I asked Miko what his impressions were. He said he was glad to have walked through his homeland. But then he added, "I was also reminded of how much I suffered in Texas."

A few years later, the most tragic time of my life developed when Nina was diagnosed with liver cancer. I was paralyzed with grief and terrified that a slow, agonizing death awaited her. I loved Nina more than anyone, and her impending death was nearly unbearable. I would visit her every afternoon at White Memorial Hospital in East Los Angeles, and each day she faded just a bit more. Her older sister, Elena, came from El Paso to say goodbye. To this day, I have not witnessed a more heartbreaking scene than the two sisters saying their final farewell.

Deep sadness enveloped me during Nina's illness. To find privacy, I would drive around, crying for long periods. However, I was more relieved than sad when Nina died. My mourning had begun as soon as we had gotten the sad news. As I write this, tears are welling up. I will never stop missing and loving Nina.

Miko, who had shared most of his life with Nina, was devastated. "Why did God have to take my little lady?" he sometimes said, wiping away tears.

Nina and Miko are the two people I most admire. I am so grateful for the love and support they provided a forlorn and suffering little boy. And I love them for the way they cared so tenderly for each other without ever verbally expressing it. It was shown in the way they looked at each other, in how Miko pampered Nina and how they almost never were apart.

꩜

As a sophomore at Cal State Long Beach, I was intent on becoming a history teacher. For years, I had read every sort of history imaginable, and the idea of teaching it seemed appealing. But those plans unexpectedly changed, thanks to an English professor named Patricio Mascorro.

He complimented me on my essays, adding that they showed "a journalistic flair." Mascorro believed my writing indicated I would do well as a journalist, and he urged me to take a news-writing class being offered by the journalism department. I enrolled with great expectations. But in an episode reminiscent of my freshman composition class, I immediately started to sink. The "inverted pyramid" format, with the most vital information compressed into a short, initial paragraph, seemed impossible to master. The professor, Ben Cunningham, was a former newspaper reporter, almost stereotypically hard-bitten. Stories he considered terribly executed were returned with a large, red letter U written on them. This meant they were unacceptable. My first assignments were returned to me with his characteristic large, red U and no critique on how to fix them. I struggled to rewrite those stories, completely in the dark as to what was wrong with them.

As with the Beebe class, my thoughts turned to dropping the course. Mascorro was mistaken. I didn't have a "journalistic flair."

One day, Cunningham stopped me after class. I had another unacceptable story in hand. "You're thinking of dropping the class, aren't you?" he asked.

"Yeah, looks like I have to . . ."

Cunningham, an intense and bearded liberal, said, "I know you're discouraged, but you should stick it out. I can tell you have what it takes. I promise, you'll pass."

I was not convinced that I could master the inverted pyramid, but Cunningham's encouragement spurred me on, and during the next several weeks, I became fascinated with journalism. At its heart, it was the investigation and presentation of contemporary history. That's how I perceived it. I had never appreciated my innate intellectual curiosity about the world near and far. And, I finally conquered the inverted pyramid. In fact, the more I used it, the more natural and logical it seemed.

Soon after completing that class, I switched my major from history to journalism and began working as a reporter for the school paper, *The Forty-Niner.* I surprised myself by how easily I took to reporting. Before graduating, I was awarded two merit scholarships, and the California Collegiate Newspaper Association named me reporter of the year.

I had become a solid student, holding steady at a B-plus average. My scholastic success earned me a campus English composition and Spanish tutoring job. I was gratified that while a few years before my writing was awful and my Spanish so-so, now I was tutoring those subjects!

During a talk with Cunningham about my future, I said I aimed to become an outstanding journalist. Once my journalistic career ended, I wanted to teach journalism at the university level. Cunningham urged me to get a master's degree, the minimum requirement to teach at universities.

While enrolled at Cal State Northridge's mass communication master's program, I got hired at the *Simi Valley Enterprise*, an obscure four-days-a-week newspaper. My beat was Moorpark, a semi-rural town some eight miles north of Simi Valley, today home to the Reagan Library.

Upon graduation from Long Beach, I naively thought I stood an excellent chance of being hired at the *Los Angeles Times.* I would have been thrilled to work there as an intern. Mexican-American reporter Frank del Olmo worked there, as had famed columnist Rubén Salazar. During my master's research, I often went to the *Times* library to review old stories. It was striking to see a newsroom teeming with white people, while the streets outside were crowded with Latinos. If ever there was a place that was in dire need of diversity, it was the *Times.* However, my many job and internship queries were not exactly rebuffed. They went unanswered. I felt the sting of racism.

I worked overtime on my degree and reporting on Moorpark and much of Ventura County. My first story at the paper was coverage of a union vote at a mammoth egg ranch called

Egg City. The workers were all Mexican immigrants, and they were to vote on whether César Chávez's United Farmworkers, or UFW, would represent them. Workers who spoke little or no English were happy to talk to a Spanish-speaking reporter. Every other reporter covering the story spoke no Spanish, so they had never been interviewed. These men and women who did backbreaking work in awful conditions reminded me of my grandparents, Nina and Miko. Stoic and inured to hard labor, all they had ever wanted were slightly better pay and decent working conditions. My grandparents, however, did not have the opportunity to join a union, nor would they dare complain to their bosses.

With this story, I was for the first time giving voice to the voiceless. They would be heard in the next day's newspaper. I was thrilled that my reporting was, at last, going to allow the workers to be heard. The Egg City employees told me they had endured threats and had their tires slashed by company security staff. The owner of the million-chicken ranch allegedly bad-mouthed the union, saying working conditions and pay would not improve should workers go with the UFW. Still, the workers stood strong. The vote was held, and workers overwhelmingly favored the union. My first story reporting the results made the front page.

In the ensuing weeks, I discovered a sizeable Mexican population that had been in the area for generations. Yet, their stories had not been told. Other reporters did not view the Mexicans as newsworthy, and there was a language barrier in the case of residents who spoke no English. They told of the harsh working conditions in the citrus orchards, racial animosity from whites and the absence of bilingual classes for their children.

Residents of Virginia Colony, a section of Moorpark, were Mexican pioneers, having settled in the town forty years earlier. All these Mexican experiences were stories I would eventually report. I was proud and gratified to bring those stories to *Enterprise* readers, confident they would find them illuminating and interesting.

But I was wrong.

My stories set off a backlash. White readers complained often and heatedly that my stories were unfairly depicting the region as a hotbed of racism and stirring up trouble. Despite the editors and me meeting with white community leaders, they were not satisfied nor were the disgruntled readers. They wanted an end to my reporting on Mexicans.

One day, a community member came unannounced to see me. In a conversation I found reminiscent of what racist southerners said about white northern civil rights workers, he said I did not understand the local Mexican population. He claimed they were uneducated and not suited for anything more than farm work. Moreover, they were better off in Moorpark than in their native Mexico. Evidently, he was unaware that many were US-born. My stories were disrupting the natural order of things and potentially fomenting turmoil.

"I understand the Mexican people," he boasted. "In fact, some of my best friends are Mexicans."

I laughed at the last comment, taking it as a joke.

The man was puzzled. "Why are you laughing?"

Soon, more than one hundred upset readers circulated a petition vowing to cancel their subscriptions unless I was fired. I was not fired, and soon the furor died down. But I was left shaken and angry at this intensely hateful, racist attempt to fire me and muzzle the press.

My journalism career would take me on a worldwide journey and provide me up-close experiences I had not imagined. The lands I would explore and describe were, of course, not at all like Pacoima. However, I would find myself inter-acting with the poor and dispossessed in Latin America, and my family and my upbringing allowed me to understand and relate to what I encountered. For instance, in El Salvador, I in-terviewed cotton pickers as they worked. I followed them along the rows of cotton. Dust rose as the workers shuffled along. The afternoon sun bore down intensely, and I could see the workers' fingers flecked with wounds inflicted by the thorns that surround cotton bolls. My grandparents had talked about those very same wounds, explaining they were unavoidable as gloved hands lacked the dexterity needed to pluck cotton from the bolls.

After nearly two years in Simi Valley, in December 1976 I took a job in New York City as an editor of a start-up Latino magazine, *Nuestro*. My 18 months there under the tutelage of former *Time* magazine editors Phil Herrera and Joe Ferrer gave me a valuable education on how to write and edit com-plex magazine stories. It was a challenging apprenticeship and one that made me a much better journalist. I wrote sto-ries about police abuse of Latinos and the ascent of Latino boxers, among others.

Sadly, *Nuestro* failed, and so I headed back; without ever seeing Stockton, California, I accepted a reporting job at the *Stockton Record*. I was dismayed as I arrived, surveyed the place, vividly recalled Manhattan and thought I had made the mistake of my life. On the bright side, Stockton, a farm-ing town some 100 miles east of the Bay Area, gave me an endless supply of juicy and enticing stories.

Most residents were poor Mexicans, Filipinos, African Americans and poor whites. The San Joaquin River runs into the town and flows out to the Sacramento River and then con-nects to the Pacific Ocean. So much of the produce grown lo-cally was shipped via the local port.

Stockton was a violent and corrupt city. In my six-month stint, I covered some grisly crimes. One involved the murder of a man shot and tossed from the fourth floor of a cheap downtown hotel. Arriving at the scene of the murder, I saw a man dressed only in briefs. He lay face-up on the sidewalk, his back bent skyward at a gruesome angle. His torso was covered with blood. It was the most horrific sight I had ever seen.

Another time, I was sent to cover a SWAT operation at a pet grooming shop. Police told me an armed man was holding some people hostage inside. A cop using a loudspeaker ordered the man to come out. But he did not emerge. I crept closer to the shop door. To my surprise, I had advanced beyond the point where the police were arrayed. I realized my predicament and took cover behind a car.

Suddenly the aluminum and glass front door started to swing open. Police fired with rifles and pistols, ripping apart the door. The hostage-taker had foolishly attempted to surrender without advising the police. He was cut down as he pushed open the door. I learned from the police that he had gone to the shop, where his estranged wife worked, to force a reconciliation.

Another memorable episode occurred when I was assigned to write a story about how restaurant inspectors did their job. The editor's idea was for me to shadow an inspector and write a story about what was involved in making sure restaurants were fit to serve the public. I called on Dan Weliber, assistant San Joaquin County public health director, to discuss the story. He looked at me quizzically and asked if I wanted an even better story than the one I described.

Pointing to several file cabinets, he said, "In there are public records. I'm going to leave the room and lock the door for an hour. While I'm gone, have a look at the files."

Surprised and intrigued, I promptly did as Weliber advised as soon as he left. These were public records, so looking at the files did not violate the law. There were dozens of files on local restaurants. The folders contained inspection reports, many detailing stomach-turning details: rodent droppings on the kitchen floor or in cutlery drawers, cockroach infestations, poultry left unrefrigerated, filthy knives, floors and walls. Many restaurants had multiple health code violations spanning years. Tellingly, there were no indications that the restaurants had been sanctioned. Some of those cited were among the finer eateries. The reports put those places in a different light.

With the publication of the stories describing the lax enforcement of health standards, the newspaper was deluged with reader letters. Most expressed outrage that such unsanitary conditions could persist. It was true that violators were just repeatedly warned and never punished. Other letters congratulated us on our exposé.

I could not have anticipated what soon followed. A county grand jury was convened, and I was subpoenaed. The proceeding was allegedly held to probe the restaurant sanitation scandal. But in part, at least, it was meant to force me to divulge my sources. In truth, there was just one human source. Everything else had come from the voluminous files. With Gannett Corporation (the newspaper chain that owned the *Record*) lawyers alongside me, I appeared at the proceeding but refused to provide any information. Dan Weliber's secret was safe.

After six months in Stockton, I took a reporting job at the *San Diego Union-Tribune*; I was there from 1979 to 1983. It exposed me to fascinating and educational field reporting. As a US-born and bred Mexican, I had no first-hand knowledge of Mexican politics and journalism. Although San Diego was just a step from the border, none of the reporters at the *Union-Tribune* were covering Tijuana, which even then was a city of about one million people. And all of Baja California was barely an afterthought.

I was hired as a general assignments reporter, which meant I did not have a specific topic or geographic area assigned to me. My reporter's sense told me that covering Tijuana and the border between San Diego County and Baja California would be a dream assignment. So I started pitching Tijuana ideas to my editor. The first was a profile on Tijuana. Most San Diegans knew it was a place to eat tacos, drink margaritas or get low-cost dental work. Others were attracted to its ever-busy prostitution business.

There was, of course, lots more to the city. Like most Mexican border cities, it drew people from all over Mexico. I learned that most did not want to become immigrants in the United States, legal or illegal. Rather, they sought to benefit from the proximity to the United States and greater job opportunities in border cities.

Since 1965, Mexico and the United States had allowed the establishment of *maquiladoras*, or twin manufacturing plants. These factories, typically with a factory counterpart on each side of the border, mainly assemble consumer and commercial goods. From Matamoros to Tijuana, there are some 3,000 *maquiladoras* employing about a million workers. The plants produce cars, auto parts, TVs, clothes, furniture, medical supplies and a vast array of other goods. Most are sweatshops or a little better, and pay is as paltry as one-dollar an hour. Goods exported are taxed only on the "value added," the value of the finished product minus the cost of the components imported to make it.

The first public figures I got to know in Tijuana were Jesús Blancornelas and Héctor "El Gato" Félix, co-owners and publishers of *ABC*, a popular Tijuana newspaper. It had a healthy circulation because Jesús and Héctor took on the outlandishly corrupt Baja California Governor Roberto de la Madrid and his cronies.

A major story had to do with the Baja California government's failure to deliver running water to large swaths of Tijuana. An aqueduct that would bring Colorado River water to the city seemed only to gobble up public funds and never get completed. Thousands of residents had to buy water from tanker trucks that filled 50-gallon tanks set in front of homes.

Matters came to a dramatic head when then President Miguel de la Madrid visited Tijuana. Residents of a dusty hilltop area called Colonia Obrera organized a protest over the lack of water. State security forces took countermeasures to ensure that the president would not see or hear the demonstrators. The president was to take a walking tour of Avenida Revolución, the tourist-tailored section of town. Police blocked streets that led to Revolución, and the ruling Institutional Revolutionary Party bused in supporters to cheer De la Madrid.

But the protestors got by the cops in enough numbers to mingle among the supporters. "We want water, Mr. President!" they shouted. "Where is our water?" The president's handlers quickly bundled him aboard a waiting bus, cutting short the walkabout.

My master's thesis had been a study of immigration coverage in two Los Angeles newspapers, the *Los Angeles Times* and *La Opinión*, a Spanish-language daily founded in 1926. Among the major conclusions was that the *Times* depended far too much on information provided by US government news sources. Typically, the US Border Patrol was cited, and its officials described undocumented immigration in apocalyptic terms. The southern border was being "overrun," an "invasion" had been unleashed, officials warned.

Of course, what was left out was the fact that this "invasion" had no apparent damaging effect. On the contrary, these undocumented border crossers primarily went right into the dirty, backbreaking jobs no one else would take. American immigration policy has long been defined by its hypocrisy. While it makes unregulated entry a misdemeanor, those who elude capture are eagerly hired by thousands of American employers.

In the fall of 1980, the San Diego office of the Border Patrol warned that undocumented immigrants had taken to throwing rocks at agents. Not only were agents at risk, but so were the Border Patrol's helicopters. The stone-throwing mobs had recently downed a low-flying chopper by directing rocks at the rear rotor, reported Border Patrol officials.

The editors and many of us reporters smelled fake news. How was it possible to throw rocks upward with enough force to bring down a helicopter? Fellow Mexican *Union-Tribune* reporter Jesús Rangel and I decided to find out.

At that time, the territorial dividing line between Mexico and the United States was quite porous. Just east and west of the port of entry there was no fence. However, that did not mean people could simply stroll into the United States, as is commonly believed. Border Patrol agents would set up a defensive human line some five hundred yards north of the border. This created a broad no-man's-land between the actual border and the Border Patrol defensive line. This in-between land served as a staging area for undocumented agents and smugglers. There were plenty of Border Patrol agents deployed, and here and there buried sensors set to detect footsteps. Agents patrolled the defensive line aboard SUVs and ATVs and even on horseback. Typically, dozens of immigrants were apprehended, while others eluded capture by finding holes in the Border Patrol line, usually with the help of smugglers.

Jesús and I dressed in jeans, sweatshirts and tennis shoes. We walked to a staging area, some one hundred yards north of the border, near the Río Tijuana canal. About seventy would-be immigrants milled about. I asked several if they knew anything about the alleged chopper downing. All replied they'd heard nothing of the incident. After an hour or so, we saw a group of border crossers quickly walk north, deep into the United States. Suddenly, they wheeled back looking shaken. Jesús asked one of the men why they had reversed course.

"Who the fuck are you?" a thuggish-looking man shouted. He pointed a long-barreled pistol at us.

"We're reporters," I replied.

"Reporters my ass!" he growled.

"Really, we are," I said, my mind whirling, trying to calculate if escape was feasible. It wasn't. The man, who I took to be a robber who preyed on immigrants, was simply too close to us. There was no escaping the big pistol.

Angrily, he ordered us to clasp our hands behind our heads and walk toward Mexico. My knees shook, as I thought the pistol-wielding fellow intended to kill us out there in the dark scrubland.

As we walked, I saw other men with pistols rounding up immigrants. I recognized one as a Baja California State Police officer named Sergio. He had been part of the Baja California governor's security detail, and we had exchanged pleasantries.

"Sergio!" I called out to him, and he immediately recognized me.

He asked the gunman to stop, and he walked over. "They're okay. I'll take over," Sergio said to the gunman. "What are you guys doing out here?" he asked.

"We're reporting," I answered. "The question really is what are *you* guys doing here?"

Left unstated was the fact that Mexican cops were rounding up immigrants in US territory.

"It's a coordinated operation with the Gringos," said Sergio. "We've been out here making arrests for a few nights."

I looked north and saw that Border Patrol agents were shining bright lights into the brush in an apparent effort to detect hiding aliens. Sergio said we had to leave. Before doing so, I asked again if the arrests were conducted with the knowledge and backing of the Border Patrol. He assured me they were.

As we walked away, we saw a line of Mexican army trucks and soldiers taking the immigrants who had been apprehended to be escorted back to Tijuana.

Two days later, our story detailing the Mexican police incursion was published. It created a predictable stir and stern denials from the Baja California cops and the Border Patrol.

A year later, after he had resigned his post, the commander of the Baja California State Police asked to have lunch with me. During our amicable meeting, he apologized for having called me a liar. He said the operation was off the books and had to be denied. It was plainly illegal to have Mexican police operate on US soil with the help of their American counterparts.

A few months later, I had another unpleasant border encounter. This one involved my then six-month-old son, Ricardo Jr. It happened on the day Ronald Reagan was elected to his first term as president. I was assigned to work that night, and my parents came down for the day. My parents and I decided to have lunch in Tijuana, just a couple miles from where I lived. I had brought Ricardo Jr. along.

In those years, a passport was not required to visit a Mexican border city. Returning, we drove up to the San Ysidro port of entry. We declared our citizenship to the immigration agent, and he was satisfied we were citizens. But he was not sure about Ricardo.

"Whose baby is that?" he asked.

"Mine. . . . That's my son Ricardo Jr."

Ricardo Jr. is and was a few shades lighter than I and had blue eyes. I understood why the officer suspected he was not my son.

"Well, can I see his birth certificate?" he asked.

"No," I replied, "I saw no need to bring it with me."

"Yer gonna have to go over to that small building and talk to the agents there," he said, pointing. "They'll check it on the computer. . . . And, you can park over by the chain-link fence."

As I walked toward the building, a tall US Customs agent strode rapidly toward me and yelled, "Hey, you can't park there!" He was within two feet of me as I began to explain what his colleague had told me. I felt tension and anger rising because of the agent's belligerence. What happened next sent me into a rage.

"I told you not to park there!" a now red-faced agent screamed. He used his index finger to forcefully poke me in the chest, punctuating every word.

"Get your fucking hands off me!" I shouted.

Instantly, agents came rushing to us. My parents got out of the car. My mother held Ricardo.

A short agent, who I took to be a supervisor, heatedly told me I was being disorderly. His southern accent, rightly or wrongly, told me I was dealing with a rabid racist. I shot back that the man who poked me in the chest was the one who needed to be brought into line.

"You need to understand we're federal officers, and you need to respect us," he demanded with a deep drawl.

"I understand you are federal officers and public servants," I countered. "But as a taxpayer, I pay your salary."

"You don't pay my salary, Pancho."

I felt gripped by a powerful fury. "Yes I do, Elmer," I answered.

My father, now himself angered, ripped into the officer. "You redneck motherfucker! Don't start that Pancho shit with us."

By this point, the agents were on the verge of assaulting us. The guy who leveled the Pancho insult had clenched his hands into fists, ready to fight at the first sign of movement. I fully expected the agents to attack. We would go down in a hail of punches, but I didn't care. In fact, deep down, I wanted to strike these racists.

The short agent then announced, "That's it. You're going to leave the baby here and go get his birth certificate."

"Go fuck yourself," I said heatedly.

"Then you're all going to jail!" he threatened.

"Yeah, yeah, just go ahead and arrest us. Believe me, you'll regret it."

Just then, a middle-aged Latino officer stepped up and asked if we had a photo of the baby. "If you do, then the baby must be yours."

My mother, consumed by nervousness, presented a photo, and just like that, we were free to go.

The Pancho guy, however, had one parting shot: "Hurry up and get out of here before we change our minds."

I had to shoot back, "Fuck you. Go ahead and change your minds!"

I've never been more enraged than I was during that confrontation. It was a needless, racist assault on a family who had done nothing wrong. I felt angry the rest of the day.

A few days later I told a federal public defender about the incident. He said we were fortunate the agents had not beaten us and then charged us with assault.

In the next couple of years, I would have other unpleasant experiences with US border officials. What I learned was that the Border Patrol and immigration agents were the scum of law enforcement. I reported a series on Border Patrol abuse and found that physical assaults and verbal abuse were so common that agents found them unremarkable.

I took what I had experienced as incentive to report and write a story on Border Patrol misconduct and brutality. My sources were mainly retired Border Patrol agents who spoke matter-of-factly about beating undocumented aliens. They argued that it was required to keep control of large groups of aliens—clubbing an alien was necessary if he even dared give an agent a dirty look.

The official procedure for returning immigrants was to book them at a detention center nearby. Detainees would be asked if they wished to be formally deported, which required a hearing or an agreement to a VR, "voluntary repatriation," which would have agents immediately return them to Mexico. However, some ex-officials told me they sometimes applied a "fence VR." This entitled agents would administering a beating away from the detention center and sending immigrants back on foot.

Vernon Jaques, a retired Border Patrol agent, was candid. "You have an officer arresting forty to fifty aliens a shift," he told me, "and that's dehumanizing. You don't view them as humans. It gets easy to haul off and whack someone alongside the head."

The "fence VR" also meant no paperwork.

Jaques added that many agents were Vietnam vets who found parallels between the war and securing the border. They saw both as unwinnable struggles, which bred anger and frustration.

"Now, instead of calling the enemy 'slopes,' they called them 'tonks.'"

Border Patrol agents still use the term today. Its derivation is unclear.

Donald Cameron, a Border Patrol officer with years of experience, voiced the "few bad apples" argument, telling me that abuse was rare and misconduct was punished. He recalled an incident in which an immigrant ran away after being arrested. "An agent chased him, caught him and ended up getting in a fight with the guy. After the agent subdued him, he socked the alien one more time. It was one sock too many, and so I suspended the agent."

In one of several Border Patrol shootings, agent Daniel Cole arrested and handcuffed undocumented immigrants Efrén Reyes and Benito Rincón. A scuffle ensued, and Cole shot the men, killing Reyes and wounding Rincón. Cole was not prosecuted.

I had witnessed and reported on police abuse, but the Border Patrol's culture of savagery was worse than what I had previously encountered.

ꙅ☯ꙅ

From May 1982 to January 1983, I researched the transborder existence of some 3,000 indigenous Oaxacans, mostly of the Mixtec people. Desperately poor, Tijuana anthropologist Victor Clark described them as "the most marginalized of marginalized Mexicans." As is still true today, many Mexicans view their indigenous compatriots with disdain and shun them. The *oaxaqueños* I began to study lived in their own society, where Mixtec was spoken much more frequently than Spanish. Most of Tijuana's Mixtec community lived at the bottom of a narrow canyon in the windswept hills above the city.

The male breadwinners made regular work forays into San Diego County and beyond, some traveling as far as Washington state. They left behind family and returned periodically to the shacks that served as home, with their dirt floors and no electricity or plumbing. Cast off furniture filled the hovels. Outsiders were viewed suspiciously and generally not welcomed. Not surprisingly, I was at first met with stony silence when I sought to speak with residents. But after a few forays, I was able to interview several Mixtecs.

Some 15 years earlier, my family and I had traveled to Oaxaca to attend the Guelaguetza festival that features folk dances from the many villages that cover the state. The gaiety on display masked a harsh reality. Later, while reporting in San Diego, I learned that the Oaxacan soil had become depleted and frequent droughts had made farming all but impossible. "It used to be we could grow whatever we wanted, but the soil got so bad we had to use fertilizer. Who could afford fertilizer?" Feliciano Guzmán asked me when I interviewed him. He and his family had migrated north ten years earlier.

Indigenous *oaxaqueños* had been traveling north in search of work since the 1940s as part of the Bracero Program, a United States-Mexico guest worker agreements. After the program ended in 1964, Oaxacans kept crossing the border. So it was that Tijuana's Oaxacan men continued to cross the border without the aid of smugglers and without documents.

The first stop for many was at the strawberry farms in North San Diego County, where I discovered workers living in hovels and in old cars in thick brush adjacent to new luxury homes. In the coming months, homeowners would protest the workers' presence. They considered the makeshift encampment an eyesore and a potential health hazard.

On a typical summer day, dozens of Mixtecs would pick strawberries for 90 cents or $1.25 per 18-pound box, depending on whether the leaves were removed. Few were able to pick more than 25 boxfuls during a 10-hour shift.

One day, the Oaxacans had just returned from a trip south, courtesy of the Border Patrol.

"It was just like in the movies when the officers came to get them," said a woman who lived in one of the fancy homes nearby. "They drove up in three or four cars and surrounded the place."

Sergio del Mar, one of those picked up, said no one even tried to run. Del Mar and his co-workers had been rounded up and returned to Tijuana so often and were so experienced at illegal border crossings that they viewed deportations as little more than inconveniences.

The farm owner, John Kobayashi, who supplied strawberries to Smuckers, simply shrugged when I asked about the Border Patrol raid. "You know, I'm not an immigration agent. These guys have been working for me for years. Unless someone tells me I must check to see if they are illegals, I won't."

As for the workers living in the brush, Kobayashi said he could not afford to provide housing. "I wish they had better living conditions. It bothers me for sure."

One of his pickers, Fernando Hernández, said, "People must think we are used to living like this because we come from Mexico. We do live in houses in Mexico. . . . Even when I picked tomatoes in Sinaloa, we lived in camps and had rooms with electricity."

The brothers Celedonio and Avelino Guzmán had just attempted their first trip from Tijuana to Kobayashi's strawberry farm. Traveling on foot, as all Oaxacans did at the time, they got as far as Bonsall in far northern San Diego County, when a group of white men intercepted them and demanded money.

"We didn't have any. Well, they got mad and one of the men cracked my skull with a club," said Avelino.

Another man stabbed Celedonio in the stomach. They were hospitalized and then US immigration officials returned them to Tijuana, where Celedonio depended on the generosity of other Mixtecs to feed him and his family while he recovered from his wounds.

"I'm worried that I may not be healing right," he told me. "All along here," Avelino said, rubbing where he had been slashed in the stomach, "I feel terrible itching deep inside. If I put a warm tortilla on the cuts, they feel better."

One day at the strawberry farm, there was no more work to be done. And a few men sat outdoors drinking beer. Some of them were drunk. Adolfo Sánchez bemoaned that the men were drinking away their earnings. Short and sun-bronzed, Sánchez had been working without documents in the California fields since 1950. His earnings, he proudly told me, had made it possible to build a home in his village.

By late afternoon, iterant vendors hawking food, clothes and radios began arriving in vans. The Oaxacans crowded around the vans, fingering the polyester pants, western shirts and boots. A man with a catering truck did a brisk business in burritos, fresh meat and beverages. He and other vendors offered credit.

"Times are tough," said the man, holding up a handful of dollar bills. "Look, nothing but ones."

Rogelio, a young Mexican from the city of Vista in Northern San Diego County, arrived in a pickup truck and invited the men to play soccer in a nearby park; several accepted the invitation and climbed aboard.

"This is something I do," he told me, "to keep the boys from drinking so much. They drink because there is nothing else for them to do when they are not working."

By nightfall, the men were back at the farm, cooking their dinners over campfires. Meat, beans and tortillas were the standard fare. Soon after dinner, the men prepared for bed. Some crowded into a wooden shack, but others had less comfortable accommodations. A few crawled under an abandoned truck trailer, and others bedded down in an old station wagon. About a dozen scattered under trees or in thick brush. They slept on old blankets.

Back in Tijuana, I spoke with Ysidro Morales, who had just returned from a stint working in Northern San Diego County. "After buying food up there, I was only able to save $50 a week," he said.

Angelino Romero said he had what was considered a good job helping build a road in Tijuana. "I earned 2,000 pesos a week (the equivalent then of about $13 dollars). What can you do with that? What choice do we have but to go north?"

∿◐◑∿

Many years after my story about the Tijuana *oaxaqueños*, I returned to the border as a *Time* magazine correspondent to report on the rise of violent nativism. Looking back, I see it as a harbinger of what was to come with the election of Donald Trump Here is the story I wrote:

Monday, Nov. 19, 1990
San Diego, California Hatred, Fear, and Vigilance
By Ricardo Chavira

Just as the sun slips toward the Pacific, they gather along Latin America's northernmost fringe. Several hundred white, mainly lower-middle-class Southern Californians arrive in dusty pickups and weathered sedans to confront what they say is a criminal invasion of America. They park single file along a marshy field on the San Diego-Tijuana border. Soon the men and women are engaged in chitchat typical of a social event. Their crimson bumper stickers proclaim WE WANT ORDER ON OUR BORDER, a demand that nearby US Border Patrol agents work hard to enforce.

Some of the 800 officers, who nightly nab upwards of 1,500 immigrants in this sector alone, buzz by in spotter choppers or patrol in four-wheel-drive vehicles, while others survey the area from hilltops.

At nightfall, the protesters suddenly switch on headlights and hand-held spotlights to illuminate a narrow stretch of the boundary. Tonight's "Light Up the Border" rally is one in a series of monthly anti-immigrant demonstrations held in a place where millions of Latin Americans and others have crossed the hills and canyons that feed into San Diego.

Four years after passage of the Immigration Reform and Control Act, the human flow it was intended to stanch is on the rise. This year an estimated 1 million foreigners will illegally enter the United States, most of them across the Mexican border. The protesters, drawn by anger tinged with xenophobia, speak darkly of the immigrants. They reject the conventional wisdom that the aliens are benign job seekers who do work that Americans disdain and that generally benefits the US economy. "We have nothing against Mexicans," says John Machan, a local courier. "Many of them are hard workers, and there should be a way for them to work . . . but then go back home. A lot of the others don't come to work. They steal, break into people's homes, bring drugs." San Diego police say they have no evidence that illegal aliens commit more crimes than the general population.

Loren Flemming, himself an immigrant from Calgary, says he has joined the demonstration to denounce a double standard. "Canadians can't come in the way these people do," he claims. "They get on welfare just by showing up at the office."

Roger Hedgecock, a former San Diego mayor, uses his popular call-in radio show to endorse the protests. He also attends the demonstrations. "We want respect for American laws," says Hedgecock. "Mexicans are violating our laws." He and others demand immediate but unspecified congressional action. Judging by the phone calls Hedgecock receives, many San Diegans share his dismay. Says Hedgecock: "I've had callers in the construction industry say, 'Gosh, I used to be a drywall hanger, and now there are no English-speaking drywall hangers in San Diego County. They all speak Spanish, and I'm out of a job.'"

Behind the angry words and glaring headlights, many Hispanics and other residents detect a resurgence of nativism. It is no coincidence, they say, that partisans are divided roughly along racial lines. While no one suggests a formal link, the protests coincide with a surge in ethnic tensions and racially motivated crimes, both locally and nationally. "There's a potential for violence in these demonstrations," says Bill Robinson, a longtime spokesman for the San Diego police department. "What we're seeing is political conservatives protesting against people who are hungry and looking for work."

The battle lines are clearly drawn. Directly in front of the border protesters, counter-demonstrators, most of them Hispanic, hold up mirrors and black plastic banners to block the lights. Aida Mancillas, a university language professor who is protesting the headlight rally, believes uneasiness about the economy and San Diego's expanding minority population fuels the demonstrations. The percentage of whites in San Diego County is expected to decline during the '90s from its current 74% to 60%, while that of Hispanics will rise from 14% to 23%. "Borders are breaking down everywhere, and it's frightening," says Mancillas. "There is a general concern that the economic standing of whites is slipping, and so the undocumented worker becomes a target of their fears." Before long, the competing protests have degenerated into shouting matches, with Hispanics chanting, "Racists go home!" while whites call back, "Wetback lovers!"

The object of much of the nativist anger is the thousands of immigrants, legal and illegal, who work on northern San Diego County farms, which last year yielded $770 million in strawberries, tomatoes, avocados and other produce. Many of the workers live in appalling squalor. As expensive housing developments continue to go up near the farms, residents often discover that they live next door to Third World-style worker encampments. "The Americans don't want us here, and so they are always reporting us to the authorities," says Longilo Miranda, 18, a worker from southern Mexico. He lives with his father in a scrap-wood lean-to. Marjorie Gaines, a city council member in Encinitas, an upscale seaside community that includes some of the encampments, charges that undocumented workers litter, breed disease, commit crimes and harass whites. Gaines claims that drunk aliens burned down a local convenience store after the owner refused to sell them liquor. "These are border toughs," she says.

Increasingly, though, it is the illegal aliens who are victims of violent assaults by whites. Armed robbers and overzealous US Border Patrol agents are responsible for countless beatings and shootings of immigrants at the frontier. But human-rights activists say San Diego's racial attacks are a microcosm of hate crimes flaring nationally. In one of several attacks involving white youths, Leonard Paul Cuen, 21, was questioned last May and remains a suspect in connection with the death of Emilio Jiménez, 12. The boy was shot as he crossed a field not far from the site of the protest and within range of Cuen's home.

Last January, farmworker Cándido Gayoso was found in a field, feet and hands bound, a paper bag over his head. On the bag was scrawled "No mas Aqui," ungrammatical Spanish for "Don't come back." The owner of a market frequented by farmhands was found guilty of assaulting Gayoso. In February, Kenneth Kovzelove, 18, was sentenced to 50-years-to-life imprisonment in the shooting deaths of two field hands. He matter-of-factly admitted killing them simply because they were Mexican.

José Pedroza, a Mexico City native, and other Mexicans congregate along a busy San Diego street to await day labor. Suburbanites in need of gardening or other chores hire the men. Pedroza says that in their search for work he and his compatriots are targets of regular abuse, some of it violent. Not long ago, says Pedroza, several white youths mugged him as he walked across a field. "They are guys who I had seen before, skateboarding and smoking marijuana," he recalls. "One of them hit me, and another one put a gun to my chest. They took all of my money, $220."

Roberto Martínez, local director of the American Friends Service Committee's US-Mexico Border Program, says he has gathered dozens of reports of unprovoked attacks against Mexicans in which robbery was not a motive. "People passing in cars throw bottles at them," he says, "or even hit them and keep going." In the newest twist, white youths clad in military garb have randomly shot Mexicans with pellet guns. Police say race appears to be the motive in many of the attacks. Theft, however, is sometimes the motive as well. Last month, Border Patrol agents arrested four youths on suspicion of robbing border crossers at gunpoint. "We come here only to work," says laborer Jesús Reyes. "It doesn't seem right for people to dislike us for that."

A staunch advocate of immigrant rights, Martínez has felt the sting of racial hatred. Two months ago, he received letters filled with racial insults. They also threatened him with bodily harm unless he dropped his pro-immigrant activities. A group calling itself the Fighters of the White Cross signed both letters. FBI agents are investigating the incidents. Meanwhile, police have beefed up patrols of Martínez's home and office. "I'm not saying the border protesters are the same ones who threatened me," he says. "But Light Up the Border has created the atmosphere for these terrorists." Rally organizers disavow any connection to white supremacists.

Martínez and other Latino activists insist that San Diego's situation demands the same kind of high-profile attention as that generated by racial killings in New York City's Bensonhurst or by anti-Semitic incidents in France. "The silence from government officials is deafening," Martínez says. "I sense that there is an indifference to what's going on because it involves people who are here illegally, and so the crimes against them are diminished." Others find an ironic contrast to Eastern Europe. "It is disconcerting to see the tearing down of barriers and greater respect for human rights over there," says Richard Castro, a member of the Mexican- American Legal Defense and Educational Fund, "while here at home the same spirit has yet to prevail."

The US-Mexico border is not monolithic. So, it is not possible to understand its complexities based solely on the Tijuana-San Diego border regions. Surely it is a part of the border where white, anti-Mexican sentiment and xenophobia are intense. Yet, the ill will is one-way. Tijuana residents typically shrug off noxious sentiments. For them, it's just part of being Gringo where San Diego meets Tijuana. Perhaps that is why among my most interesting assignments was a long series on the US-Mexico border. I would learn that the San Diego stretch of the border was an anomaly and not even remotely representative of the 1,954 miles it covers.

Photographer Jerry McClard and I traveled the entire border, documenting life in this unique region shared by Mexico and the United States. Time and again, I saw firsthand that the border did not fully divide the United States and Mexico. Most of the border, the 1,000 miles in Texas, is comprised of twin cities, one in the United States, the other in Mexico. Family, personal and economic ties fused the two nations where they met, creating what scholars call the borderlands and Mexicans simply refer to as *la frontera* and border residents as *fronterizos*.

We completed the assignment in the late summer of 1982. Mexico was suffering a financial crisis, and undocumented immigrants were streaming across the border. Yet, American border residents were unconcerned by immigration. Instead, they fretted about Mexico's economic health. Many were worried that a financially unstable Mexico could cause a social upheaval to their south. But more than anything else, we discovered a genuine spirit of good neighborliness, bi-nationalism and cross-border ties, despite Washington's beefing up and militarizing the border. US efforts have not dampened the cross-border connections that give the region its vibrancy and uniqueness.

Starting in the 1980s, the number of undocumented Mexicans and Central Americans set off alarms in Washington, DC. The hardening of the border would have repercussions.

Xenophobia and nativism gripped parts of the United States and helped ensure the election of Donald Trump in 2016. Trump's policies notwithstanding, the flow would have slackened by itself. Job-seeking immigrants would have stayed home as employment dried up north of the border. In fact, that was what happened. The number of Mexicans crossing into the United States had by 2019 fallen to its lowest level in many years. Mexican immigration has always been largely a function of supply and demand. When there are plenty of undesirable jobs—fieldwork, beef and poultry processing, kitchen work—Mexicans will trek north to fill them. When jobs are scarce, few Mexicans leave home.

Unregulated immigration is a multi-faceted industry. At least 100,000 Border Patrol and Customs and Border Enforcement agents are employed. "Coyotes," as people smugglers are called, make millions of dollars annually bringing immigrants into the United States. No question, immigrants benefit to some extent. Employers hire them for jobs that pay many times more than what they would earn back home. But their increased earnings are in large part offset by the much higher cost of living. Large sectors of the American economy depend on cheap Mexican labor to remain profitable.

From late 1979 until late 1983, I completed many reporting trips along the US-Mexico border and traveled often to Mexico City. There, I reported on that nation's politics and nascent grassroots democratic movements. I wrote hundreds of stories based on countless interviews.

I got to know Jesús Blancornelas quite well. When we met towards the end of 1979, most Mexican journalists were under the control of the authoritarian government. Many received regular bribes to write only positive stories about the government. They pretended the outlandish official corruption did not exist. Not Jesús. He wrote scathing investigative stories detailing Baja California state corruption. He denounced the bribes and kickbacks that plagued the state and he exposed the criminal collusion between police and drug traffickers.

The state government decided to shut down his newspaper, *ABC*. Officials worked with a corrupt truckers' labor union, paying staffers—janitors and truck drivers—to join the union. They made outlandish demands of the paper, including steep salary increases. Jesús and his business partner Hector "El Gato" Félix could not afford to pay what union members demanded, and so the union went on strike. But because only a few staffers were union members, the newspaper kept operating. Citing an obscure state law, Baja California officials authorized a forcible closure of the newspaper.

Jesús called me a few hours before the threatened closure. Some of my colleagues and I arrived in time to watch as dozens of club-carrying members of affiliated unions forced their way into the newspaper's offices and forcibly dislodged the staff. *ABC* ceased publication forever. Félix went into seclusion, but Jesús moved to San Diego. We kept in touch, and he confided to me that soon he, Félix and a few staff members would issue a new publication in San Diego and have it surreptitiously distributed in Tijuana. This experience dramatically epitomized the depth of Mexico's authoritarian grip on the press.

The editors named their new paper after the last letter of the alphabet, an oddly sardonic distinction from *ABC*. In doing so, Jesús said, "We have gone from the start of the alphabet to the end, where we will make our stand. We mean to say we will not retreat." *Zeta*, a weekly tabloid, soon became the Tijuana's top-circulating newspaper. It took on government corruption and the worrisome growth of Tijuana's drug mafia, while it covered hard news and the arts. With a new governor elected in Baja, Jesús returned to Tijuana and presided over the tabloid's growth.

In *Zeta,* Jesús and Félix, who wrote a weekly column by-lined El Gato Félix, Felix the Cat, relentlessly reported on the spread of drug trafficking and drug-related activities. Félix alleged that Jorge Hank Rhon, son of a former Mexico City mayor and owner of the city's racetrack, was a major money launderer. He confided in me that he'd received death threats. Laughing, Félix brandished a rifle and said he was ready.

On April 20, 1988, assassins killed Félix with several shotgun blasts as he sat in his car at a traffic stop in Tijuana. Jesús published a weekly notice accusing Rhon as the man who ordered Félix's murder: "Jorge Hank Rhon: Why did your bodyguard Antonio Vera Palestina kill me?" Rhon has denied any connection to the attack.

Sometime in early 1996, I ran into Jesús at a conference. We had not seen each other in a few years. A tall man accompanied Jesús. He was a bodyguard Jesús had hired after receiving many threats from drug gangsters. I knew that Jesús had to be living with a grave threat to his life.

On Thanksgiving Day, 1997, assassins working for the Tijuana Cartel struck. Jesús and his bodyguard, Luis Valero Elizalde, were en route to the airport, when an SUV suddenly stopped at an intersection, blocking Jesús's Ford Explorer. A man emerged from the SUV and fired a shotgun blast at the vehicle's windshield. The bodyguard began to speed in reverse, just as AK-47 automatic rifle fire began riddling the vehicle. Valero used his body to shield Jesús.

A freak accident saved Jesús. A bullet ricocheted, striking the shotgun-wielding killer in the eye, killing him instantly. The other assassins, apparently thinking they were under attack, fled. Valero was dead. He was hit seventeen times, and Jesús suffered four gunshot wounds, none fatal. Following the attack, the government assigned a permanent military security squad to protect him and his family.

The last time we met was at a Mexico City restaurant in late 2003. A soldier patted me down and sat just feet from me during the dinner. Jesús said he would keep writing about the drug gangsters but complained that security concerns kept him housebound most of the time. He was effectively a prisoner in his own home. Jesús died of stomach cancer on November 23, 2006. In the years leading up to the attack and afterward, Jesús received many journalistic awards. Upon his death, the Committee to Protect Journalists called him "the spiritual godfather of modern Mexican journalism."

Drug gunmen killed two other Mexican journalists I knew well. Francisco Ortiz Franco, who wrote about Tijuana drug trafficking, was murdered in 2004 in a drive-by as he sat in his car with his two children. Manuel Buendía, a nationally renowned newspaper columnist, had cultivated close relations with presidents and the National Security Directorate, or DFS, the nation's shadowy political police responsible for murdering hundreds of leftist activists and snuffing out nascent guerrilla movements. I befriend him, and he often offered me insights into the Mexican government. I, in turn, told him what I learned from American officials.

During one of my 1982 reporting trips to Mexico City, Buendía invited me to dinner. We met at his office in the Zona Rosa section of the city. Just before we left for the restaurant, he strapped on a shoulder holster with a .38 caliber pistol in it. "There are people that want to see me dead," he said. "I'm not sure I can stop them."

I asked who wanted to kill him, but he waved his hand and said he was not prepared to talk about it. I did not doubt his word, but I could not imagine who would want him dead.

In a May 4, 1984 column, he wrote that the country's drug traffickers were expanding production and distribution. He added that this would not be possible without the cooperation of government officials. This was a bombshell. No one had ever publicly suggested there was a connection between the nascent drug mafias and the government. Several days after publication of his column, he touched on the topic again. A gunman shot Buendía in the back at close range in a Mexico City parking lot on May 30, 1984. He died instantly, and soon purported gunmen were arrested.

It was obvious that the *sicarios* did not act on their own. Someone had ordered the assassination. Buendía's family and associates pressed for justice, and finally in June, 1989, police arrested José Antonio Zorrilla Pérez, former head of the DFS. Zorrilla was sentenced to 35 years in prison, but he was released for health reasons in 2013. As for the DFS, it succumbed to its gross corruption, human rights violations and ties to Mexico's drug mafias. It was disbanded in 1985. Mexicans had endured DFS abuses for years and would also face years of economic turbulence.

❦

It was early 1982 when Mexico plunged into a financial crisis. The government had borrowed heavily in the late 1970s, when oil prices were high. Mexico, a major oil producer, had bet that petroleum revenue would service the debt. But a global recession struck, and Mexico's oil sales plunged.

In August 1982, Finance Minister Jesús Silva Herzog told the US and International Monetary Fund that Mexico could not service its foreign debt of $80 billion. The next month, President José López Portillo in a fiery speech announced nationalization of the banks to halt capital flight. Washington had to organize a $3.5 billion aid package. Nevertheless, Mexico would face economic woes for years to come as it faced other peso crises.

Mexico's financial problems pushed hundreds of thousands of its citizens north into the United States. In turn, Washington focused on the tempering and further militarization the border.

This fortification of the border caused a change in immigration. For years, getting into the United States without papers hadn't been easy, but it was manageable enough to allow single men to periodically head north for work stints. The circular migratory flow was now greatly constricted, so Mexican breadwinners were forced to bring their families north with them. Crossing the border was now fraught with the risk of apprehension.

In April 1982, I came across a story I found incredible. Journalism would expose me to events stranger than fiction. This story was about the illegal adoption of Mexican babies. It seemed the stuff of urban legend, and it first caught my attention with the 1978 publication of *The New York Times* story about a legal dispute concerning an adoption in San Diego of an illegally trafficked Mexican baby. One of the lawyers involved tipped me off to the larger problem of black-market adoptions. He put me in contact with San Diego's district attorney, whose office was investigating the criminal activity. It was a major case of human trafficking involving the buying and selling of Mexican infants.

I was provided with names and contact information of six Mexican women who had given away their newborn children. All six women I contacted agreed to interviews. They were young, poor and unmarried. Most had responded to Tijuana newspaper ads that said an American couple wanted to adopt a baby. Those who responded to the ads believed they were too poor to care for their newborns. Some also lived far from their families who might have provided support, but others did not want relatives to know they had become pregnant out-of-wedlock. None of the women thought they were selling their babies, but rather relieving themselves of an unbearable burden. Abortions were illegal, dangerous and expensive in Mexico.

When expectant mothers called the number listed in the ads, a woman would answer in Spanish and tell them that she represented the adoptive parents. She would ask personal questions, such as the women's age, occupation and address. If all seemed in order, the women would meet with the purported representative in Tijuana or other Baja California locations. The baby broker would size up the mothers-to-be, looking for indications that the women were in poor health or prostitutes and appeared sincere about going through with the transaction.

In exchange for agreeing to give up their babies for adoption, the women were told that prenatal care and delivery costs would be covered. The representatives, always young women, said the mothers would also receive a few hundred dollars as compensation. Shortly after the babies were born, the representatives, Mexican women who were US citizens, would pay the mothers and take the infants to San Marcos, a city in northern San Diego County.

At that time, Americans who crossed into Mexican border cities were not required to show a passport when reentering the United States. Border agents simply talked to those who presented themselves at ports of entry and determined if the persons were American or legal residents. Thus, the women couriers would explain to the agents that they were citizens, as were the infants they had with them. They were waved through.

San Marcos resident and tax preparer Dora Díaz Green was, according to the district attorney, head of the illegal operation. A few times, Díaz and an alleged associate, Heather

Springer, smuggled expectant mothers from Tijuana into San Diego.

One of the women who surrendered their babies was an undocumented immigrant, twenty-year-old Patricia Alvarez of Carlsbad in northern San Diego County. She told me her father, Silvino, approached Díaz, who had helped him with a separate immigration matter. He reportedly sought advice from Díaz because he and his daughter did not have enough money to cover prenatal and birth expenses. According to Alvarez, Díaz offered to take custody of the infant in exchange for her covering those expenses. Alvarez and her father agreed, and after giving birth to her daughter, Adriana, Díaz took the baby. A few months later, Alvarez said she regretted her decision and sought Adriana's return Also, Silvino was angry because Díaz had failed to cover Adriana's medical costs.

Finally, Díaz took Alvarez to the Vista home of Thomas and Juanita McMillan. There, Díaz showed Alvarez an infant girl and told her she was Adriana.

"I could tell it was not Adriana, and I never told Mrs. Díaz to give Adriana away," Alvarez said. "She was supposed to keep her."

Díaz insisted it was Adriana and that it was now too late to take her away from the McMillan's, because they and the baby had bonded.

Alvarez went to local authorities, who executed a search warrant for the child at the McMillian home. An infant was recovered, but, as Alvarez had said, it was not Adriana. The baby's mother was Norma Alicia Montes of Tijuana. According to Montes, she had replied to a Tijuana newspaper ad and Díaz and Springer had come to see her. Montes gave birth to Iliana in Tijuana on March 1, 1980. Twenty days later, the women came to pick up the baby. Montes, a Mexico City native, said, "I was breastfeeding the baby and wanted to feed her that afternoon. They came that night and took her and told me they would take care of the adoption paperwork."

Montes said she was relinquishing her baby out of economic necessity but refused several times to accept money from the women. Reluctantly, she accepted forty dollars.

The McMillans refused to disclose many details of what happened next, but on March 3, "a third party" (neither Díaz nor Springer) delivered Iliana to their home. The couple, married for thirty-two years at the time, had one child, a 20-year-old daughter.

Mrs. McMillan, tall with salt and pepper hair, recalled they had visited a Tijuana orphanage. She said, "This little boy about five came up to me and hugged my leg. He wouldn't let go. I was shocked that he couldn't talk. The people there told me they kept contact with the children to a minimum so it wouldn't be hard on children when they had to leave."

When baby Iliana was delivered to the McMillan home, Juanita said she didn't have the heart to turn away the child. "I understood that this child had no one to care for her." Soon, she began to worry that she had no documents giving her custody, so she gave Díaz $400 to set matters right.

It turned out that Adriana, Alvarez's daughter, was in the care of Díaz's daughter. She returned the baby to Alvarez. Surprisingly, no one was charged. The DA's office concluded the only crime they could prosecute was the operation of an unlicensed adoption agency, a misdemeanor. They chose not to prosecute.

Federal immigration authorities acknowledged that the law was violated when the babies were smuggled into the country. However, they noted that prosecution would involve the deportation of the infants. As I learned was typical in such cases, the well-being of the children was what mattered most. Deporting small children to Mexico meant they would be taken from a loving home and placed in a Mexican orphanage.

CHAPTER SEVEN
The Big Leagues and Central American Lessons

IN SAN DIEGO, I started writing occasional stories for *The New York Times*. Non-staff reporters, as I was, are stringers. I wrote several stories that received prominent display in the *Times*. Encouraged, I formally applied for a staff position. The assistant national editor wrote back, coldly informing me that I did not have the writing or reporting skills to work at the *Times*. Of course, I disagreed. Indeed, I had proven my ability by having my work published in the legendary newspaper already. Before I had left *Nuestro* magazine in late 1978, I met with Frank Trippet, a recruiter for *Time* magazine. Over the next two years, I had occasional meetings with Trippet and other recruiters, but none resulted in a job offer. The big mainstream media purportedly wanted a more diverse workforce. Based on my experience and the numbers, the diversity drive was more rhetoric than substance. The media brass thought that hiring a few journalists of color equaled diversity.

In addition to *Time*, I applied to *Newsweek*. By 1982, I had been a journalist for eight years, producing spot news, profiles, features and a lot of economic reporting on Mexico. In September of 1982, Richard Duncan, *Time*'s chief of correspondents, called to invite me for an interview at the magazine's New York offices. I accepted the invitation. Just days before I was to leave for New York, a *Newsweek* editor, Michael Ruby, phoned me. He was in Los Angeles, and asked to meet with me to discuss working for the magazine as a correspondent.

I arrived in New York, excited and a bit intimidated by the prospect of interviewing for a "big league" job. For an entire day, I went from one interview to the next and had lunch with Duncan. With the interviews over, I expected Duncan would either offer me a job or condolences. Instead, Duncan simply said he was sure I was talented enough to work for *Time*, and he said goodbye and wished me well.

This meant I had not landed the job, I was certain.

But two days later, Duncan called to offer me a job as a Mexico City correspondent. I would work with the bureau chief in reporting on Mexico and Central America, which under Ronald Reagan had become a major foreign policy issue.

Days after Duncan's call, Ruby called me to offer a New York interview trip. I politely declined, of course, explaining I'd just accepted a job with his magazine's rival.

Time editors assigned me to work in the Los Angeles bureau for three months. They explained my temporary stint would be used to train me in *Time*'s reporting style. I quickly learned that editors expected much deeper and more plentiful reporting, compared to newspapers. Reporting also had to reflect a point-of-view. That was taboo in newspapers at that time.

What they did not tell me was that I was a probationary hire. When I learned this at the successful end of my LA assignment, I was angry but relieved. It made me angry to know that the editors harbored doubts about my ability. I was a proven veteran and an excellent reporter.

I believe my probation was a racist act. In the future, I would discover that many white *Time* correspondents with much less experience than I had were hired without a probationary period.

In January 1984, my wife Carol and my two children, Ricardo Jr., 2, and Marlena, 10 months old, moved to the Mexican capital. The next two years were among the most remarkable of my life.

Within a day or two after we arrived, I was assigned to report on land reform in El Salvador. It was an ill-timed assignment, as we had not yet unpacked or found a place to rent. Still, I set off for San Salvador without a clue of how I would be able to report the story. I did not know anyone in El Salvador, and the story was challenging. The government had begun an effort to give some landless peasants farmland.

I needed to interview Salvadoran government and US embassy officials as well as peasants. El Salvador was in an enduring war between the government and five leftist rebel groups allied in the Farabundo Martí National Liberation Front, or FMLN. Martí, a government-executed hero, had been a legendary patriot and communist revolutionary. Fidel Castro in 1979 had met with the commanders of the various factions in Havana and helped convince them that they would be stronger as a united group, with each faction maintaining its own leaders and members. The FMLN was formed the following year.

El Salvador, among Latin America's smallest nations, is poor. Many Salvadorans lived in slums, impoverished villages or on coffee plantations. I once visited a plantation and found workers living in huts on the property. Their hovels did not have running water or electricity. There were no schools.

A handful of wealthy families—some put the number at twelve—unofficially ruled the country in collaboration with the military.

El Salvador also had a history of political turmoil. In 1932, the military killed between 10,000 and 40,000 peasants fighting to eliminate social and economic inequality. Farabundo Martí, the head of the Communist Party of El Salvador, helped lead the uprising. The government had him shot after the rebellion was put down. Indigenous people suffered genocide.

El Salvador remained buried in poverty for decades. By the late 1970s, the country again was in political turmoil. José Napoleón Duarte, a former student activist and mayor of San Salvador, would prove instrumental in future events. Duarte ran in the February 20, 1972, presidential election but lost to Arturo Armando Molina in a fraudulent contest. Duarte was said to have received most of the votes. Leftist military officers who supported Duarte attempted a coup in March, 1972. The coup failed, and Duarte was arrested. After enduring torture, he went into exile in Venezuela, but later returned and became foreign minister of a civilian-military junta.

Duarte was the junta's spokesman following the assassination of Archbishop Oscar Romero on March 24, 1980, but never revealed why the government did not investigate the murder of Romero, who had been an outspoken government critic and an eloquent advocate for the poor. "I will not tire of declaring that if we really want an effective end to violence," he once said, "we must remove the violence that lies at the root of all violence, structural violence, social injustice, exclusion of citizens from the management of the country, repression. All this is what constitutes the primal cause, from which all the rest flows naturally."

A gunman assassinated Romero as he celebrated Mass. In his final sermon, he had called on Salvadoran soldiers to obey God's order and stop carrying out the government's policy of repression. Pope Francis canonized Romero as a saint on October 14, 2018.

On December 22, 1980, José Napoleón Duarte became the head of state. The FMLN, formed two months earlier, responded by launching a "final offensive" on January 10, 1981. The offensive failed. It also brought the regime immediate US military aid and military advisors. During the 1980s, El Salvador received $4 billion, and soon fifty-five American advisers were unofficially running the war.

Duarte's Christian Democratic Party lost control of the national assembly, and the ultra-right ARENA party ousted him as president. Conservative Alvaro Magaña was president until 1984, when Duarte was elected.

During my first reporting trip to El Salvador in January of 1984, I traveled to the countryside to assess the nation's land redistribution program. Farmland was being broken up into agricultural co-ops. Peasants would be allocated land to be held and farmed collectively. It was a traditional "hearts and minds" effort designed to make peasants sympathize with the government and not the guerrillas. However, I found that the farmers lacked money for supplies. Promised loans had not been provided, and so the co-ops were inactive. Some farmers seemed afraid of me, insisting that all was well. It took me a few weeks to figure out what caused the reticence. I wore guayaberas and Ray-Ban sunglasses, giving me the appearance of a government official or security agent. I switched to T-shirts.

Government spokesmen I interviewed acknowledged that the land reform program was not operating smoothly but insisted the loans would soon be provided.

Unexpectedly, I got a rare glimpse of the war. I met an executive of the national telephone company while having difficulty sending a telex. Once that was sorted out, the official and I talked about the conflict. The government and the guerrillas, he said, were evenly matched. He seemed exceptionally knowledgeable. The FMLN were superb guerrilla fighters, he said, and the government forces were holding their own, thanks to American counterinsurgency training. It was an accurate assessment.

He invited me to dinner at his home. I accepted, and later that evening we boarded a small bus. He lived with his mother in the hillside slum of Soyapango. I had expected him to live in a middle-class home and not the tiny, sparsely furnished house where his mother served us dinner.

Later we stepped outside, and several young men came up to us. They greeted the man and he introduced them to me.

"He's a friend," he told them, referring to me. "You can speak freely."

They said Soyapango had endured lethal government repression. The army's death squads had in recent months arrested and never returned several young men. They were now among the "disappeared," people arrested, tortured, killed and their bodies disposed of in remote places. Lake Ilopango was a favorite for disposing bodies.

"But we have taken measures to protect ourselves and our community," the telephone executive said. "Go ahead, guys. Show him."

They scampered off and returned with an assortment of firearms, including AK-47 rifles, carbines and handguns.

"Now, when the death squads come, we have a welcome for them," said the man.

Everyone laughed.

"In time, there will be a national FMLN offensive," he continued. "Right here in the capital, that offensive will be decided. If we take San Salvador, the war is over."

I could not have anticipated what I witnessed. A national offensive would be launched years later, and, in fact, help bring the war to an end.

In the meantime, I worked hard to understand the nature of the Salvadoran conflict. I contacted the rebels and the country's security forces. From 1984 to 1986 and again in the late 1980s, I would spend many days and nights with combatants and commanders of both sides.

One day in early 1984, I hired a taxi and went to Usulután Department, one of several provinces where the FMLN was active. (El Salvador refers to its provinces as departments.) After a couple of hours on the highway, we came to a rebel checkpoint. It was manned by two fighters armed with AK-47 assault rifles. I explained to them I was a journalist and wished to interview rebel commanders. One of them apologetically said he was unable to forward the request, as he had to remain at this post. So, I conducted an informal interview with him and his comrades.

I had read a great deal about Latin America's leftist guerrillas, including Che Guevara. But I never held out any hope that I would meet one of the combatants that leftists had romanticized. I was also an avid student of the Mexican Revolution; it fascinated me that millions could take up arms to overturn the established order. Though my family had been on the wrong side of Mexico's revolution, nonetheless it was part of my heritage.

The men appeared to be not much older than twenty, but they said they had been fighting the government for three years. They had joined the rebel cause, they said, to improve the lives of the poor.

Back in Mexico City, I contacted the media representative of the Democratic Revolutionary Front, or FDR, the rebels' political arm. A German, Paolo Leurs, agreed to meet me. I proposed an extended trip with the FMLN for a *Time* story. Paolo was not encouraging, noting that the guerrillas were wary of outsiders. He suggested I attend an upcoming dinner in Mexico City, where several FMLN commanders would be available to talk.

Among them was Ana Guadalupe Martínez, the daughter of a prominent Salvadoran family. Her father was a pilot in El Salvador's air force. As a teenage student, Martínez had become active in Salvadoran leftist causes. In 1973 at the age of 19, she joined the clandestine People's Revolutionary Party or ERP. Martínez had taken part in urban guerrilla actions until security forces captured her in 1976. Her whereabouts remained unknown for nine months. During that time, she was imprisoned and tortured in a secret detention center. In 1978, she wrote a book detailing her experience as a political prisoner and describing the detention center.

Martínez was freed after ERP combatants had kidnapped a prominent Salvadoran magnate, Roberto Pomo, and freed him in exchange for Martínez's liberation. After a year of exile in France and Algeria, Martínez rejoined the ERP and became an influential commander of the organization. The ERP was by far the most militarily potent member of the FMLN.

Martínez and I chatted about the war and the FMLN's constant challenges in keeping an irregular fighting force fed, equipped and armed. I told her that government officials said the rebels were coerced into joining FMLN ranks by threatening to harm their families.

"That's really crazy propaganda!" Martínez said, laughing heartily. "Becoming part of the struggle is a long process. First, a potential comrade must demonstrate true commitment. There must be a strong desire. If we grabbed youths and put guns in their hands, they would drop them and run away during their first combat. We help new members develop a deep political awareness of what the war is about. Then they work in support roles. Only later are they trained to fight, and that process lasts months. Then they fight."

When I explained the angle I wanted to take in my story, Martínez said she liked the idea but added that the guerrillas had to be extremely selective in allowing journalists to spend extended periods with them. According to her, enemy intelligence operatives sometimes posed as journalists. Indeed, the CIA had years ago given some agents covers as journalists.

I would later learn that the FMLN leadership read my stories, focusing on whether I betrayed any political bias or was unfairly critical. I would have to gain their trust, and that would take nearly two years.

Several months later, I acted on a tip that a coastal village in Usulután was a key logistical supply point for the FMLN. All five factions operated there. On a hot summer day, Cindy Karp, a *Time* photographer, and I drove to the village. We found Salvadoran Army medics there administering vaccinations. Karp and I wandered through the village asking if they had contact with the rebels. The peasants all claimed that they had never even seen guerrillas.

An old man offered us slices of watermelon and invited us to sit in the shade of his hut. Convinced there were no rebels to be found, I was about to head back to San Salvador when a young man rode up on horseback. He carried himself with the confidence of someone in a position of authority.

"I am David, and who are you?" he asked, looking at us intently.

I replied that we were journalists who wished to confirm what we'd been told about the village.

"That is true, and I am the person responsible for the coordination of supplying our comrades in the interior," said David.

He dismounted and let out a shrill whistle. Dozens of armed rebels emerged from the surrounding brush and peasant homes. Many were young women who wore makeup, an incongruous detail. Still more incongruous was how the rebels were able to maintain a presence just a few hundred feet from government soldiers.

David said he had to ask nearby commanders for permission to grant us an interview. He rode off and returned some 30 minutes later. He recounted that supplying the guerrilla armies was a struggle. Small boats would ferry weapons, gear and food from a larger craft to shore. In the village, mules were loaded, and guerrillas made the risky trip up to eighty miles into the mountain strongholds.

The rebels also got arms, supplies and even uniforms from the Salvadoran Army after their frequent clashes. Salvadoran and American officials accused the Sandinistas of supplying the guerrillas. The guerrillas contended they had a few supply sources, but never denied Nicaragua aided them. Years later in Havana, I visited a rehabilitation center for wounded FMLN combatants, and officials there said they provided training. Cuban officials denied supplying weapons.

෫ඁ෨

I was already tense that day in May, 1984, when several Salvadoran soldiers leveled their assault rifles at *Time* photographer Matthew Naythons and me. We had traveled to Metalio in Sonsonate Department to report on death squads. A source said that an army death squad was terrorizing the seaside town. They occupied a stone house. Naythons was driving our rented car. As we neared the house, I asked him to slow down. He did not, and so the soldiers rushed from behind a wall, leveling their assault rifles and shouting for us to stop and get out of the car.

"Fucking Matthew!" I muttered.

Once I had satisfied the soldiers that we were journalists and not guerrillas, they showed us into the house. Here is a portion of the June 1984 story I helped report for *Time*:

He seems the very model of military rectitude. Sitting straight as a dagger behind his steel desk, hands clasped in front of him and mustache neatly trimmed, Sergeant José Antonio Rivas explains that he is the "maximum authority" in Metalio, a Salvadoran seaside village of 6,000. Several members of his ten-man army unit listen, fingering their weapons, as Rivas boasts that Metalio remains untouched by his country's cyclones of violence. "This is a very peaceful place," he says with a smile, his gold-capped teeth glinting in the light. "We treat the civilian population well, so we, in turn, are well treated. I am friends with everyone. Ask people. They will tell you."

What the people tell is a far different story. According to some Metalio residents, Rivas and his crew make up one of the country's dreaded death squads, responsible for more than 200 killings during the past four years.

The terror comes not just from the horrible ways in which people die, but from the utter randomness of who is killed. Motives can range from suspicion of "subversion" to jealousy over a girlfriend to settling a grudge to no reason at all. Fear has bullied Metalio into an eerily subdued place of whispers and furtive glances. "Rivas and his men are animals... no, worse," says a young man softly. "I wish I could tell them what I really think of them, but that would be like asking for a death sentence."

Confronted with the accusation, Rivas moves uneasily in his chair. "I have not touched anyone," he says. He insists that not a single homicide has occurred during his four years at Metalio. Glancing around at his men, Rivas adds, "We are all clean. We have not harmed anyone."

The village of Metalio symbolizes one of the most daunting challenges facing President-elect José Napoleón Duarte: how to handle the country's death squads, those bands of killers, some with links to the military, that have terrorized the Salvadoran people. . . . A vociferous critic of the murderous crews, Duarte pledged during the campaign to set up a commission to investigate the most notorious killings.

Duarte's progress will be carefully monitored by Capitol Hill, where many legislators have tied their support of further military aid for El Salvador to progress in diminishing the violence. Congressional outrage has been fueled by the Salvadoran failure so far to bring to trial the accused killers of four American churchwomen in 1980 and two US land-reform advisers in 1981.

Duarte's task is complicated by the fact that so much is unknown or unprovable about the squads. Even the death toll is a matter of debate. Tutela Legal, the human rights office of the Archdiocese of San Salvador, claims that during the last six months of 1983, 2,615 civilians were killed "by the army, security forces and paramilitary squads allied with them," up from 2,527 during the first half of 1983.

This year, the organization contends, the tide is still rising: 241 dead in January, 269 in February, 407 in March. Though State Department officials do not contest Tutela Legal's overall statistics, they point out that the group lumps together all civilian casualties, including Salvadoran civilians killed during combat. Says a State Department spokesman: "There are two distinct problems. There are people killed by the military and paramilitary forces in bombings and shellings. We can't verify that every bomb hits the right target, but this is very different from dragging people out of their houses."

The State Department declines to combine all civilian deaths under one label while a war is going on. Its analysts put the 1983 total at 1,686. . . . Though the toll hit 100 in March, Administration officials claim the long-term trend is downward. . . . While President Reagan has suggested that the left is sponsoring squads to smear the right, both the US embassy and Tutela Legal put civilian deaths attributable to the guerrillas at a fraction of those assigned to right-wing packs.

Nicolás Carranza, head of the treasury police, admits that some of the intelligence-gathering cells under his command evolved into hit squads, but he denies direct knowledge. National Police Director Colonel Carlos Reynaldo López Nuila insists that he knows nothing about the murders, but nonetheless, suspects are tortured and killed in police compounds. Even Defense Minister Vides Casanova is not untainted: from 1979 to 1983 he served as director of the national guard.

Death gangs run by the security forces are more visible in the countryside, where, as in Metalio, they can brutalize an entire town. Rivas and his men allegedly don civilian clothes and masks before conducting a nighttime hit, while other times they show up at a house in broad daylight and full uniform to take someone away for "questioning." A favorite dumping ground is a shallow estuary nearby, but sometimes the burial technique is grislier. Several heads were once discovered stuffed in cloth bags and neatly aligned in a field, while the bodies were scattered around the town. Rivas reportedly told one person of how ten bodies from Metalio were heaped in a nearby village last year, prompting the military commander to complain, "If you are going to kill them in your area, dig your own holes."

Many of the murders are carried out by clandestine teams from the intelligence-gathering departments of battalions called Section 2 (S-2), specially trained soldiers who make their rounds dressed in civvies and often wearing wigs. They rely on town spies, or *orejas* (ears), to tell them of suspicious persons, who are then picked up for what is often a fatal interrogation. Says a Salvadoran who served in a battalion until last month: "It is not good to ask about them because they will even kill other soldiers who they think are too curious."

The ties between the police forces and the death squads are rooted in Salvadoran history. Created in 1912, the national guard often acted as a private security force for the country's landowners, who helped to pay the salaries; when peasant uprisings got out of hand, the landlords organized bands of vigilantes to assist the guardsmen. In 1932, when Farabundo Martí, the father of El Salvador's revolutionary movement, led a revolt, paramilitary squads were sanctioned to aid the army in squashing the rebellion. The estimated toll: at least 10,000. The lines between official and illegal violence blurred further after the National Democratic Organization (ORDEN) was formed in the mid-1960s. ORDEN's dual purpose was to teach peasants about the evils of Communism and train them to watch out for subversives. But under the direction of a fistful of national guard intelligence officers, the group had deteriorated into a ruthless militia numbering between 50,000 and 100,000. One of the commanders: Roberto D'Aubuisson.

Violence assumed the proportions of a national policy in the 1970s . . . ANSESAL, the Salvadoran national security agency, targeted victims, while ORDEN carried out the killings. Military and police intelligence officers were in touch with both groups, and occasionally they received assistance from right-wing political organizations.... Out of this explosion of terror came a death squad trademark that is branded forever in the psyche of the nation: *mano blanca*, a pair of painted hands splattered across a door or wall announcing a fresh kill. The reformist coup of 1979 brought an official end to ANSESAL and ORDEN, but by then most army battalions and police brigades had their own intelligence departments devoted to tracking down and often eliminating "subversives."

D'Aubuisson has never been conclusively linked to death squad atrocities. He retired after the 1979 coup, but within weeks he was appearing on television, his time paid for by rich landowners, naming opponents inside and outside the new government as "subversives." A disturbing trend developed: some of those he mentioned were murdered shortly afterward. Calling D'Aubuisson "a pathological killer," former US Ambassador Robert E. White has accused him of masterminding the March 1980 assassination of Archbishop Oscar Arnulfo Romero. White could never prove his charge, but allegations continue to haunt D'Aubuisson and his associates.

After the war ended, the United Nations Truth Commission for El Salvador and the Inter-American Commission on Human Rights concluded that D'Aubuisson gave the order for Romero's assassination.

During a 1984 interview in his San Salvador home, D'Aubuisson exploded in a fit of rage when I asked if he had anything to do with Romero's murder.

"Only a communist would ask me that question," he shouted. "Why don't you ask me about how I am working to keep El Salvador from becoming another Cuba?"

His hulking bodyguards glared at me and inched closer to where I was seated. For a few moments, I thought I would be assaulted. Chain-smoking and gulping coffee from a Thermos, D'Aubuisson remained on edge throughout the interview.

The death squad members were masters at instilling fear. Sargent Rivas, noted in the *Time* story above, managed to make me quite uneasy. The source who had tipped me off about Metalio said many death squad victims were dumped on the beach.

"Have you had a chance to tour our town?" Rivas asked me after the interview.

I replied I had not but would do so in the future.

Suddenly, Rivas said amiably, "Oh, you can't leave without visiting the beach. Come on, let me take you there."

Chilled, I begged off.

∽◌◌◌∾

Returning to San Salvador after a day of reporting, I had another harrowing encounter, one of many I would experience in Central America. My rental car broke down, stranding me in the countryside. I flagged down one of the pick-up trucks that served as rural public transportation. When we came to an army checkpoint, a soldier ordered all of us passengers and the driver out and to present national identity cards. I told the soldier I didn't have a card and was about to show him my US passport. He angrily pointed his rifle at my stomach.

"Get over there with the rest of them," he said, motioning to a slope on the side of the highway.

There were about five men, face down with their thumbs tied together behind their backs. One craned his neck to look at me. He appeared terrified. The soldier ordered me to lay face down with the other men. I was certain that if I joined the men on the ground, I would be arrested and possibly tortured and killed. I told the soldier I was an American, and that was why I didn't have a card. But I did have a military-issued card identifying me as a journalist and my passport to show. I explained what the documents were, and he let me get back in the truck.

Between 1984 and 1986, when I reported often on El Salvador, I would learn that the Salvadoran Army's intelligence officials and soldiers actually comprised the death squads.

Non-military vigilantes were a tiny minority.

The American and Salvadoran governments skillfully promoted the notion that death squads were shadowy vigilantes or just committed garden-variety acts of violence that had nothing to do with politics. The *Time* story, despite my best efforts to shape the narrative, repeated this misleading version.

In reality, American military advisers and CIA agents posted to El Salvador to help direct the war were complicit in the death squad activity. The death squads were nothing more than an extension of CIA policy and Salvadoran military intelligence, making them an integral element of the nation's counterinsurgency strategy.

This was to be expected. After all, the American counterinsurgency operations had long included the use of death squads. In Vietnam, the CIA coordinated the Phoenix Program, an assassination campaign aimed at destroying the Viet Cong's civilian support structure. It was in effect from 1965 to 1972 and resulted in the assassination of between 26,000 and 41,000 suspected supporters.

There were 55 American military advisers deployed to Salvadoran military bases. From there, they largely directed the war. The advisers were allowed to carry weapons but were not to engage in combat. The FMLN, however, charged that the advisers routinely fought alongside Salvadoran troops. In addition to the advisers, some 50 additional American soldiers served in support of the government's efforts to defeat the rebels.

During the war, Washington lavished some $4 billion in aid, most of it military. The American embassy held military briefings for journalists, usually conducted by the head of US military advisers, Army Colonel James Steele. He had served in Vietnam and was a counterinsurgency expert who years later would train Iraqi paramilitary forces. One day before a briefing, I encountered him in an embassy bathroom. He griped that it was hard getting Salvadoran troops to fight effectively. I asked him to explain. Steele said that earlier that day he had visited an army outpost. Soldiers told him they had murdered several guerrilla prisoners. I thought the killings had upset him. But he said, "The morons didn't even interrogate them first."

Salvadoran President Duarte called José Alberto Medrano, alias "El Chele," "the father of the death squads, the chief assassin of them all." I interviewed Medrano on March 22, 1985. Founder of ANSESAL and ORDEN, the retired military man and idol of the far-right said that he formed the organizations as part of an ideological struggle with communists operating in the Salvadoran countryside.

"You have to understand," said Medrano, seated on his patio, flanked by two bodyguards, "that Castro had just taken power. We were in a struggle here to keep from becoming another Cuba."

Medrano was known as a tough commander, yet he implausibly claimed that he was unable to control the wanton killing of civilians that marked his career. The Kennedy Administration provided him and select troops with Green Beret training, and under President Lyndon Johnson, Medrano was given a three-month tour of Vietnam to learn how counterinsurgency worked.

He said that the CIA kept Salvadoran military intelligence informed of leftists who traveled abroad, including to Cuba. "We used this information to take appropriate action."

Medrano was also on the CIA's payroll.

The military extrajudicial killings of armed rebels, Medrano argued, were necessary. "The enemy was other Salvadorans, so Geneva did not apply. The soldiers just executed those they captured."

Medrano said he knew the FMLN wanted to kill him. "I'm an old man now, but when I was working, I did a lot of damage to them. They are not ever going to forget."

As he walked me to my car without his bodyguards, I felt he was exposing himself and me to attack.

Chillingly, a guerrilla hit squad ambushed Medrano the very next morning as he drove in San Salvador. The .45 caliber pistol he always carried lay beside him. A Salvadoran newspaper photographer gleefully presented me with a photograph that showed a bloody Medrano slumped over the wheel of his vehicle. I went to Medrano's home to offer my condolences. But I also had an ulterior motive. I was concerned that El Chele's family might conclude that the timing of the interview and his murder were not just a coincidence. It sounds crazy now, but in El Salvador, with lethal violence all around, I thought it prudent to call on the family. They thanked me for my visit, and I was relieved.

In early December of 1984, I received news that my request to visit FMLN territory had been approved, some 18 months after I had asked Ana Guadalupe Martínez for permission. Just a few days after Christmas, I would be traveling to Morazán Department, an area controlled by the People's Revolutionary Army, or ERP. Journalists Lucia Annunziata, Cindy Karp and Jon Lee Anderson would also be included.

Starting the trip was a difficult challenge. The army had roadblocks on the road that led into the rebels' mountain redoubt and was not allowing journalists or any non-residents to pass. I left for Morazán on the morning of December 27, 1985. As we drove toward the checkpoint, I saw that it was unmanned. I sped up, and as I passed the roadblock, a group of soldiers who were some 50 yards from their posts yelled for me to stop. I sped up and kept going.

Here is the January 20, 1986, *Time* story I produced after the trip:

> Crossing to the northern bank of El Salvador's Torola River is like entering a different country. The neatly uniformed government troops who man checkpoints south of the river are replaced less than a mile down the road by rebels in mix-and-match uniforms and civilian clothes. A guerrilla painstakingly writes down travelers' names, addresses, ages

and reasons for coming. Having passed inspection, the visitors drive up the rutted, overgrown road to Perquín, where they are shown the bomb-damaged house in which they will stay, stark evidence of the danger that envelops the 15,000 to 20,000 people who live in northern Morazán. But despite the hardships the war has imposed, the portrait that emerges from a visit behind rebel lines is of an area struggling desperately to return to normality.

Nowhere is this more evident than in Perquín, a coffee and lumber center that in 1980 had a population of 5,000. When the ERP stepped up its guerrilla war, Perquín was repeatedly overrun by battling government and rebel troops, and by 1983 it was a bombed-out ghost town. Today, as those who fled have slowly and steadily returned, it is again home to 4,000 people. Most say that regardless of who is in control, they would rather live in a war zone than in refugee-choked cities.

The guerrillas have carefully nurtured the repopulation of northern Morazán by restoring basic services that collapsed when the government abandoned the area to the rebels. There is still no electricity or telegraph service. Buses have not been seen for five years, and consumer goods are scarce. But the rebels, through civilian "directorates" that now run the towns, have reopened schools, many of which had not conducted classes for four years. While most of the new teachers are recruited and paid by the directorates, four in Perquín are government employees. One of them, Esperanza Varela de Guevara, 47, moved back to Perquín with her husband a year ago. "When we moved away people accused us of being on the side of the guerrillas," she said, "and when we moved back, we were accused of being army spies. We are just caught in the middle."

Like people who live under military occupation anywhere, those whom visitors can talk to in northern Morazán express views that range from overt cooperation with the rebels to resigned tolerance. One center of support is the area around La Joya, where more than 900 residents [along with residents of nearby El Mozote] were killed in late 1981 in an assault by government troops. Villagers now flee at every approach of the military, whose last attack they say came on Christmas morning.

The town's 200 or so inhabitants were preparing to observe the holiday quietly when seven planes of the Salvadoran air force swooped in low, dropping several bombs and strafing the area with machine-gun fire. "That was President [José Napoleón] Duarte's Christmas present to us," remarked María Cruz Amaya, who says she spent most of the day hiding in the brush. As it happened, no one was hurt in the raid. Indeed, Armed Forces Chief of Staff General Adolfo Blandón later denied to *Time* that there had been any recent air attack on La Joya. Such charges, he said, were a "trick" by the rebels to "ruin the prestige of the armed forces."

Despite the air raids, peasants today are safer from the ravages of large-scale fighting than they have been for years. The army's effective aerial counterinsurgency program has forced the rebels, in Morazán and elsewhere, to regroup into small units of ten to 15 fighters. The guerrillas have made few territorial gains in the past three years; they control perhaps 10% of tiny El Salvador's territory and 70,000 of its 5.4 million people. But they are still capable of major destruction, as they proved last week when the ERP

launched a midnight strike on Juay, a government-
controlled town in western Sonsonate province.
While no one was killed, an entire block was left in
ruins when fire from a bank hit by antitank rockets
spread to surrounding buildings.

Insurgent leaders say that with the breakdown of
peace talks a year ago, they are even more intent on
waging a prolonged conflict designed to destabilize
the Duarte government and sap military morale.
Their tactics, as detailed by a top ERP official in
Morazán, will be as blunt and brutal as ever: urban
warfare, including kidnappings like that last fall of
Duarte's daughter Inés; economic sabotage, like blowing up power stations; and the outright murder of
U.S. advisers and officials. "In the long run, killing
Yanquis is a form of undermining Reagan's policies,"
declared the rebel official.

The story did reflect many of my impressions and omit-
ted some facts. Editors gave the story an anti-rebel tenor, the
result of *Time*'s longstanding conservative bias. I found for
the most part civilians supported the ERP. They appreciated
the medical and educational services the rebels provided.
Surprisingly, many guerrillas were deeply religious Catholics
and worked as catechists. They held religious services. In
turn, civilians fed many of the troops. In contrast to my trip
with the Contras, I never went hungry, nor did my colleagues.

During trips to contested regions, I found an interesting
phenomenon. Coffee plantation owners grossly underpaid
their workers. FMLN commanders had met with owners to
review their books and set more equitable pay for those who
cultivated, picked and dried the coffee. Rebels burned down
the farms of owners who refused to go along. "I asked the
army for protection," one recalcitrant owner told me. "They

posted troops on my property for a week or so, but then they said they had to leave. It was not possible to give me permanent protection, so now I pay the sons of whores." I asked him why he did not simply abandon the farm rather than comply.

He replied that even by paying higher wages, his farm was quite profitable. Greed, not economic necessity, motivated owners to pay so little.

Perquín and another nearby town, San Fernando, had suffered a great deal of government bombing. Most of the buildings were in ruins or damaged. Even a grade school in San Fernando had been destroyed. Among the rubble, I found a brass plaque that proclaimed that the school had been built thanks to the Alliance for Progress, President Kennedy's ambitious program to foment economic progress in Latin America. The Kennedy Administration was to invest many billions of dollars in the effort, which was envisioned to last twenty years. Now, American-made bombs had destroyed a school built using American money.

We also visited the site of the La Joya massacre. As most of those killed lived in El Mozote, the massacre is best known by that name. El Mozote was a small mountain village that the Salvadoran army discovered supported the ERP. On December 13, 1981, the elite, American-trained Atlacatl Battalion led by Lieutenant Commander Domingo Monterrosa ordered the massacre of up to 900 civilians, including many women and children. Ghosts now haunted the site, said residents who were afraid to be there at night.

The survivor and witness, Rufina Amaya, in an interview with me in 1984 at a Honduran refugee camp, said that the soldiers rounded up all the villagers. Sensing what was to come, she slipped into the brush while the soldiers were distracted. A handful of villagers managed to flee before the soldiers arrived. Soon, the killing began with soldiers machine-gunning some villagers and slitting children's throats. Many women and girls were raped. The bodies were burned.

She recounted how she watched soldiers decapitate her husband, Domingo. "I could hear my son Cristino calling for me," said Amaya. "He was yelling, 'Mama they're killing me.' I wanted to run to him, but I knew I could not save him and would be killed, too. I decided I had to survive to tell what happened there."

Her daughters María Dolores, María Lilian and María Isabel, ages 5 years, 3 years and 8 months old, were also murdered.

"The killing went on for hours, and so did the burning of bodies. After a long time, I crawled far away from there."

El Mozote epitomized the war's savagery and was among the worst military atrocities committed in modern Latin America. The accused killers have been on trial since 2016. The US government has failed to provide documents related to the massacre.

ᥱᦡᥕᥳ

I was surprised to find Paolo Luers, the German FMLN spokesman and former journalist, in Perquín. He and several Spaniards and a Belgian priest, Rogelio Ponseele, were there in support of the ERP.

"If I am truly committed to the cause," Luers said. "I need to put my life on the line and not just sit behind a desk." He described his year in the mountains as grueling and risky. "I had never fired a weapon until I got here," said Leurs. "We have had some fierce battles and have hurt the army many times." Smiling, he confessed that he badly craved a beer.

Luers produced several pro-FMLN mini-documentaries to build support for the revolutionary cause. Radio Venceremos—

"Radio We Will Win"—the FMLN's radio station, operated near Perquín. However, it was a highly mobile operation to avoid being hit by the military, which tried to destroy it. The station provided objective news accounts of battles, acknowledging its own casualties.

Many of the ERP combatants were former university students from San Salvador. Most told of engaging in student anti-government protests and being jailed as a result. They had known of friends and other students who had been "disappeared," snatched by government forces, almost certainly tortured, killed and their bodies dumped where they could not be found. And so, they literally disappeared.

A portly, middle-aged peasant and ERP leader who went by the pseudonym Benito Juárez—an iconic Mexican president—recounted how he had become radicalized. "Starting in the early 70s, a lot of us poor people took part in protest marches," he said. "All we wanted was a democratic government that would look out for the poor and not just the wealthy. These were peaceful marches, but the security forces attacked us. People were killed just for marching. So, I decided to join the armed struggle."

Several adolescent women combat veterans not only fought, they handled communications between units as well. They spoke in code using Motorola walkie talkies. Male guerrillas said the young women were fearless and fierce in combat. Some of the young fighters were orphans who the ERP had informally adopted.

On our last day with the guerrillas, a young woman commander visited us. She used the code name "Celia." A member of a wealthy San Salvador family, Celia became radicalized while attending the University of San Salvador.

"As I hope you have seen, this is an authentic people's war," she said. "All of us are here fighting to create a truly democratic nation, one that cares about the poor, who are the majority in El Salvador."

Celia confirmed what I had learned. The FMLN, in reaction to intensified military assaults, had broken up into smaller and more mobile fighting units. What I did not know then was that the rebels were secretly and slowly preparing for a major battle in San Salvador. This was still several years in the distance.

For the first time, I had spent days talking with men and women who were fighting and willing to die solely for what they believed in. It was outside my experience to meet people who gave all of themselves without any financial remuneration. Not a single soldier I had known previously fought strictly out of conviction. I felt that, whatever the merits of their cause, the FMLN had a fighting chance of achieving outright victory or at least forging a new nation.

As someone who encountered systematic racism and marginalization in the United States, with ancestors who had suffered even more, I could not help but sympathize with the rebels. They were underdogs who every day put their lives on the line. Ultimately, the weight of American aid, weapons and generous technical assistance would deny the guerrillas victory. They would have to settle for a draw and a negotiated peace.

New Year's Eve, 1985, was among my most memorable. It is not widely known that the rebels abstained from alcohol. But they were all for partying on New Year's Eve, and so a lively celebration was organized. Hundreds of guerrillas converged on Perquín with the rebel musical band Los Torogoces de Morazán providing the entertainment. Men and women rebels, their weapons shouldered, danced through the night. It was a striking scene. Other combatants were given guard duty and were deployed over a wide area. Our hosts noted that the army might seek to take them by surprise during the festivities.

❧

In early 1989 while I was assigned to *Time*'s Washington bureau covering diplomatic affairs, an FMLN contact called me. She said the group's high command, including ERP chief Joaquín Villalobos, recognized as the most powerful of the leaders, wanted me to visit rebel-controlled areas. The trip would produce significant news, she assured me. I would also be one of the few journalists to interview Villalobos later that year.

In mid-February 1989, I arrived in San Salvador and waited for word on how to proceed. I received a phone call advising me to call on two nuns at the Metropolitan Cathedral of the Holy Savior in downtown San Salvador. I was further instructed to bring enough clothes and personal items for a few days. Two Spanish nuns received me and drove me to Santa Ana, El Salvador's second-largest city.

The nuns unnecessarily stressed that I should not disclose their involvement in the FMLN cause. I knew well that revealing their role would get them killed. I chose not to ask them why they were taking such an enormous risk in connecting me with the rebels. Their actions spoke for themselves.

We stopped at the city's outskirts. One of the nuns pointed to a barely visible clearing in the brush. "Go through there," she said, "and you will find the comrades waiting for you."

Some one hundred feet into the brush, a smiling man holding an AK-47 greeted me. He was, I would learn, Cirilo, an ERP commander who would be killed in combat a few months later.

This is the story I reported and wrote for *Time*:

El Salvador Revolt Under the Coconut Palms
FMLN rebels prepare for their boldest assault since 1981
Monday, Mar. 20, 1989
By RICARDO CHAVIRA

El Salvador's Santa Ana volcano juts majestically over a verdant carpet of coffee bushes, coconut palms and banana trees, and the occasional clump of peasant shacks. Nine years of civil war have racked vast portions of the country, but Santa Ana and the rest of western El Salvador have hardly been touched. Now all that is changing. Hidden beneath the foliage, several hundred guerrillas of the People's Revolutionary Army (ERP), the strongest of five factions that make up the 10,000-member Farabundo Martí National Liberation Front, have begun battling government forces for control of the economically vital region. "Cirilo," the western regional commander of the ERP, explains, "Our interest is to lead the people toward insurrection. They are already clandestinely organized, and now we are moving to arm them."

Cirilo is with a group of some 30 heavily armed fighters camped on a coffee plantation just seven miles from Santa Ana's provincial capital, the site of a major army base. In recent months ERP regulars and dozens of new peasant militias have attacked military outposts, ambushed patrols, and even briefly taken a town near the Guatemalan border.

The guerrillas' bold entry into the region, together with a sudden surge in FMLN urban violence is a graphic demonstration of what even the Bush Administration privately acknowledges is the FMLN's improved military prowess.

Despite the infusion of $3.4 billion in American aid over the past eight years, the Salvadoran government is not even close to winning the civil war. Troops killed most of the guerrilla leaders in the west eight years ago, forcing the FMLN out of the area. The rebels' return underscores their new strength and the army's inability to vanquish them permanently.

The FMLN's military aggressiveness contrasts sharply with the peaceful image the rebels have projected in recent weeks. FMLN leaders surprised American and Salvadoran officials in January with a dramatic offer to lay down their weapons and participate in national elections. In exchange, the rebels wanted the March presidential vote postponed for six months. That offer set off a flurry of counter ERP proposals and talks between the FMLN and political-party representatives. State Department officials, who quietly met with a rebel spokesman to discuss the initiative, were so intrigued that they encouraged the Salvadoran government to negotiate with the guerrillas. For a time, it seemed as though the rebel plan could provide a way out of the war.

But like past attempts to bargain, the proposal fell victim to intransigence and political shortsightedness, as Salvador's civilian and military leaders squabbled over whether, how and when to include the guerrillas in the electoral process. There is little doubt now that the election will be held as scheduled— March 19—without rebel participation.

Stung by their diplomatic setback, the guerrillas are prepared to unleash what even Bush Administration officials believe will be their boldest military assault since the failed 1981 "final offensive." US intelligence officials say the FMLN, in preparation for the push, has recruited several hundred new fighters from among refugees in Honduran camps. The officials expect the offensive within weeks.

The guerrillas sound determined to fight unless a newly elected government proves unexpectedly willing to reopen negotiations. Warns Cirilo: "We have a genuine desire for peace. But that should not be mistaken for weakness." Schafik Jorge Handal, head of the Salvadoran Communist Party and one of the FMLN's top five *comandantes*, agrees. "If the military says no to our plan, then that indicates their intention of defeating us militarily," he says. "That would oblige us to respond, and the product would be a deepening of the war." Roberto, a veteran ERP combatant is more direct: "If the elections are held March 19, our plan is to block them. This is a war to the finish between us and the oligarchs."

Far to the east of Santa Ana, in Usulután province, the ERP has consolidated its hold on another mountainous corridor, populated by nearly 200,000 peasants. Three years ago, the insurgents there were under frequent military attacks. Civilian support was minimal. Today government troops dare only sporadic attacks, and they are frequently beaten back by peasant militias fighting alongside regular combatants. "We have established political control over the area," says "Raúl," the rebel commander, "and now we are moving toward military control as well." He and other guerrilla leaders have lately obtained AK-47 assault rifles. They say the guns were bought from the Nicaraguan Contras; US and Salvadoran authorities insist that the Sandinistas supplied them. "The fact that we have these weapons is an indication of our development," says Raúl.

Peasant support is crucial to the kind of rural-based war the FMLN is fighting. The impoverished farmers of Usulután, for example, supply the rebels with food, information and labor. Says a civilian supporter in Santa Ana: "The moment a soldier asks you the whereabouts of the guerrillas, and you lie and say you don't know, from that moment you are collaborating with the guerrillas. And there are thousands of us like that." The coming guerrilla offensive seems likely to prove a pivotal test of the government's military strength. US officials doubt that the FMLN can inflict a major defeat. But a senior State Department official adds, "However real or illusory the chances for peace, they are now gone. Now the only alternative for El Salvador is more war." That is the last thing battle-weary Salvadorans want.

Connecting with the Usulután rebels required another contact. He was the leader of a peasants' rights organization in Usulután Department and secretly worked with the ERP. The middle-aged man introduced himself only as Fermín. Soon after I arrived at his countryside office, we boarded a pick-up truck and headed deep into Usulután.

Fermín said that if we encountered a military checkpoint, he would tell the soldiers I worked for him. Perhaps an hour after we began our trip, we came to such checkpoint. The soldier in charge knew Fermín from other encounters and did not ask about me. Late in the afternoon, we arrived at a village. I followed Fermín to a house, and he introduced me to a couple and their children. "This is the visitor I told you about," Fermín said to the man and his wife. They smiled and nodded, and Fermín said that I would be in contact with ERP guerrillas the next morning.

The couple laid out some blankets on the earthen kitchen floor. I spent the night sleeping fitfully as fleas feasted on me. Early the next morning I was awakened by two young guerrillas. They escorted me up into nearby hills where an ERP camp had been set-up.

Raúl, the commander, was confident of victory, in part because he and his fighters—some twenty were in the camp— had inflicted heavy losses on government troops. "Here, we are only two kilometers from an army base," he said. "The *quilos* know we are here but they are afraid to attack us."

Some six months after spending several days with the ERP, I interviewed the group's top *comandante*, Joaquín Villalobos. The rebel leader was the man most wanted by Salvadoran security forces, and so he rarely sat down for interviews.

On September 27, 1989, we met at a luxury hotel in Mexico City, across the street from the city's upscale Perisur shopping center. The interview was notable because Villalobos expressed a desire for a negotiated end to the war. The youthful-looking *comandante* dressed in slacks, a sports jacket and open-neck shirt. He affirmed that a prolonged war "no longer corresponds to the reality of the world. If a revolutionary asked me today what to do, I would say, 'Conspire to launch a short-term war.'"

This was an unexpected change in rhetoric. Villalobos clearly was signaling a desire to reach a negotiated end to the conflict. "We can't at this time aspire to an armed revolution that the Soviet Union will subsidize." He also said the rebels would accept multi-party elections and recognize the winner of the elections.

After years of dodging the accusation, Villalobos admitted that Nicaragua had supplied the FMLN with weapons.

Salvadoran President Alfredo Cristiani told a fellow *Time* correspondent that he, too, wanted an end to the war, adding that American financial support should be converted to economic support to help the nation recover from years of conflict.

It was not to be. The United States provided El Salvador with $90 million in military aid in fiscal 1990; in comparison, recently in 2019 US economic aid totaled $47 million.

Despite Villalobos's conciliatory words, as my March 1989 story suggested, the FMLN did, in fact, launch an all-out offensive. It was launched on November 11, 1989, with some 3,000 rebel combatants moving on San Salvador, where they linked up with fighters already in place. In addition to San Salvador, the offensive targeted San Miguel, Santa Ana, Usulután and Zacatecoluca. Several fixed targets were hit, including President Cristiani's residence and the capital's First Brigade barracks.

The key objective was the taking of San Salvador, which had never been attacked. The rebels spent years preparing for the offensive. They had discreetly purchased many homes, which they reinforced to act as strongholds. Arms and ammunition had also been smuggled in.

The rebels took the military by surprise and held the upper hand during several days of fighting. They occupied large areas of the capital, including the wealthy Escalón neighborhood and the Sheraton Hotel. It appeared for a time the FMLN would triumph. But the hoped-for broad popular uprising did not materialize. To further blunt the offensive, government forces used indiscriminate aerial bombing. They carried out widespread arrests and murder of perceived rebel supporters; this included six Jesuit priests at Central American University, their housekeeper and her daughter. Members of the Atlacatl Battalion had raided the campus and killed them in cold blood.

The offensive failed to overthrow the government, but it cleared the way for peace negotiations. The government and Washington now understood that a military victory was far from certain. The FMLN shared that view.

Cirilo, the guerrilla leader I had interviewed near Santa Ana, was killed in the fighting. His family asked me for photos of him taken just months before his death, which I provided.

Lieutenant Colonel Domingo Monterrosa authorized the El Mozote massacre. He was the darling of the Salvadoran armed forces and the adversary the FMLN regarded as the most formidable. He was that and more, not the least which was a very able propagandist, beloved by his troops. I saw the former side of him in my April 1984 interview, when he was the commanding officer of the Third Infantry Brigade of San Miguel.

Monterrosa had welcomed me effusively when I arrived at his headquarters. The government was winning and had the rebels on the run, he insisted. He showed me several papers that he claimed were captured FMLN documents. They described, he said, deep concern among the rebels, who feared their struggle was stalling.

He was a graduate of the US Army's School of the Americas, where for fifty-four years many Latin American soldiers, including Manuel Noriega, were trained. FMLN leaders regarded Monterrosa as a formidable adversary.

Abruptly, Monterrosa asked if I had plans for the day. I did not, and he invited me to accompany him to visit soldiers in a combat zone. We traveled aboard Monterrosa's Huey helicopter. Our destination was Cacahuatique, a mountain in Morazán the army used mainly for communications.

We landed close to a group of about twenty soldiers. There were two dead, encased in body bags, soldiers killed in combat the day before. Monterrosa sighed. "Boys, of course, we are sad to lose companions," he told the somber soldiers. "Unfortunately, this is part of the war. These men have fallen, but we are still standing ready to fight even harder."

The pep talk continued for a few more minutes. One soldier with whom I spoke afterward, however, was angry and frustrated. "The guerrillas hit us and run away," he said. "They won't stand and fight. They are cowards."

I noted that hit-and-run tactics were central to guerrilla warfare. He simply nodded.

Monterrosa gathered the soldiers in a circle and using a stick drew in the dirt a patrol route we would follow. Naturally, I had not planned to go out in search of rebels, but it was an opportunity to see Monterrosa in action. He directed the soldiers to divide into two groups, march in opposite directions, looking to flush out and engage guerrillas, and then meet toward the bottom of the mountain.

I went with Monterrosa's patrol. About an hour in, automatic rifle fire crackled for several seconds. I dove to the ground. Monterrosa and his soldiers just knelt on one knee and chuckled at what they said was my overreaction. I laughed good-naturedly, but even today I believe my maneuver was highly prudent. A prone human body was much harder to hit than one that was kneeling.

For the next two hours, Monterrosa stopped periodically to chat with farmers. He casually asked about the guerrillas. The farmers were polite but restrained. None offered any detailed information. "My dogs were barking a lot the other night," said one. "The boys must have been passing through."

The guerrillas were typically called los *muchachos*. But the rebels called each other "*compañeros*" or "*compas*."

More than a year later during my Morazán visit with the guerrillas, we visited some of the same farms. On that occasion, the farmers happily greeted the rebels. Most offered detailed information about government troop movements. One of the ERP leaders reminded the farmers that it was wise to criticize the rebels. "That way they don't imagine that you help us."

A farmer said he liked giving the soldiers false information. One of the rebels agreed, adding that it was important they provide the soldiers with some information. "If you never have anything to say, they will mark you as collaborators. The soldiers know we pass through here often."

The twin outings gave me a clear picture of guerrilla warfare and the government's challenge in attempting to counter it. The people were with the rebels and not the military.

Monterrosa was killed on October 23, 1984, when his helicopter crashed in Morazán near Joateca. Days after the crash, the FMLN claimed one of their commando teams had downed the aircraft by concentrating their fire on the rotor. This was a tactic the rebels had used before, but Luers and other rebel officials on Radio Venceremos maintained that they killed Monterrosa using a well-planned trap. Monterrosa was obsessed with destroying the station and had always insisted that the station operated from Nicaragua, but, in fact, it broadcast from Morazán, the site of his death.

"For many days we had been criticizing and mocking him," Leurs told me. He said they even suggested that Monterrosa was gay, a stinging insult in Salvadoran culture. "We calculated that this would make him even more eager to destroy us."

The rebels said they had devised an ingenious plan to lure Monterosa in. Radio Venceremos went silent for three days, leading some military leaders to believe the station had finally been knocked out. Never had Venceremos stopped transmission. Then, the guerrillas abandoned a back-up transmitter and other equipment. Monterrosa and his fellow soldiers took this as proof that Radio Venceremos was no more. The rebels, though, had hidden explosives in the transmitter. One fuse was radio-controlled; the other was set to activate when Monterrosa's chopper reached a certain altitude.

Monterrosa triumphantly flew to what he took to be Venceremos' remains. Several other commanders were with him when he had the booby-trapped equipment loaded onto the chopper. Minutes after take-off, the aircraft exploded. While some soldiers in communication with the pilot said he reported a malfunction after take-off, eyewitnesses said the chopper exploded, which would indicate an attack.

✑

After the rebels and government had battled to a draw, UN-brokered talks were held in Mexico City's Chapultepec Castle. On January 16, 1992, a treaty was signed by both parties. Government representatives were present, as were representatives of each of the five factions of the FMLN, among them FPL commander Salvador Sánchez Ceren, who would serve as El Salvador's president from 2014 to 2019.

In all, the war cost the lives of at least 70,000 people and caused an estimated one million more to flee the country. While the FMLN became a political party and had two of its candidates elected president, it had to accommodate itself to political realities. That meant adopting some neo-liberal policies in exchange for International Monetary Fund and World Bank loans. Today, El Salvador is beset by gang violence and stubborn poverty.

CHAPTER EIGHT
Guatemala: Killing Field of the Americas

MY REPORTING IN CHIAPAS on Guatemala's war refugees made me afraid to visit the country. As often happened, however, my journalistic curiosity trumped my fear, and so in early June, 1984, I organized a trip that began in Managua and ended in Guatemala City.

Minutes after landing, I got in line at Guatemala City's La Aurora Airport to clear immigration. A man and a woman in civilian clothes grabbed each of my arms and ordered me to go with them.

"What's this about?" I asked nervously.

"It's just a routine matter," the woman said.

They led me to a small room with a table, where my opened suitcase lay. I was asked to sit on one of three chairs, and the man, who identified himself and his companion as "security agents," asked why I had come to Guatemala. I replied that I was a correspondent on assignment for *Time* magazine.

From the suitcase, the woman pulled out copies of Sandinista publications. She asked why I had them.

"Because they helped me understand Nicaragua, where I have been recently."

"Okay," said the man. "Now I want you to tell us why you are really here."

This "routine matter" was becoming a threatening interrogation.

"Please let me call my embassy. I have an appointment there, and I need to let them know I will be late," I said. I did not have an appointment but decided a strategic lie was called for.

"There's no need for any phone calls," said the female agent.

"But I'm being held, and I want the people at my embassy to know," I said.

"Oh, you are not being detained," she assured me. "All you have to do is tell us the truth and you can go."

I started to fear the worst. Suddenly, the man closed my suitcase, picked it up, and he and the woman left. Several minutes elapsed. I feared security goons would soon take control of my interrogation. Instead, the couple returned and asked me to follow them. We walked to the sidewalk in front of the terminal. There was my suitcase. The man handed me my passport, which was stamped, and he told me I was free to go and hoped I enjoyed my stay.

In fact, my nerves were on edge the several days I was in the country. I was on the security radar and concerned that authorities would pick me up for more questioning at some point. My fear was well-founded. At least 342 journalists had been murdered and 126 were disappeared between 1960 and 1996 during Guatemala's civil war. My boss, Dick Duncan, had told me he had received written death threats while reporting there.

Nicholas Blake, an American freelance journalist I knew, disappeared in March 1985 while in Guatemala. Blake and I had breakfast a few months before he disappeared. He told me he planned to hike through El Quiché Department to report on the war. Blake invited me to come along.

"Nick, that's a crazy idea," I told him. "It's way too dangerous. No way am I going there. You shouldn't go either."

He chided me for being overly cautious. Intending to interview the head of the insurgent EGP, Blake hiked into Quiché with fellow American Griffith Davis. After they had disappeared, Blake's family, wealthy Republicans from Philadelphia, sought to learn his fate. Guatemalan and American government authorities knowingly and falsely blamed the guerrillas for murdering Blake and Davis.

Private investigators determined that a self-defense patrol captured the men near the village of Santa María Nebaj, shot them to death and burned their bodies. No one was punished for the crimes.

Guatemala was by far the most dangerous Central American nation for Americans. Reports in the 1980s documented the torture and killing of various American journalists and even religious by the Guatemalan military. In most cases, the US State Department's response was timid or non-existent.

The day after my arrival, I interviewed General Manuel Benedicto Lucas García brother of late Guatemalan President Fernando Romeo Lucas García and himself the ex-head of the army's general staff. He was the embodiment of the government's savage repression. He achieved notoriety during his brother's rule from 1978 to 1982, overseeing "Military Zone 21," a clandestine location used for the detention, torture, rape and execution of civilians. In 2012, the remains of hundreds of indigenous people were unearthed there.

As were many Guatemalan officers, Manuel Benedicto was a graduate of the US School of the Americas, which in the 1970s and 1980s had trained many future dictators in the repressive techniques that have been universally censured. While Manuel Bendicto enjoyed impunity for many years, finally in 2016, at the age of 83, he was charged with the crimes of illegal capture, detention, rape and torture of 19-year-old Emma Guadalupe Molina Theissen and for the crime against humanity of enforced disappearance of her 14-year-old brother, Marco Antonio Molina Theissen.

On May 23, 2018, Benedicto Lucas and several other ex-officers were found guilty and sentenced to fifty-eight years of prison.

At the time of my interview of Benedicto, he had suggested we meet over lunch at a Guatemala City restaurant. When I arrived, I walked to the booth where he sat with three other men. He smiled and motioned for me to sit next to him.

"Not too close," he warned, pointing out an Uzi machine gun at his side. "You know a lot of people would like to kill me." Several friends sat at nearby tables as security for him.

He started by chatting at length about his farm in Alta Verapaz Department. In recent weeks, he said, his security team had captured and killed a guerrilla assassination team. He then bantered with his friends in the restaurant. The Lucas García family were wealthy landowners and rabidly anti-communist. Curiously, Lucas and his friends conversed in K'iche, one of twenty-four Mayan languages spoken in Guatemala. Lucas said even non-Mayans such as himself were fluent in K'iche because so many Mayans did not speak Spanish.

I asked him about accusations that he had violated human rights.

He did not deny the allegations and instead seemed to relish his savage legacy. "I make no apologies for killing the communists who wanted to take over my country. The EGP were tough killers themselves, who wanted to create another Cuba." (The EGP was one of four armed guerrilla organizations collectively called the Guatemalan National Revolutionary Unity.)

Lucas García breezily justified human rights abuses as unavoidable. "See, the communists are following the Vietnam model. They mix civilians with combatants, thinking we won't act to avoid killing civilians. But they have been mistaken."

It was a disturbing interview. Seated next to me was a mass assassin who felt no qualms about taking innocent lives.

At the time, the war was concentrated in the far northern Quiché Department. The military had a major presence in the mountain village of Santa María Nebaj in what is known as the Ixil Triangle. The Ixil Maya have lived in the region for hundreds of years. I visited the village twice to better understand the conflict. By 1983, the EGP had been weakened, the result of relentless genocide of indigenous supporters, scorched earth policies and forced recruitment of "civilian defense forces."

The Ixil had borne the brunt of the savage counterinsurgency campaigns begun under the rule of Gen. Efrain Ríos Montt. His government determined that many Ixiil were EGP supporters. In response, starting July 8, 1982, the government launched "Operation Sofía," in which the 1st Battalion of the Guatemalan Airborne Troops was ordered to exterminate so-called subversive elements in Quiché. There was no apparent effort to selectively murder civilians; it was ethnic cleansing.

Even before Operation Sofía, the genocide was underway. In April of 1982—close to the time I reported on the Guatemalan refugees in the Chiapas jungle—there were 3,300 civilians killed, according to the Guatemala-based International Human Rights Center. During the Ríos Montt period, which spanned 1982 and 1983, government troops had already killed as many as 75,000, mostly within the first eight months between April and November 1982.

President Reagan admired the dictator, whom he met in 1982. Complaining that Ríos Montt was "getting a bum rap on human rights," Reagan called him "a man of great personal integrity," adding that Ríos Montt advocated for social justice. "My administration will do all it can to support his progressive efforts."

I made two reporting trips to Nebaj, one in June 1984, and the second in November 1985. Two American journalists, Francisco Goldman and Jean-Marie Simon, accompanied me on the first trip. Driving on unpaved roads for several hours, we wound our way into the highlands, through many Mayan villages and across creeks. The towering green Cuchumatanes mountains, sprawling fields lush with wild vegetation and villagers dressed in colorful traditional clothing had me in awe. At the same time, I knew that this was a land where thousands had died just in the last few years. That knowledge chilled me and would not allow me to revel in the natural beauty I was seeing.

We arrived at Nebaj, tucked between mountains, and arranged to stay in a rustic boarding house. Dinner had already been served, so we walked to a convenience store nearby to find something to eat and drink. Loud Andean music and the sound of men laughing filled the room as we picked out bags of chips and soft drinks that would be our dinner. Suddenly, two soldiers staggered into the store, evidently from a back room. They were quite drunk; one had two Uzi machine guns, one slung over each shoulder. He eyed us angrily.

"Who are you?" he yelled.

None of us spoke. We were stunned.

Finally, I replied that we were American journalists.

"Oh, so you're here to help the communists, huh? All you sons of whores do is write bad things about us and good things about the communists," he said, now standing menacingly in front of us.

I realized our lives might be in danger. The army was notorious for its murderous savagery, and we were two hundred miles from the capital in a remote village. It was dark, and a drunk, armed and belligerent soldier was confronting us. We had to extricate ourselves from this ugly situation.

"You are right," I blurted. "A lot of journalists don't tell the truth," I said, lying through my teeth. "This is my first time in Guatemala, and I want to find the truth and report that."

The soldier calmed down but remained wary. "Who are you going to interview?" he asked.

We had arranged to speak with the area military commander. "Oh, we have an early morning appointment with your commander."

The soldier then invited us to join him in the store's backroom and the source of the noise we had heard. When we politely declined, the soldier stubbornly insisted we accept his invitation. We stepped into the small room, where several soldiers sat on crates, drinking a popular sugar cane alcohol known by its brand name, Venado. Once we had sipped a few drinks, our hosts happily allowed us to leave. Back at the boarding house, I felt uneasy. We had told the soldiers where we were staying. What if they decided we were really guerrilla sympathizers who ought to be killed? They could have murdered us with impunity.

The next morning, we drove a few miles to a "Development Center," a government-supervised settlement inhabited by Mayans forcibly relocated there. By grouping them in one place, the thinking went, the civilian population would be cut off from the rebels. Denied popular support, the guerrilla struggle would die off. This was a copy of the "Strategic Hamlets" implemented by the United States and South Vietnam. It backfired in Vietnam when it bred popular resentment.

General Oscar Humberto Mejía Victores, president at the time of our visit, had authorized the creation of the centers and put them under the supervision of the military high command.

I interviewed families in the newly created center. All said they were unhappy to have been relocated, and they lived in fear of the soldiers.

"We lived on our farm in the mountains," Juan Domínguez, the father of four children and a subsistence farmer, told me. "When the soldiers came to take us away, they said we had been helping the guerrillas. That is a lie. We are Christians and don't believe in communism. When the guerrillas came, we had to give them some food, but it was very little because we barely had enough for ourselves."

Domínguez and others complained that the small farm plots they had been assigned were incapable of producing enough food to live on. They said the government provided them with some additional food, but it too was insufficient.

The men were required to join "self-defense patrols," militias that were supposed to act as the eyes and ears of the army. Manuel Benedicto Lucas García had created the patrols. All of those assigned to the patrols with whom I spoke were unwilling participants.

"We have to capture other *campesinos,* or the government says we are not doing our job," one member told me. "But we don't want the guerrillas to think we are fighting them."

On May 24, 1982, the army ordered patrol members to execute eleven other center members in San José Sinaché, in Quiché Department. Their crime? They complained about having to serve.

The Inter-American Commission on Human Rights found in 1985 that the development centers and self-defense patrols resulted in the violation of the right to personal security and freedom.

My next trip to Nebaj would be one of the most emotionally wrenching experiences of my life.

I arrived at the village one afternoon in early November 1985. I planned to interview residents about the second round of presidential elections. They would create the first civilian government after some thirty years of military rule.

Over the years, I had reported many pre-election stories that were meant to gauge public opinion and detect candidate preferences. However, the largely Ixil Mayan population seemed largely unaware of the election. I explained to residents that a new president would be elected, and a civilian would hold the post.

Almost everyone I talked to, after hearing my explanation, had little reaction. They said they were more concerned about seeing an end to violence and hoped for economic betterment.

Within minutes after arriving at my boarding house, two small boys and a little girl, Ixil Mayans, approached me. "We can wash your car," the larger boy offered.

I replied that the unpaved streets were muddy, so washing the vehicle would be a waste. Undaunted, he offered to shine my boots. Again, I noted that mud everywhere made this a needless task.

"How about we show you the town? We are very good guides."

I did not say the village hardly required guide services. It was clear that the tiny trio was in great need. The mountain air was cold, especially in the early morning and late afternoon. The girl was barefoot and wore a tattered dress and a thin sweater. The boys wore T-shirts but no sweater or jacket.

Manuel was the larger boy, the other his brother Martín. The little girl, María, was their sister. They did not know their ages. I guessed that Manuel was about nine, Martín, seven and María three-years-old.

I asked about their parents and where they lived.

"The soldiers killed our parents," Manuel said. He did not want to say anything more about their deaths. He went on to tell me they supported themselves by doing odd jobs around the village and lived in a room they rented. There were no relatives or responsible adults to look after them.

I was horrified and overcome with sadness. How was it possible that these three little children had to make their way in the world all alone? I had to help them. While I thought of what I could do, I asked them to go buy us some snacks and soft drinks at a store. When they returned, I gave them the equivalent of five dollars. The boys were overjoyed.

There was a Catholic Church orphanage in the village, and so we walked to it in the hope that the kids could be taken in. But a priest said there was no room for them. He added that the war had left many orphans, some of whom had to fend for themselves, just like these. The priest said that as far as he knew, the few orphanages in operation were full.

Manuel asked if I had any more work for them, and I told them I would the next day, Sunday. I was leaving Sunday afternoon. When I stepped outside early Sunday, the children were waiting for me. It was market day, and I told the boys I wanted to buy María some shoes. The only footwear on sale for little girls were plastic sandals. I bought María two pair, and she happily put on a pair right away.

Next, the boys pulled their sister aside and began talking to her earnestly in Ixil. She soon started crying.

I asked Manuel what was the matter.

"Are you married?" he asked.

I was puzzled by the question, but answered yes.

"Do you have children?" he then asked.

"I have a son and a daughter."

"How would you like to have another daughter?" asked Manuel. "We cannot take care of María, so maybe she could live with you."

I was surprised, saddened, confused.

María covered her face with her forearm and sobbed. My mind raced as I struggled to think of how best to help these children. I knew that adoption would be difficult, time-consuming and not a sure thing. I was certain I could not leave the children in their present condition. But what could I do?

I told the boys that María was not happy about being separated from them, and so adoption was not possible. I asked how much they paid in rent and food. Based on that figure, I gave Manuel the equivalent of one-hundred and twenty dollars, more than most local working people made in six months. He was thrilled. I instructed him to hide the money well, not tell anyone about it and spend it carefully.

That afternoon, I said goodbye to the children, feeling that I had not done enough. My heart told me I should have taken them with me and placed them in a secure environment, a stable home. On the other hand, I consoled myself with the knowledge that I had provided immediate relief and that, realistically, I wasn't able to do more. When I think about them now—I have never forgotten Manuel, Martín and María—I feel I should have done whatever was necessary to adopt them. And because I didn't, I feel guilty.

The Guatemalan civil war that began in 1960 and ended in 1996 with the signing of a peace treaty. Some 200,000 had been killed and 40,000 gone missing during the conflict.

Guatemala is a stunningly exotic nation, filled with natural beauty. But it is also a haunted country, a place overflowing with memories of savage atrocities. Most of the guilty have eluded punishment. And today, Guatemala is bleeding people. Since October, 2016, some 264,000 Guatemalan parents traveling with their children and unaccompanied minors have presented themselves to the US Border Patrol. Violence in much of Guatemala has prompted many to leave, but hunger and malnutrition in the northern departments of El Quiché and Huehuetenango have pushed still more north to the United States.

Reflecting on my time in Guatemala, I understand I witnessed an ongoing humanitarian catastrophe. My hope is that this tortured nation can find the path to enlightenment and social justice.

CHAPTER NINE
Cuba and Its Impossible Revolution: Myth and Reality

FIDEL CASTRO'S BROAD SMILE belied the grim and defiant speech he would deliver to a crowd of some two hundred dignitaries, Cuban officials and foreign journalists at Havana's El Cacahual Mausoleum, the resting place of independence hero Antonio Maceo.

I was among the journalists grouped some seventy feet from the Cuban leader on December 7, 1989. The sixty-three-year-old Castro had come to honor the thousands of Cubans who had died fighting in Angola and elsewhere abroad. Angolan President José Eduardo dos Santos accompanied him. On the eve of Angolan independence in 1975, Cuba had intervened militarily in support of the People's Movement for the Liberation of Angola, or MPLA. They were at war against right-wing forces, backed by the apartheid South African government.

Cuban forces stayed in Angola to support the government in its struggle with the National Union for the Total Liberation of Angola, or UNITA. South Africa supported UNITA. Cuba eventually committed 55,000 troops to the war in Angola against South African forces and their allies. At least 2,000 Cubans had died in vanquishing the South Africans.

Fidel stood on stage and began his address by recounting the long and bloody struggle in Angola and elsewhere in Africa. He spoke with a mixture of solemnity and good cheer. Then, he grew thoroughly somber as he turned to the demise of the socialist world. Of this major political shift, Castro said, ". . . we can only expect negative economic consequences for our country."

The consequences would include an end to substantial Soviet aid and in two years leave Cuba near economic collapse.

This was the second day of my first trip to Cuba. I was intensely focused on Fidel. He had with his tenor and words created a heavily dramatic atmosphere. His imposing physical stature and expressive gestures that day made him a captivating speaker. Of course, Castro was among the most charismatic leaders in modern history. Seeing him in action, however, gave me a concrete sense of how he was able to reshape a nation.

Castro, further lamenting communism's fall, said, "Imperialism and the capitalist superpowers cannot hide their euphoria over these events. They are persuaded, not without reason, that the socialist camp is virtually nonexistent at this time."

Focusing on Cuba, he thundered, "Yankee imperialism believes Cuba will not be able to resist and that the new situation created in the socialist camp will enable it to inevitably make our revolution collapse. Cuba is not a country in which socialism arrived after the victorious divisions of the Red Army," Castro noted, referring to Eastern European nations that came under Soviet control following the Second World War.

"In Cuba, we Cubans forged socialism through an authentic and heroic struggle," he said, leaning forward. "Thirty years of resistance to the most powerful empire on earth, which wanted to destroy our revolution, are a testimony of our political and moral strength."

Fidel, as Cubans usually called him, dressed in his customary green fatigues, warned of what awaited the island should it discard the revolution. "We owe everything that we are to the revolution and socialism," he said. "If capitalism returned someday to Cuba, our independence and sovereignty would disappear forever. We would be an extension of Miami, a simple appendix of the Yankee empire."

Castro invoked President John Quincy Adams, who in April of 1823 established his "Ripe Fruit" foreign policy in relation to Cuba:

> There are laws of political as well as physical gravitation; and if an apple severed by its native tree cannot choose but fall to the ground, Cuba, forcibly disjoined from its own unnatural connection with Spain, and incapable of self-support, can gravitate only towards the North American Union....
>
> There is no foreign territory of greater significance to the United States than the island of Cuba.... It has come to take on momentous importance for the political and commercial interests of our union.

Fidel, pounding the podium, proclaimed, "The disgusting prophecy of a United States president of the last century, when they were thinking about annexing our island, would be fulfilled ... An entire people will be willing to die today, tomorrow and always to prevent this from happening."

The speech would be among Castro's most memorable because it underscored the government's determination to remain at its core communist, despite the ideology facing extinction. Even today, with the implementation of some capitalist and free-market measures, Cuba is one of the few nations that firmly embraces communism.

As a longtime student of Latin America, I had for years wanted to visit Cuba and see for myself what the hemisphere's only communist nation looked and felt like. During my several days there, and over the next thirty years of traveling to all parts of the island as a journalist, academic and husband of my Cuban wife, Yoleinis, I would discover a small nation that not only has a major presence on the world stage, but is at least as complex as the United States. Being Mexican was a great advantage, as Mexico is widely beloved and admired in Cuba.

Much has been written about Cuba's rich and turbulent history, its momentous revolution and the island's acrimonious and even violent relationship with Washington.

Cuba's most significant, accurate and interesting story is told by its people. Thus, this chapter profiles some of the people who make Cuba what it is today.

The Original Revolutionaries

I spoke to Rolando Bezos one summer afternoon in 2013 as he steered his Soviet Lada sedan past the Museum of the Revolution, a building in the grand style of a nineteenth-century opera house. He sighed, recalling the bloody battle that broke out there fifty years earlier. Bezos, then an idealistic university student, belonged to an armed group that shook Cuba for several violent hours.

"Today it is almost impossible to accept that I was involved in such things," he said, a look of wonderment coming over him.

Angular with stringy hair and thick glasses, Bezos, now 84, scratched out a living prowling Havana's tumbledown streets, searching for tourists who needed a ride. Bezos is a cousin of Miguel Bezos, Jeff Bezos's adoptive father.

Starting in 1957, he was a comrade-in-arms to Fidel Castro, then battling to overthrow the Fulgencio Batista dictatorship. Castro and other rebels waged war from the Sierra Maestra Mountains in the east. As a member of the Revolutionary Directorate, Bezos and his companions formed an urban cell that organized protests and engaged government forces in numerous clashes. In one gruesome incident, Batista agents captured several Directorate members on a downtown street and immediately executed them. That atrocity and years of cruel dictatorship fueled an uprising that could not be extinguished.

Bezos and some eighty comrades were determined to avenge the crime. They spent only a few weeks plotting Batista's assassination. On March 13, 1957, the student insurgents launched a mid-afternoon armed assault on the presidential palace and a radio station.

The dictator learned of the plot but did not know when the attack would come. He stationed extra guards at his palace, now the elegant museum. Batista also had reserve troops posted nearby. The attackers arrived in cars, piled out and rushed the palace, shooting. Government reinforcements soon arrived, while another wave of attackers became locked in a street battle far from the residence.

The attack was snuffed out, leaving thirty-five rebels and five soldiers dead. Bezos said he spent the rest of the insurrection in jail. He and his comrades were freed on January 9, 1959, the day Castro's army rode into Havana.

Cruising through central Havana, Bezos criticized the government. "Look at this place," he said, waving at the blocks of decaying and crumbling buildings, some in ruins.

"What kind of government can't keep its capital from falling apart? This symbolizes how Fidel and his boys took a beautiful ideal—the creation of true democracy and prosperity for people living in misery—and turned it into crap," he said in a tone of raw disgust.

Nearby, in a quiet University of Havana office, Clinton Adlum was also back at the scene of his own youthful revolutionary deeds. A little older than his lifelong friend Castro, Adlum was dapper and lean and spoke English in the clipped accent of his Jamaican parents. Some 100,000 West Indians had settled in Cuba during the early 1900s.

Adlum, too, risked his life for a new Cuba. As a university activist, he defied Batista's death squads, responsible for thousands of killings. After graduation and with the anti-Batista movement growing, Adlum landed a job at the officer's club on the US Naval Base at Guantanamo. Soon, his real occupation was to spy on the movements of Batista's army and air force, which used the base for resupply. The activity indicated planned government offensives, valuable intelligence for the insurgents.

Courtly and ever-smiling, Adlum would go on to a career in espionage for the Cuban government. In 2004, he expressed with delicacy and whimsy his own disillusionment at modern-day Cuba: "As a black man who grew up poorer than you can imagine, I knew we had to change Cuba. I never doubted that the revolution would triumph. When it did, we all got swept away with this utopian notion that you could discard every bit of capitalism," said Adlum, smiling broadly. "You know what? We even did away with things as basic as inventory control or any serious accounting, saying that the new Cuban man and woman could be trusted not to steal. That alone was enough to bring the economy to ruin."

Spanish-born Eloy Gutiérrez Menoyo, another participant in the insurgency, looked across the gargantuan Plaza of the Revolution one drowsy afternoon in 2004. It was the site of mass rallies where Castro delivered stirring speeches soon after the Revolution's triumph. In those days, a million or more people would converge to hear their leader denounce the deposed regime and promise democracy and economic development. Gutiérrez, a wiry chain-smoker, who died in 2012, said he never imagined he would return to this revolutionary shrine.

His parents were active Republicans in the Spanish Civil War and fled to Cuba in 1945 following Francisco Franco's rise to power. He and his brother, Carlos, were among the March 13ᵗʰ group that sought to kill Batista. Carlos, who helped lead the attack, was killed. Eloy escaped and made his way to the Escambray Mountains. There, he formed a guerrilla force allied with Castro's called the Second Revolutionary Front of the Escambray.

Gutiérrez fought valiantly. His soldiers, having vanquished Batista's last troops, marched into Havana through what would become the revolution's plaza, just ahead of Castro's own forces. Nevertheless, within a couple of years, Gutiérrez broke with the government. He charged it had betrayed the struggle's democratic ideals by veering into communism.

Alienated and angry, Gutiérrez moved to Florida. There, he rallied exiles and formed Alpha 66, a group dedicated to the violent toppling of the Cuban government. From bases in Florida and the Bahamas, Alpha 66 launched armed raids, mainly shooting up commercial ships in Cuban waters.

In December 1964, Gutiérrez and his followers landed in Cuba, intent on fomenting a popular uprising. Instead, government troops captured all the invaders within a few weeks. Officials convicted and jailed Gutiérrez. He was imprisoned for twenty-two years. Gutiérrez said prison guards frequently beat him, breaking numerous bones.

Upon his release and return to Florida, the combatant became a man of peace, calling for dialogue between Castro and his enemies. Ostracized by hardline anti-Castro activists who shunned talks in favor of force, Gutiérrez lived in Havana since 2003, openly pursuing a quixotic and unsuccessful goal: the creation of an opposition political party.

During our chat, he described Cuba as an economic and political wreck, the consequence of a "bankrupt" dictatorship. "On January 1, 1959, our island seemed to have vanquished all of the forces of evil," said Gutiérrez. "We had a slogan that was on everyone's lips: 'Liberty with food and food without terror. . . . The food never materialized, and the liberties denied have become intolerable."

Bezos, Adlum and Gutiérrez scarcely knew each other. However, they agreed that Cuba was undergoing a profound transformation, even as Fidel Castro remained in power. It was becoming a new, tough and, for the first time in its 110 years of sovereignty, truly independent nation.

For a time, the change appeared to be a true transformation. Castro was politically weaker than he had ever been. He and his government had seen their hold of the country ebb, as years of economic crisis and political isolation sapped the government's strength. The state's ability to stoke the economy, generate international trade and provide new jobs had tumbled since the early 1990s, a trend that continues. Today, Cuba is in the midst of a severe economic crisis, perhaps its worst in modern history.

However, several years ago, trade with Hugo Chávez's Venezuela and a boom in American tourism, thanks to the Obama Administration's normalization of ties, gave the economy a boost. But now, Venezuela's dire economic and political crisis and the Trump Administration's return to outright hostility toward Havana have left growing numbers of Cubans, living hand-to-mouth, forging their own economic reality. Many thousands of other Cubans are in nightmarish limbo at the United States-Mexico border, hoping for political asylum in the United States. The Biden Administration has yet to define its Cuba policy.

During a June 2018 trip to the island, I found people in a somber mood, compared to the year before. My in-laws, Edy Vega and Jorge Mena, told me that the combination of food scarcity and high prices had made life harder than it had been in many years. Since then, conditions have deteriorated further with the rationing of many goods. Gasoline and diesel fuel have all but disappeared, with motorists waiting in lines to gas up. Long lines for food that demand hours of waiting are now common. Our family sends my in-laws money that ameliorates their situation.

I have seen Cuba in profound economic distress. That was in August 1993, when I reported and wrote a series on the crisis that hit following the end of Soviet aid. It was what Fidel warned about in his December 7th speech.

The characteristic tropical shroud draped over Havana was charged with an eerie buzz. Everyone in the capital seemed to sense tension, as though something momentous, perhaps catastrophic, was in the offing. Night and day, people of all ages hung out in the streets. Some gathered in groups, speaking guardedly. Others sat alone, staring at the ground or toward the Caribbean Sea that stretches to Florida. They all seemed to have turned out for an impending event, one that had yet to define itself.

Cuba was in what officials called "a special period in times of peace," or in its briefer, more euphemistic term, "the special period." What made the days and months "special" was an economy that shriveled by a third in only three years. It was the most calamitous financial collapse the world had seen in decades.

The crash was sparked by the dissolution of the Soviet Union, Cuba's primary benefactor. Moscow had bought Cuban sugar and sold Cuba oil at subsidized prices, resulting in the equivalent of roughly three billion dollars of annual aid. With that help gone overnight, Cuba's centralized and hugely inefficient economy was just barely functioning. Most factories were closed, leaving hundreds of thousands of workers with nothing to do but while away their time outside. Shortages of everything from basic food items to electricity and gasoline and school supplies unleashed a muted desperation among Cubans, especially those in control of running the country.

"We are in danger of the Revolution collapsing," said Angel Pino, a foreign ministry official who had just returned from a tour of duty in Cuba's Washington diplomatic mission.

One fact summed up the magnitude of the crisis: Cuba, heavily dependent on imported oil, had just three days' worth of reserves left. The country was all but broke.

"Vietnam, seeing our situation, offered to donate a shipload of rice, recalled Armando Brinis, one of many officials charged with keeping the nation afloat. "I thought it was wonderful news until I figured out we did not have the money to pay for the shipping costs."

Olga Fernández, a foreign ministry official, invited me to dinner at her home. Relying on candles to light the dining room—the power had been out all day—Olga served a large avocado split in half. Olga, her husband Claude and I savored it. I expected a main course, but the avocado was all that was served. Olga said nothing. I understood there was not anything else *to serve*.

Thousands of other Cubans slipped into the sea on crude rafts, hoping to avoid sharks and deadly exposure to reach Florida and economic rescue. The exodus grew, as Cuban officials did little to stop it, explaining that patrol boats lacked fuel.

Cuba analysts saw the moribund economy, the burst of rioting and the mass human outflow as clear evidence that the Castro regime was on its last legs. Journalist and longtime Cuba watcher Andrés Oppenheimer even wrote a book, *Castro's Final Hour*, describing the looming collapse of the island's political system.

Although conventional wisdom suggested that outcome, the government Fidel Castro had created, now badly battered, would still be standing more than twenty years later. Castro built a reputation on his ability to overcome adversity and turn setbacks to his advantage. This time, he relied on his brother Raúl, head of Cuba's armed forces, and economics minister Carlos Lage to make what for communist Cuba were major changes. Raúl had transformed the military into a self-sufficient organization by having soldiers farm. Lage was widely respected as an economic genius, but one who had to work within the strict limits of socialism. Now, Castro gave them a larger say in resuscitating the country. Lage, once considered a possible successor to Fidel, was later sacked for reasons that are unclear. It is rumored his ambitious maneuvering for the post cost him his job. In a written statement released when he was dismissed, Lage wrote, "I recognize the errors committed and assume responsibility."

In July, 1993 Cubans were suddenly allowed to circulate dollars, prompting an infusion of millions in remittances from family and friends abroad. Cuban leaders courted foreign investors, and soon there was a boom in the tourist industry. As suddenly as they were approved, dollars ceased to legally circulate. In their place, Cuban officials introduced the convertible peso or CUC. The traditional Cuban peso remained but was not accepted at stores that sold imported goods. In October, 2019, Cuban authorities legalized the use of ten foreign currencies, including the dollar. It all made for a monetary maze.

Foreign vacationers poured in, drawn by the island's pristine beaches and little-known Spanish colonial towns and cities. Cuban citizens, meanwhile, were permitted to open private restaurants and establish other small businesses. Farmers were encouraged to sell their produce at special markets where supply and demand set the price.

While remaining socialist at its core, Cuba embraced a hodgepodge of economic reforms, averting collapse and even regaining some lost ground. However, the current economic woes, which include increased and severe rationing of consumer goods and electricity compounded by tightened American sanctions, suggest greater hardships up ahead.

The Chronicler

It was 1953. The country was stirring with reports of rebellious university radicals intent on toppling the Batista dictatorship. No group had succeeded in forging ties to working-class Cubans. Instead, the agitators were almost exclusively students or intellectuals. Fidel Castro, a recent law school grad, was among those organizing violent opposition. He would be among the first to strike a blow against Batista.

Castro and his fellow revolutionaries, including his brother Raúl, hatched a foolhardy plan to take over La Moncada military barracks in Santiago de Cuba. From the start, the assault was a fiasco. Fidel and his guerrilla companions were lightly armed, some with puny .22 caliber rifles, and were haphazardly organized. They faced a well-armed garrison with excellent defensive positions behind high concrete walls.

The attack was launched on July 26, 1953, now known as the Day of the Revolution and commemorated with a huge parade. But there was little to celebrate after the assault was easily turned back. Government soldiers shot and killed several of the rebels. Seventy of the attackers, including the Castro brothers, were captured. Some had been wounded; reportedly many prisoners were tortured.

Rookie reporter Marta Rojas was working in her native Santiago de Cuba, the nation's second-largest city on the eastern end of the island. She was at a carnival with friends when they heard popping noises. "I thought, *It must be fireworks,*" she recalled. But then she and the others, also journalists, ran toward the sound and witnessed the historic event. She turned in her story to *Bohemia,* a magazine. That story and others Rojas would write were censored.

Trials for Castro and his co-conspirators loomed. It was certain they would be found guilty and likely be sentenced to long prison terms. But in what would be a trademark practice, the future national leader played his prison time for all it was worth, organizing political meetings behind bars and plotting his defense. Largely through the power of his commanding presence—he stood over six-feet and was broad—and charisma, he became a celebrity prisoner.

When the trials began, Marta was in the courtroom. She and others present would see history made. Castro, who as a student radical at the University of Havana had a reputation as a rousing orator, he was also a lawyer. As soon as the trial began, Castro objected to one thing after another, often winning concessions. Rojas recalled that the judge seemed overmatched by the quick-witted and legally skillful Castro.

His golden moment came during his summary statement, what would come to be called his "History Will Absolve Me" speech, a four-hour-long and devastating indictment of the regime. In detailing the grotesque corruption, routine brutality and crushing economic inequality, Castro was justifying his armed assault on Batista's dictatorship.

"When we talk about 'the people,' we are not referring to the well-off and conservative sectors of the nation" proclaimed Castro, "for whom any repressive regime, any dictatorship, any despotism is convenient; who kneel before whichever master . . . What we understand by 'the people,' when we speak of the struggle, is the great unredeemed mass, who are cheated and betrayed, who long for a better, more dignified, more just homeland . . . who are moved by an ancestral thirst for justice because they have suffered injustice and have been mocked generation after generation."

Castro predicted that the regime would collapse. The future Cuban leader was sentenced to fifteen years in prison. But his fame and legendary stature were assured. The son of a well-off farmer, Castro became the symbol of hope for a Cuba free of Batista. In prison, he and his fellow revolutionaries plotted their next move. Political pressure led Batista to release Castro and the other prisoners on May 15, 1955.

Castro headed for exile in Mexico City. There he organized what he was confident would be a triumphant return and rapid armed toppling of the Batista government. His ideology was leftist and of a nationalist bent. The communist Castro either had not yet evolved or was in the closet. Biographers are not sure which it was.

For Rojas, the Moncada trial forged a lifelong professional relationship with the future world figure. "I was, extremely impressed with him," she recalled. "Here I was, a young woman from a city far removed from Havana. Covering the trial, listening to him speak, I concluded I was seeing a future leader of my country."

History would bring them together again.

Fidel returned on December 2, 1956, with eighty-two of his followers, among them the legendary Argentine revolutionary Ernesto "Che" Guevara. They had sailed from Veracruz, Mexico several days earlier aboard a decrepit pleasure boat, "Granma," so named by the American who sold it in honor of his grandmother.

It was a disastrous landing. Government soldiers hit them almost as soon as they came ashore. Several of Castro's followers were killed and most of the survivors scattered. As he and a few followers lay in tall grass, their weapons lost, Castro declared that victory was within grasp.

In an implausible turn in fortunes, Castro and his followers regrouped, recruited peasant fighters in the Sierra Maestra and developed into a credible fighting force. Castro and his comrades had only rudimentary military training in the Mexican mountains, and none had ever engaged in combat. Before long, they had overrun military outposts. The victories added weapons and supplies to his army. Equally important, the rebels released prisoners they had taken in battle, showing they were compassionate.

Intrepid Rojas, pursuing the story of the insurgency, took to the mountains and found Castro and his guerrilla army, which numbered no more than several hundred.

One day in 2005, she showed me dozens of black and white photos of Fidel and his army. In most, Fidel was wearing dark, horned-rimmed glasses and a beard, giving him a beatnik look. He seemed happy, smiling and greeting campesinos.

The time in the mountains, talking to the hearty farmers about the Cuba he hoped to create, battling the Batista forces, was his happiest. He was several years away from the Cuban missile crisis, the CIA's cruel war on Cuba and the everyday travails of running a country considered by some a pariah.

Almost before anyone knew it, the revolutionaries swept down from the mountains, chasing Batista's soldiers before them. In the middle of a gala 1959 New Year's Eve celebration, Batista, his family and inner circle boarded a Miami-bound plane. The next day, *los barbudos,* or bearded ones as all called the unshaken guerrillas, paraded into Havana. A new Cuba was born.

The first few months and years of the revolution were without question Cuba's most dramatic, heady, violent and patently historic. Rojas had a front-row seat as the island was convulsed and intoxicated by the raw power of revolutionary fervor. Enemies of the state were executed, the old capitalists overturned, uprooted.

"We all seemed to know we were living through a profound and historic time," said Rojas. "The Cuba we knew, the one we had grown up in, was gone, and a new way of life would take its place."

With dizzying speed, Cuba and the United States not only severed diplomatic and economic ties, Washington imposed an asphyxiating trade embargo, still in place today. It also launched a CIA-directed war, highlighted by the Bay of Pigs fiasco. "Operation Mongoose" was the CIA's clandestine offensive against revolutionary Cuba. The effort featured numerous attempts to assassinate Castro, economic sabotage and destabilization of the government. Its foot soldiers were pulled from the ranks of anti-revolutionary Cuban immigrants who operated from the CIA's covert Miami station. By law, the agency was banned from having domestic outposts. But when it came to Castro-ruled Cuba, the United States was to develop a fast-and-loose attitude.

Castro's Cuba, meanwhile, was morphing from a classically bourgeois, white-ruled Latin-America society into an egalitarian, multi-racial socialist system. The barriers of race and class were taken down, Rojas said.

In what would be a historic shift, Cuba forged an alliance with the Soviet Union and its communist client states. "It meant that we would be involved in the Cold War much more emphatically," said Rojas. "Being socialist and not bowing down to Washington meant we would be treated as danger-

198 / *Ricardo Chavira*

ous outcasts. The ties to the Soviets meant we were an even greater threat."

The Cuban Missile Crisis reshaped Cuba. The United States for the first—and so far, only—time came to the brink of the nuclear holocaust after Cuba successfully urged the Soviets to set up nuclear missile sites aimed at the United States. The Soviet move was meant to counter America's own sites in Turkey pointed at the USSR and to deter further US aggression against Cuba.

President John F. Kennedy and Soviet Premier Nikita Khrushchev were on a collision course, with neither one willing to back down. Unless there was some movement, the Cold War adversaries might obliterate each other.

"In the historical accounts, nobody seems to have taken note of what we in Cuba were going through," Rojas said. "We were facing extermination. The missiles were here. The United States would have attacked the sites."

At the Hotel Nacional in downtown Havana, Luisa, an employee, pointed out on a model the bomb shelters tunneled into the cliff on the grounds. "I was a child, and we were brought to the tunnels," she said. "Our teachers told us we would have to go there if war started. It is not something you forget."

The crisis was settled when the United States agreed not to invade Cuba in exchange for the Soviets removing the missiles. Kennedy also secretly agreed to remove American missile installations in Turkey. Rojas chronicled all this early drama on the pages of *Granma*, the government's daily newspaper.

Cuba in the coming years would take on a world stage presence far greater than its size. As an exponent of colonial liberation and Third World revolution, Cuba became embroiled in numerous insurgencies well into the 1980s.

The revolution took an unexpected turn, when in early 1965 Guevara disappeared. Having led the literacy campaign and trained many of the soldiers who repelled the Bay of Pigs invaders, Guevara was assumed to wield great power. But he had grown alienated from the Soviet Union and indirectly said so in a speech and explicitly in private, writing that the Soviets had "Forgotten Marx." Castro, however, was determined to remain linked to the Soviets. His split with Castro was never revealed at home and is not widely known even today.

During Guevara's absence from Cuba, Castro publicly read a letter purportedly written by Che in which he bid farewell to Cuba and renounced his Cuban citizenship. He did not reveal his future intentions. In secret, Guevara and a contingent of Cubans sought to lead a Congolese insurgency. When that attempt failed, Guevara took on what would prove a foolish mission to spark armed struggle in Bolivia. Guevara was unsuccessful in forging an alliance with Bolivian leftists. Bolivians, despite their dire poverty, were not willing to engage in an insurgency. Still, Che forged ahead, unaware that CIA and Bolivian special forces were tracking him.

The campaign was a fiasco that ended with Guevara wounded but captured alive by Bolivian troops under the leadership of CIA operative and anti-Castro Cuban Félix Rodríguez. Bolivian President René Barrientos ordered Guevara's execution.

Guevara's death elevated him to revolutionary martyr status. Decades after his death, his face and identity are known worldwide. El Che was powerfully charismatic and inspirational, Rojas said. His miscalculations in the Congo and Bolivia were simply the product of revolutionary zeal and, thus, understandable.

Ever the intrepid reporter, Rojas secured an assignment to cover the Vietnam War as a guest of the Viet Cong. It would prove a dramatic period in her life.

"I was in Vietnam for several months, all of them in the South," she recounted, her eyes twinkling as she recalled the daring journalistic adventure. "All of it was amazing. There was always the danger of attack. The first time I heard planes overhead, I hit the ground looking for shelter. The Vietnamese laughed and told me that the bombs would have hit before I heard the planes."

The most searing memory she brought back was the knowledge that a Third World people could withstand the force and fury of the United States. "This was a lesson that I shared all over Cuba. We had not suffered anything as they had. It really opened our eyes to what the Americans could do to a poor country and what that country, if united, could do in response."

Rojas chronicled her country's armed and logistical support for liberation movements, primarily in Africa. The experience further amazed her and deepened her pride in Cuba. "When we came to help black Africans fight white South Africans, we saw how unequal the struggle was and we determined to do what we could to make the fight equal."

Castro and other Cuban leaders dispatched thousands of Cuban troops to Angola. There they met head-on white South African troops intent on wiping out the black African National Congress guerrillas affiliated with Nelson Mandela and their Angolan patrons. Several Afro-Cuban veterans of the war told me that they felt a strong connection with their African allies. "We are the same people, we just lived in different countries," said Rafael Mesa, one of the veterans.

The Cubans, who suffered thousands of casualties, were key to fighting the Afrikaners to a draw. That, in turn, led to a negotiated settlement that involved the United States, South

Africa and Cuba. It ensured the end of the fighting and withdrawal of Cuban forces. American diplomats involved in the talks, who I interviewed during my time as a diplomatic correspondent, were astonished that the Cubans honored the agreement.

Today, Rojas, now in her nineties, spends her time writing historical novels. Through the years of economic hardship and non-stop hostility with the superpower just to the north, Rojas has kept remarkably good cheer. To be sure, she has modest perks her legendary stature affords her. For example, she has a new, if tiny, Korean car and permission to travel abroad. But Rojas remains seemingly unaffected by what she has witnessed and lived through.

She laughed at the improbability of a small, underdeveloped nation casting such a large international shadow. "I guess that has been our destiny because we Cubans are people with a dramatic history. From the time the Spanish arrived more than four hundred years ago, we have gone from one momentous event to another. The only thing we don't know for sure is what the future will bring. But it will for sure be sweeping and change Cuba once again."

The Spy

As a student at the University of Havana in the early 1950s, Clinton Adlum was a schoolmate of Fidel Castro. But unlike the tall, strapping and white Castro, Adlum was a smallish black man. That meant that Adlum, a Guantánamo native, lived in a world quite different from Castro's.

Cuba was virulently racist. There was no Ku Klux Klan or lynchings, but Jim Crow-like practices were a fact. Blacks were banned from many public places, and it was virtually impossible for any to achieve professional success. Sports and entertainment were the only fields open to them, just as was true in the United States. Black Cubans were disproportionately poor, often desperately so. Open animosity and suspicion greeted blacks whenever they found themselves in white Cuba.

Upon graduation with a business degree, a rarity for a black man, Adlum went job-hunting in Havana. He was turned away everywhere he applied. "I remember that the American companies, like Chase-Manhattan, were the most open in showing me the door without so much as an interview. There were no black people in white-collar jobs, and I would not be an exception," Adlum said. "Even classmates who were sympathetic told me I was crazy to try finding a decent job."

Eventually, he found work as assistant manager of the officers' club at the US Naval Base in Guantánamo. "I kept track of inventory and made sure the service was good. I was really overqualified, but that was the best job I could find here in those years."

But Adlum was able to parlay the job into much more than seeing to it that American officers were fed and served drinks. He, like many other young, educated Cubans, chafed under the rule of the Americans' puppet, Batista. Adlum would not say if he took the job simply because it was all that he could find, or for the exceptional fringe benefits it offered. In fact, through clandestine contacts, he was recruited to spy on Cuban government operations at the US base. Batista's troops and planes were resupplied at Guantánamo, and Adlum secretly passed along the information to the guerrillas.

It was valuable intelligence because it signaled government military operations. Adlum spied for several months, but he picked up signs that base counterintelligence agents were suspicious of the unassuming assistant manager. He then slipped away and went to the Sierra Maestra Mountains, where he fought during the last months of the war.

Soon after Castro assumed power, Adlum was given a diplomatic post in Suriname, then a Dutch dependency. Largely rainforest and not of any apparent strategic importance, it would seem an odd posting for a country with a modest-sized diplomatic corps. Cuba, however, faced challenges in the political atmosphere just after the revolutionaries began their rule. Latin America was in a ruinous state, thanks in large part to dishonest, dictatorial regimes. Poverty and misery were a way of life for most in the region, and there were no signs that anything would change. The United States was reasonably content to overlook these injustices so long as it was able to extract the oil, coffee, bananas and whatever else its big companies desired without any interference.

Cuban revolutionaries were determined to shake things up, just as they had done in their homeland. They were convinced that other nations could oust dictatorial regimes and transfer power to the masses. Many African lands were European colonies. Liberation meant not just toppling indigenous governments but breaking colonial shackles as well. It was in that context that Adlum went to Suriname. The backwater, even under benevolent Dutch colonial rule, was ripe for revolution—or so the Cubans thought.

Adlum strongly hinted from time to time that his real work had little to do with diplomacy. In reality, he was a spy and agent of influence, a person whose mission it was to learn everything and create friendly feelings toward Cuba. He joined a robust network of Cuban spies assigned diplomatic posts all over the world. In Suriname, Adlum quietly began offering political guidance to would-be insurgents. Eventually, a leftist, pro-Cuban government led by Desi Bouterse took power.

Adlum's tour in Suriname was followed by stints in several other countries that Cuba considered important. Among his most interesting was an eight-year stay in Baghdad. There he got to know Saddam Hussein and other key members of the Baathist Party. "They were extremely secretive men and very disciplined in what they chose to say," he noted, smiling.

"In those years, we Cubans and the Iraqis had the common experience of having to contend with a superpower, the United States, who wished to see us disappear. Later, that would change for a time during the Iraq-Iran war," said Adlum. "It was amazing and instructive to see how the North Americans could turn around and support Iraq with intelligence information and secret aid. Then came Desert Storm, and again the United States was bent on destroying Iraq. We did our best to warn them. We told them, from our experience, you can tease the lion, but you can't poke him. Saddam thanked us for our advice, and the rest is history."

Adlum's last tour was in Washington as a political officer and press attaché at his country's diplomatic mission. We got to know each other in 1989 while I was a diplomatic correspondent with *Time*. I was constantly reporting on a wide range of foreign policy matters. Consequently, I was assigned to report on an unusual trial just completed in Havana. It had significant foreign policy overtones.

Arnaldo Ochoa, a popular division general in the Revolutionary Armed Forces, twin brothers Antonio "Tony" de la Guardia, a colonel in the interior ministry, and Patricio de la Guardia, a general, and two other security officials had recently been shot by a firing squad. Their crimes were varied, but the most serious involved drug dealing and corruption, specifically taking bribes from Colombian cocaine traffickers. Several other officials have over the years been arrested or banished into obscurity after it was learned they used their position for personal gain. Former Foreign Minister Roberto Robaina, for example, was sacked and sent to a re-education center when it came to light that he and his wife engaged in off-the-books business deals with a Mexican governor charged with drug trafficking.

At about the same time the drama played out in Havana, Adlum was carrying on a cat-and-mouse game with American intelligence agents in Washington. It was a struggle to keep Panamanian strongman Manuel Noriega in power. While the Cubans had no illusions about the general's brutish and venal nature, he served their purposes by allowing them to bank and buy American goods in Panama.

Adlum and a handful of operatives in Washington and Panama City were advising the dictator in organizing popular armed resistance to the expected American invasion. But when the 82nd Airborne and more than 20,000 other US forces—some based in the country-invaded Panama on December 20, 1989, resistance was weak and disorganized. Cuba had lost a valuable outpost, and Adlum accepted the setback with a philosophical shrug.

The colorful Adlum, supposedly beyond his diplomatic duties, struck up a romantic relationship with an African-American woman foreign service officer based at the US State Department. He has always insisted that it was strictly an affair of the heart. My frequent suggestions that he benefited from pillow talk were always greeted by hearty laughter—but no denial.

Adlum did perhaps his most beneficial work on Cuba's behalf by cultivating close ties to African-American communities around the United States. The Rev. Jesse Jackson and actor Danny Glover were among the prominent blacks who became his friends. His farewell party at Cuba's diplomatic mission, which I attended, drew African-Americans from all over the United States.

Today, beleaguered as ever, the revolution survives. It has a new leader, Miguel Díaz Canel, but it still is Castro's Cuba. And Cubans are still acutely aware of the dictatorial nature of their government. Yet there is almost no speculation about wholesale corruption of the kind so common in Latin America. "The revolution has been unwavering in enforcing discipline," said Adlum. "To be frank, it has many faults, but tolerating corruption or allowing outsiders to buy government influence is not one of them."

Returning to the topic of the armed forces arrests, trials and executions, Adlum said they shook the government to its core. "This was an extremely grave situation. It exposed that we had lost control of some things. We had key officials making deals with (drug lord) Pablo Escobar," he said. "It gave our enemies a golden opportunity to say we were involved in drug dealing."

The incident also fed rampant speculation that the Castro government was coming apart. Journalist and author Andrés Oppenheimer used the affair as the basis for *Castro's Final Hour*. In it, Oppenheimer contended that the Ochoa scandal was only one of many fatal missteps that gave the government at most "a few years" before it collapsed.

Adlum smiled at the wild miscalculation. "Cuba is a small country, and that sometimes leads even smart people to think it's a banana republic. What they don't keep in mind is that we have honed our political survival skills to a very high level, thanks to Washington's incessant efforts to undermine us. Our opponents have nothing to lose. We have everything to lose. That explains why the revolution continues to exist. It's why Cuba continues to make its way in the world."

The Returnee

Cuban-Americans older than 80 typically recall pre-Castro Cuba as an emerging nation, rich with consumer goods and career opportunities. Cuba was the first Latin American country to enjoy color TV broadcasts, they boast, clear evidence of its enviable standard of living. Whatever the merits of luxury TV, it is true that Cuba in the 1950s had a healthy and growing middle class.

The trouble was that it had an even larger and faster-growing underclass, millions who lived in dire poverty. Successive governments were content to see most Cubans destitute and marginalized. Millions of peasants were virtual serfs, and the urban poor confronted chronically high unemployment and paltry pay. The old immigrants, who formed the economic and political elite, could afford to view their Cuba as a place of luxury and promise.

For old Cubans who stayed in their country, the memories are entirely different. Alfonso González, who died in 2013, was one such Cuban. For him and others of his era, crushing poverty and hopelessness plagued Cuba several decades ago. They offer the flip side to the Miami version of Cuba's halcyon days.

González, who operated a Havana bed and breakfast establishment, was born into poverty. When he was eight, his father died, leaving his mother to raise him and his two younger brothers in Havana.

"Our situation was not good," González, a gregarious retiree, recalled. "My mother was illiterate, and the only job she could find was taking in laundry. She was from the country, where only the wealthy lived well. In Havana, my mother could get the most work, but as much as she tried, we were not making it."

An uncle in Tampa stepped in to offer help by having Alfonso live with him. It would mean a ten-year trip and the start of young Alfonso's lifelong love affair with the United States.

For decades before Miami became the center of Cuban life in the United States, Tampa filled that role. Its many cigar factories drew thousands of Cuban tobacco workers. Some migrated between Havana's plants and Tampa's. Easy immigration regulation made the trips possible. Many Cuban cigar makers, among them González's uncle, decided to settle in Tampa, and within the city, Ybor City developed as a predominantly Cuban community.

Young Alfonso rapidly adapted to his new environment, learning English and developing an easy familiarity with mainstream culture. His uncle was married to a Sicilian, who spoke no Spanish. So, the boy, unlike most Cuban immigrants, used Spanish sparingly. "In a lot of ways, I got to be a regular American kid," González said with a grin.

He sold newspapers after school. After the United States joined the Allies in the Second World War, his paper sales skyrocketed. "I remember that when the United States started winning, my sales went up even more," said González, who sent almost all his modest earnings to his mother.

Soon after graduating from high school, however, new circumstances forced him to return home. His uncle's son married and brought his bride to live in the house. "All of a sudden," González said, "the home was pretty crowded, and the situation felt awkward. I knew it was time for me to leave."

It was a bittersweet homecoming. While glad to be reunited with his mother and brothers, he confronted the same bleak reality he had left. His mother remained mired in poverty, doing laundry.

"I had a dream of going to a university, but we had no money. I was 18, and my duty was to work to help my mother." An uncle who owned a grocery store provided a job that paid one peso a day. González worked six-and-half days a week and slept in the store to provide security.

He would labor at the job for five years, always giving his mother most of his pay. During that period, González recalled, he had to make a trip to a provincial city. "I took the train, and it was the first time I had been out into the country. It turned out to be a shocking experience. Every place we stopped, hundreds of people would crowd around the train. They were dressed in rags—not even real clothes—that just hung from their skinny bodies. They were begging for anything at all. What I saw scared me. So, when I hear that old Cubans in Miami say that everything was wonderful in those days, I get really indignant."

González went to work for another uncle who owned a bar. His pay, however, remained the same: 30 pesos a month. A brother, meanwhile, took a job like his. Now both were contributing to their mother's welfare.

"It was a constant struggle for all of us. Many, many Cubans were in the same situation. We would work as hard as we could, and we stayed poor," he said.

In a bid to land a better job, González, then 23, took night business classes and landed a secretarial job with Remington-Rand, an American business machine firm.

"I felt I had hit the lottery," he said laughing. "You see, I got my salary doubled to 60 pesos a month."

The good fortune lasted just six months. His American bosses fired him when they decided his job and others were expendable. He next went to work selling life insurance door to door, a job that produced little income.

"Most people," he said, "worried about today and tomorrow. Worrying about dying was too much of a luxury."

Finally, González caught a break. His brother worked as an accountant at an air conditioning factory and brought González on board as an assistant accountant. Not long after starting his new job, Castro took power. One of the immediate consequences was that González got a large raise. He was now earning 138 pesos a month.

There was more. With the new revolutionary government advocating education, González's bosses urged him to get a college degree. He did so by studying nights.

"For the first time in our lives, we as a family had enough money for little luxuries, like lunch at restaurants. But the most important thing is that we were able to buy our mother a refrigerator, the first one she ever owned," said González. With a degree in hand, he was making 250 pesos a month as an accountant. In time, he came to head the accounting department.

"We had some good years as a country," González argued. "Yes, it was the result of the Soviets helping us. Still, our jobs paid us enough to buy what we needed, and there were many things to buy. Once the Soviet Union died, we almost did, too."

The disastrous economic collapse took a terrible toll, he admitted. "Almost overnight there was nothing to eat, nothing in the stores. I remember we would brew orange tree leaves because we did not have coffee. We were eating once a day, and not very much."

Looking over the last decades, the former Tampa resident said he learned that Cubans are incredibly resilient: "Just look at how we overcame Spanish colonial rule, American domination and attempts to subvert the country. We are a small country and island, with few natural resources. We have many problems. Which Latin American country does not? Still, here we are still standing. People here do not die for lack of medical care. Even in your country people must worry about how they will pay medical expenses. I do not know what the map looks like, but I do know we Cubans will find the road to prosperity and build a better country in the coming years."

As for Americans, González had only good things to say. Indeed, he hosted many Americans at his bed and breakfast. "I have the American people in my heart forever. They received me warmly when I was a young boy. The government is a different story. I do not confuse the American people with their government. The day is not far off when we Cubans and Americans will be reunited in friendship."

The People on the Hill

In the United States, only multi-million-dollar homes offer the majestic view afforded from the heights of Havana's Puente Grande neighborhood. The soft, rolling hill, rising 200 feet above the street and topped with a plateau, allows residents to see a broad stretch of the Cuban capital and the Atlantic beyond. The Almendares River and an abandoned brewery form Puente Grande's eastern border. But as in the rest of Latin America, the hills above a city are not desirable and they are left for poor people and squatters. Puente Grande is such a place.

A warren of cinderblock apartments with shabby patios and dozens of tiny, cramped homes cover most of Puente Grande, named for the large bridge that spans a wide wash a few blocks away. Footpaths connect homes and aging apartment buildings. They also connect lives, and the few hundred residents all know each other and criss-cross the neighborhood to stop by for unannounced, casual visits. Neighbors offer visitors tiny cups of coffee over conversations about family, friends, work or neighborhood gossip. Sometimes, useful information is passed along, such as what's for sale on the black market.

The lives of Puente Grande residents are uneventful, filled with work and occasional neighborhood gatherings. Vacations away from Havana or even nights out on the town are beyond the reach of most Cubans, and the Puente Grande residents are no different.

Based on my numerous trips to Cuba, I consider Puente Grande to be representative of the country today. It is home to a broad cross-section of Cubans, from laborers and government bureaucrats to students and retirees. Most have basic needs covered: food, shelter, medical care and a steady if paltry income. And that's it. For some, what they have is enough. Many others yearn for more, much more.

Cuba historically has loomed much larger than its actual size. Its many shortcomings and its advances frequently are magnified. Cuba's reality routinely is distorted because it is viewed through an ideological prism. In some important ways, Cuba is unique among Latin American nations. And in others, it's surprisingly similar. It is not a nation of prisoners, nor of blissful folk.

Estansilao, better known as Tani, is a construction worker who lives with his wife and two children in a roomy, rough-hewn house with a large yard. A gregarious hard drinker, Tani has for several years been an independent laborer, working mostly for foreigners who want homes built or remodeled. He makes the equivalent of several hundred dollars a month, a fortune for Cuban workers. Still, he yearns for the days when the Soviet Union and Cuba were allied.

"After the Soviet Union collapsed, everything turned bad About the best hope we have today is opening the economy more to foreign investment, letting lots more capitalism take root."

Tani stroked his chin when I asked him the question I do of every Cuban who is even mildly unhappy about the state of affairs: "Would you leave your country for good?"

His answer: "I think sometimes that I should because I don't have job security. The foreigners could at any time stop hiring me. In the United States, you can always find work."

He lets out a loud sigh, plainly in turmoil at the idea. "But I hear from my relatives in Florida that, yes, you can live much better there. But it's not like you're going to be a rich man. The first ones who left were university educated, doctors, lawyers and large landowners, so they were experienced at making money. A lot of us are *guajiros*, country folk, who are not really prepared to handle capitalism. My kids are still young, and it is for them to have a better chance in life that I would go. But how? You must raft your way all the way to Florida. So, is it even a realistic proposition? I have my doubts."

Tani is typical of hardworking Cubans nearing middle age. They are convinced that for years Castro proved adept at leveling the economic playing field at home, even as he adopted most of the traits of the traditional Latin strongman. Cubans derive a great deal of pride from the equality that sets their society apart from most Latin American nations.

In a stuffy upstairs apartment in Puente Grande lived Aída, Alfredo and Isabel Pérez. Aída and her husband were old and sickly. Isabel, their 52-year-old daughter also suffered from a host of illnesses, including rheumatoid arthritis, that made her miss work at the Commerce Ministry several days a month. The trio spent much of their time arranging medical appointments, going to them and then resting from the exertion required to travel to medical offices.

The camaraderie they shared with neighbors to some extent offset the Pérez's dreary existence. Their door was always wide open, as much a concession to the heat as an invitation to visitors. Several times a day a neighbor would look in on the family to see how they were faring. Often, they would stay for a visit. "We Cubans who stayed in Cuba retained the habit of just dropping in on people," Aída said, laughing. Her son, Pedro, was living in Miami. During a six-month stay with him, she was taken aback by the custom of friends and relatives calling ahead before visiting each other. "That is just so formal and not like we Cubans. The revolution was supposed to have changed everything, but to me, it seems like those who went to Miami changed far more."

Before the revolution, Alfonso and Aída owned a prosperous grocery store and lacked nothing. But when private businesses were banned in the early 1960s, the government expropriated Alfredo's store. He was then employed as a clerk at his old store, which was now in government hands. Alfredo shrugged to accept the turn of events. He simply said he needed a job and figured it best to stay in a line of work he knew.

A lifelong friend who runs an illicit mechanical repair shop worked for Alfredo when he owned his store. Years later, he had Alfredo run daily errands for a modest fee. "Only in a crazy communist country could a successful shop keeper have his store taken away just because the government hates capitalism," the friend said with a wan smile. "In most places, you would have to fail, go bankrupt, or commit a big fraud to lose your business. But here you have Alfredo, reduced to running little errands."

Alfredo and Aída were able to visit their only son, a Soviet-trained engineer, just once. As a boy, he was a model revolutionary and exemplary student who earned a scholarship to the Soviet Union. The incongruity of a Cuban spending five years in the Soviet Union studying engineering only to earn his living in Florida is commonplace today. Adding to the incongruity is his Uzbek wife, whom he married and brought back to Cuba.

"Pedro has a huge house, about 20 times bigger than this apartment," said Aída excitedly. "It's so clean, you would not believe it," she continued, her eyes wide, perhaps seeing the immaculate palace in her mind's eye. "There, they have everything. My son and daughter-in-law begged us to stay. But after six months we came home."

I asked why they returned. "Well, it's complicated. Whatever our defects, this is still our country," Aída said, as she set up for the evening game of dominoes. "I have a daughter who would be here by herself."

Aída looked back, nostalgic for the times before Castro's rise. "We were of the comfortable class before the revolution. Our house was large and full of luxury goods. I had maids. Now, look how filthy I keep this apartment. I don't have the strength to clean. My son sends me money, but I don't have the desire to go out. Many of us, after so many years in a system that just drains you, are tired all the time."

In 2012, housing authorities moved the Perezes into a much larger ground floor house in the Playas section of Havana. Sadly, in the course of two years, Isabel died of a heart attack, her second. Alfredo died a few months later from a stroke. I visited Aída shortly after the deaths. She burst into tears when she saw me. Aída was consumed by grief. Fortunately, her son was able to secure a humanitarian visa, and she is living with him now in Miami.

Another informant, Manuel, leaned against his vintage Mercedes Benz sedan, enjoying the balmy Sunday afternoon. A budding businessman, Manuel was a private chauffeur. I was taking photos of sugar cane workers to accompany a news story, when he called me over.

"Look," he said, pointing at a drunk, disheveled black man reeling toward us. "This could mean trouble."

The man's boozy grin didn't seem to convey danger. He stopped and asked what I was doing and where I was from. That set off a friendly chat, yet Manuel, arms across his chest, just glared. Oblivious to my companion's grimace, the drunk wished us well and continued weaving along the side of the highway.

"Did you see how drunk and unkempt he was?" Manuel spat out. "That's how most of them are. They are drunks, lazy and shameless. And there's a reason why the prisons are full of blacks," he said loudly. "You are not from here, and you don't know these people. But whenever there's a crime, we say, 'For sure it was a black man.'"

Certainly, I had heard the comment more than once. Sometimes, blacks themselves, half in jest, said the same thing. I had the sense it was a jab at the racist generalization.

"I'm not saying that all blacks are like that," Manuel said. I half-expected him to add that some of his best friends were black. "Some are educated and behave themselves."

As we drove off, I asked Manuel how he would feel about his daughters marrying an educated, well-behaved black man.

"I would rather die than see that," he said. "Can you imagine having little mulatto grandkids running around?"

Such stories were common in the virulently racist pre-revolutionary Cuba. But with the revolution's triumph, discrimination was supposed to have been swept away.

"The reality," said María Fragua, "is something else."

Ms. Fragua, a black historian, married a white man a few years ago and moved to his neighborhood. "I was the only black person there. So, when my relatives and black friends came to visit, our neighbors wanted to know who they were and what they were looking for."

What the two stories illustrate, say Cuban authorities, is that while Castro and his government greatly improved the lives of blacks by ending official discrimination, informal racism survives in this heavily black nation.

"There is no official racism here anymore," said Adlum. "But there is still a culture of racism. The mistake was to think that just by having everyone integrated, racism would fade away."

African slaves were brought to Cuba for three centuries, and slavery wasn't abolished until 1886. During those years and beyond, blacks were barred from white schools, neighborhoods, social clubs and other institutions. Afro-Cubans endured high unemployment rates, and when they found work were relegated to the lowest-paying, most arduous jobs.

Months after taking power in 1959, the revolutionary government outlawed housing and workplace discrimination, banned all-white country and social clubs and, perhaps most significantly, granted free universal access to higher education.

Fidel Castro, signaling the changes, announced that "in the schools, white and black children must be together so that later the white man and black man will be in a position to earn their living at the same workplaces."

Pablo Díaz, a black foreign ministry official, said the government had never so directly taken on racial discrimination.

"You can't overestimate the positive impact that had on blacks. My family was very poor, and before the revolution, nobody even dreamed of attending a university. Today, we have engineers, economists and doctors in my family. And there are many, many other black families who experienced the same change."

Gisela Arandia, a University of Havana researcher, said that blacks were not entirely singled out by race but by circumstance: "Because they were so marginalized, blacks and mulattoes made great advances in the early years of the revolution."

In a more controversial undertaking, the Castro government sent thousands of troops and advisers to African nations. About 70,000 African students were brought to Cuba for free education. But many here say the government has made no further moves to root out subtle, intractable racism. Some blame the government's Marxist bent.

Ms. Arandia added that discriminatory practices stem in part from the centuries-old tradition of distinguishing between blacks and persons of mixed white and black ancestry, or mulattoes. "You have many people here who don't think of themselves as black, [but] who in the United States would definitely be black. So, you don't have anything like the level of black consciousness that you do in the United States. It also means you limit the possibilities that race will be discussed frankly."

Ms. Arandia, who has studied race relations, said that Cuban racism shows itself in many ways. In the burgeoning tourist industry, management jobs mainly have gone to non-blacks. Blacks largely are relegated to menial jobs, such as kitchen helpers and hotel maids. And, the crushing economic crisis that has engulfed Cuba since 1989 has hit blacks disproportionately hard.

"Just look around here," Ms. Arandia said as she sat in the patio of the luxurious Hotel Nacional. "All the people working behind the counters are white."

Black actors and actresses frequently find themselves playing servant and slaves roles. "We see these racist images that don't reflect reality. We have thousands and thousands of black professionals who are not portrayed in the media."

While no statistics are available, experts here say most of those imprisoned for criminal offenses are black.

"The army is heavily black, but blacks get only so far in rank," Ms. Fragua said.

For all the evidence of racism, visitors to Cuba often are struck by how fully integrated Cuban society seems to be. Cubans of all hues mingle in public and social gatherings, and intermarriage is not unusual. "In that regard, we are further along than the United States," Ms. Arandia said. "There, blacks and whites generally don't sit down together. I've had African-Americans visit here, and they just don't understand how this happens."

Only now has the government started to reflect the island's diversity. Half of the six vice presidents of the ruling Council of State are black, including the first vice president, and three are also women.

"In truth, from 1959 to today is a very short time to cure an illness that is centuries old," Ms. Arandia said. "Cuba and every other country on Earth has to get beyond race. If we do, there will be no problem."

Cuba is one of the world's most surreal and illogical countries. Plainly there is nothing cut and dried. I spent many months in Central America when it boiled over with grassroots insurgency and in Panama when General Manuel Noriega ran the country thuggishly. In those places, things were pretty clear, there was unmistakable logic. Bad, cruel and power-hungry people were in charge. Logically, they generated angry enemies, people willing to die—and who did die—in the hope of radically changing their country. Elsewhere around the world, human rights champions who stood up to dictators in the Philippines, Egypt, Libya and in most of the European communist nations were legion.

Cuba has none of that. The anemic dissidents on a Washington dollar are the only semblance of an opposition. Simply, there is no organized opposition. Even those who receive US government financial support bicker, and Cuban counterintelligence operatives have infiltrated them.

Cuba experts dismiss the lack of a true opposition as simple fear. I strongly disagree. Cubans are not timid or fearful folk. Díaz Canel is not a bloodthirsty or cruel dictator. The government maintains tight controls, but activists are not murdered or disappeared as in other Latin American dictatorships. Some, like blogger Yoani Sánchez and the Ladies in White, openly denounce the government.

I have come to view Cuba as unique among nations.

Few are satisfied with the state of the nation or their own situations. Cubans worry mostly about having enough to eat, and that is often a challenge, given that jobs generally pay no more than the equivalent of seventy dollars a month. At the same time, many Cubans own their homes, have no credit card debt—there are no Cuban credit cards—pay just a few dollars a month for utilities and have free universal health care. College educations are paid for by post-graduate employment in a government ministry.

Cubans do not express a desire for multi-party elections. Their prime concern is improving their economic status, preferably without having to emigrate. I learned long ago that most Cubans want to remain in Cuba and hope that somehow the economy becomes robust. A minority want to leave and often do.

Visitors to Cuba often look for "the real Cuba." No doubt they mean the Cuba that's not on a tour itinerary, but off the beaten path. Critics of Cuba travel—those who criticize tourists for seeing only the beautified sites and not the neighborhoods that cover Havana's 261 square miles—say the "real Cuba" is ugly and depressing.

No question, residential Havana is a mix of small, modest homes on streets dotted with potholes and upscale, leafy, elegant neighborhoods such as Miramar and Siboney.

My native Los Angeles in 2019 drew a staggering 50 million visitors, the seventh consecutive year that number increased. At the same time, according to the *Los Angeles Times*, "The number of those living in the streets and shelters of the city and most of the county surged 75%—to roughly 55,000 from about 32,000—in the previous six years (Including Glendale, Pasadena and Long Beach, which conduct their own homeless counts; the total is 58,000).

So, what's the point in drawing these comparisons?

It's simply that every city has a set of alluring sites meant to attract tourists. Those tourists typically don't travel long distances to see how average people live. Certainly, visitors to my hometown would not want to survey the long lines of tents and tarps that crowd parts of downtown Los Angeles.

So, where is the "real Cuba?"

It's not a place. It's the people.

Broadly generalizing about people is uncomfortably close to stereotyping. Still, it's no exaggeration to say Cubans are open, extroverted, generous, animated, hardworking and value family and friends. They long for material goods, but those things don't define their happiness.

My in-laws are representative of many Cubans. They live in an old home of some 500 square feet, work incredibly hard for little money. Their furniture is well-worn, the TV a 17-inch affair that depends on a rooftop antenna (no satellite or cable). They have a limited Internet connection with a used smartphone I gave them, but no computer. Fans are all they have to combat the tropical heat.

Their house faces a narrow passageway. Neighbors yell greetings through the open door. They stop in without an invitation. That's quite normal.

My Cuban family laughs a lot, sighs at life's daily hardships, like the random shortage of food items, and they dream of expanding and improving their home, which they own. My in-laws, Edy and Jorge, have never owned a car and never will. They don't often buy clothes. Vacations are rare and follow a tight budget. They usually have ample food— though it usually requires scouring Havana markets—and ready access to medical care. Their utility bills total the equivalent of a few dollars.

Like many Cubans, they don't wish to leave for the United States. They know life in the United States has its own challenges. Word-of-mouth offers an accurate depiction.

While predicting what will happen in Cuba is tricky, I believe that it will become steadily more capitalistic. There is no way it can remain rigidly state-controlled without falling into a deep economic crisis. Above all, Cuba will survive.

CHAPTER TEN
Panama: What Washington Wrought

MANUEL NORIEGA regarded me with expressionless, heavily lidded eyes, giving him a sinister appearance. A greasy sheen covered his pock-marked face. The acne scars had stuck him with the nickname *Cara de Piña,* Pineapple Face. It was an incongruously mocking moniker for a ruthless dictator.

Noriega, commander of the 12,000-member Panama Defense Forces and effectively the nation's ruler, had agreed to a rare formal interview. It was just days before Panama was to hold a presidential election, ending 16 years of military rule.

The May 6, 1984, electoral contest was in large part the result of American pressure to restore a semblance of democracy in Panama. With the Panama Canal gradually being ceded to Panama, Washington did not want an outright dictatorship to be on the receiving end.

Diplomats and political activists, however, told me that Noriega would tolerate a civilian president, but he would remain in control behind the scenes.

"So, you are the reporter from *Time,*" Noriega said as if asking for confirmation. "I expected a Gringo," he chuckled.

Despite the momentary show of good cheer, I sensed this would be a challenging interview.

The election pitted Arnulfo "Fufo" Arias, a nearly blind octogenarian of the Democratic Opposition Union against Nicolás "Nicky" Ardito Barletta, the forty-five-year-old candidate of the military-backed National Democratic Union. Arias, an ardent anti-Communist, had the unusual distinction of being elected president three times—in 1940, 1949 and 1968—only to have the military oust him after every election.

Working-class people on Panama City's streets were pleased with the prospect of having a truly civilian democratic government, yet they feared electoral fraud.

"The elections are just a show," said store clerk Julio Escalante. "Noriega is not going to let go of the power he has. He has worked too hard to let it go just like that."

Arias, with his longtime antagonistic relationship with the military, was drawing large and enthusiastic crowds. Ardito Barletta, by contrast, was a drab ex-World Bank vice president, who many Panamanians said would be Noriega's puppet. His rallies often were sparsely attended.

Noriega furrowed his brow and clasped his hands together when I told him what my reporting had found. "The defense forces will continue to be involved in the nation's affairs," he said. "Some people imagine that I personally will control the government. The truth is that we in the defense forces are stepping back from politics. We will just be poised to ensure public order and, if necessary, safeguard the canal."

A senior American diplomat in the region had assured me that Panama was a crucial transshipment point for cocaine and marijuana smuggled from Colombia to the United States. My source further asserted that many of Panama's banks and businesses were laundering millions of drug-tainted dollars. I didn't expect a truthful answer when I asked about the allegations. Nor did I expect his somewhat menacing response.

"Who told you these things?" he asked sternly. "Give me their names."

I replied that an American official had spoken to me on the condition that he remain anonymous.

"You should be careful about repeating lies. I have worked closely with the American government for many years, and nobody has ever told me what you're saying. The root of the drug problem is in your country."

He then made a bizarre allegation: "The Jews in Las Vegas control narcotics trafficking, but they are untouchable."

When I asked him to elaborate, he simply said that I should do some investigative reporting in the United States.

I asked if he and the defense forces had a favored candidate.

"Of course not," he said. "It is a decision for the people to make."

American diplomats in Panama made clear that Washington favored Ardito Barletta over Arias, who they criticized as an erratic, unpredictable populist. Ardito Barletta would be a steady and capable president who, with his financial experience, would be able to tackle Panama's economic woes, which included a $3.7 billion foreign debt, high unemployment and a severe housing shortage. It struck me as an odd preference, given that Arias was so ardently anti-communist and admired Ronald Reagan. In time, I would come to understand the American stance.

My interview with Noriega ended abruptly when an aide handed him a message. He stood up to excuse himself. Tony, as his friends and associates called Noriega, was not physically imposing, standing some five feet six inches. He was a pint-sized strongman in a tiny country. Yet just five years later, he would bring down the wrath of the US 82nd Airborne and thousands of American troops.

The 1989 invasion was impossible to imagine, given that Noriega was in large part a Washington creation. A Panama City native, Noriega was born into poverty in 1934. His godmother raised him in a one-room apartment. Reportedly, he was the illegitimate son of an accountant and his domestic employee. A *mestizo* of indigenous, African and Spanish origin, early on he was drawn to the military.

One of his brothers, Luis, introduced him to socialist politics, and for a time Noriega was a minor political activist. Described as serious and studious, he won a scholarship to the Chorrillos Military School in Lima, Peru. Upon graduation in 1963, he returned to Panama, joined the National Guard and was commissioned as a lieutenant colonel. He was fortuitously posted to Colón on the Atlantic Coast; his commander was Omar Torrijos, a future charismatic dictator. Torrijos became his patron and mentor, seeing to it that Noriega took several courses at the infamous US School of the Americas. By 1966 he was an intelligence officer, monitoring labor union activists.

Arias won his third term as president in 1968 after running on a populist platform. He ran into trouble when he sought to reorganize the National Guard. Torrijos and other military commanders ousted Arias from the presidency after he had served just eleven days. A military junta took control of the country, with Torrijos effectively the head-of-state. A year later, Torrijos survived a coup attempt, thanks to Noriega's steadfast loyalty. He was rewarded with the job of national intelligence chief. In that role, he ruthlessly disrupted and repressed political opposition to what was an outright military dictatorship. For the next 15 years, Panama would have several civilian puppet presidencies. The real power would always be in military hands.

It was Torrijos who was able to realize the long-held dream of Panamanians to gain sovereignty over the canal. On

September 7, 1977, Torrijos and President Jimmy Carter signed a new treaty that would gradually grant Panama complete control of the canal on December 31, 1999. The Canal Zone would no longer exist as of October 1, 1979.

On August 1, 1981, Torrijos was killed in a plane crash. There was no apparent successor, so Noriega and other officials competed for the position. Noriega emerged victorious in 1983 and took control of the National Guard. He brought together the armed forces to form the Panamanian Defense Forces. He also formed a paramilitary force called Dignity Battalions. They would act as shock troops whenever opposition demonstrations were held.

Investigative journalists and scholars have established that the CIA recruited Noriega in 1970. He had been passing along intelligence for years, and the agency saw him as an invaluable asset. Noriega gathered intelligence on Cuban officials and Central American leftists, including the Sandinistas. By the mid-1970s, Noriega was significantly involved in drug trafficking. Specifically, he allowed Colombian mafias to use Panama as a transshipment point for northbound drugs. Panama-based banks were permitted to launder billions of drug-tainted dollars. However, American officials who were aware of Noriega's transgressions did nothing to stop them and did not publicly disclose what they knew.

Noriega and Torrijos had provided weapons to Sandinista rebels fighting to overthrow Nicaraguan dictator Anastasio Somoza. After the Sandinistas took power, Noriega sold weapons to Salvadoran guerrillas. Several FMLN commanders told me that most of their communication equipment, primarily Motorola walkie-talkies, were bought in Panama.

According to declassified US government emails, Noriega had offered to help the Reagan Administration attack Nicaraguan installations, thus aiding the Contras. In return, Noriega asked for help in cleaning up his image. In an August 23, 1986, message from Oliver North to National Security Adviser John Poindexter, the Iran-Contra star urged acceptance of Noriega's offer.

"You will recall that over the years Manuel Noriega in Panama and I have developed a fairly good relationship," North wrote.

Poindexter the next day replied with an e-mail message authorizing North to meet secretly with Noriega. "I have nothing against him other than his illegal activities," Poindexter wrote.

North and Noriega, according to the declassified documents, met in London on September 22, 1986, to discuss the creation of a commando training program in Panama for Afghan rebels and the Contras. Israel would offer unspecified assistance.

Noriega was receptive to North's idea of sabotaging key economic targets, including Nicaragua's electrical system. When the Iran-Contra scandal broke, the plans were abandoned.

Beyond a doubt, American officials were aware of Noriega's illicit activities and, as Poindexter said, did not approve of them. But they decided to overlook his crimes so long as he continued to provide useful intelligence and assistance. This was not particularly unusual. In the Cold War atmosphere, American policymakers decided that Latin American strongmen would not be brought to heel so long as their politics aligned with Washington's. With the Cold War raging, Noriega forged fruitful ties with Communists and the United States. It was not an easy feat.

Leading up to the May 6, 1984 elections, I interviewed dozens of Panamanians in the capital and in Colón. There was a sense of nervous anticipation. Most of the people I interviewed expressed mild optimism that at long last Panama would have a democratic government.

But it was not to be. The National Tabulating Board began to hand-count hundreds of thousands of ballots on election day, but by day's end, there were no announcements of partial results. Some 26 hours after polls closed and with still no electoral results released, Arias backers took to the streets. They fought with Ardito Barletta supporters, and before long the violence spread.

Several American reporters and I took a taxi to the scene of nighttime rioting several blocks from the Legislative Palace where votes were supposedly being tabulated. Gangs, apparently from both sides, had barricaded streets and were looting nearby shops. Some rioters I managed to interview said they were protesting the defense forces' attempt to steal the election from Arias. No police or soldiers were at the scene, so the rioters ran amok.

Intense automatic rifle fire suddenly crackled from the roofs of surrounding tall buildings. I saw the muzzle flashes, but it was difficult to tell if the gunfire was directed toward the mobs. Still, everyone scrambled, some yelling as they dashed off. In a panic, the other reporters and I sprinted toward our waiting cab, which was starting to depart without us. We clambered aboard and asked the driver to take us to the Legislative Palace. On our way there, we spotted several heavily armed men in civilian clothes. They were crouched behind a wall with their backs to us, seemingly in wait for someone or something.

Juan Tamayo, a *Miami Herald* reporter, ordered the driver to stop. In unison, the rest of us asked him why he had given the order. He said he was going to interview the men. The others and I told him that it was a crazy idea. Alarmed at the possible consequences of Juan's action—arrest or death— we urged him not to get out of the cab. He laughingly dismissed our warnings, exited the car and walked toward the men with his hands raised. The frightened driver said we should drive away. We insisted he remain parked.

When Juan was about 50 feet from the group, he called out to them, but I could not make out what he said. Slowly, one of the men turned around and pointed a pistol at Juan, then fired a thunderous shot above his head. In reaction, Juan jumped straight up as though he had been propelled. He then scrunched his torso far down, evidently to make himself a smaller target. His hands still raised, Juan turned around and waddled slowly back to the cab. The gunshot had given us all a fright. The toll on that night of rioting was one dead and 41 wounded.

We arrived at the Legislative Palace to find officials sitting at desks idly shuffling papers. It did not appear that ballots were being counted. One of the workers said they were simply waiting for ballots to arrive.

With no winner yet declared, I left Panama two days later, convinced that there had been vote tampering. Ten days after the election, and with thousands of voter fraud allegations filed, Ardito Barletta was declared the victor with a margin of just 1,700 votes. With his candidate installed as president, it seemed that Noriega had strengthened his hold on power.

Some two years later, however, *The New York Times* reported that Noriega had the Panamanian Defense Forces (PDF) engage in widespread electoral fraud to ensure Ardito Barletta's razor-thin win. The CIA and American Embassy staff in Panama were aware of vote-stealing soon after it had occurred. That knowledge did not prevent Secretary of State George Shultz from attending Ardito Barletta's October inauguration. His attendance was an unmistakable sign that Noriega could steal an election and enjoy Washington's unspoken acquiescence.

Shultz in public remarks said that Panama's new leadership meant "a new opportunity for progress." He called Ardito Barletta "a longtime and respected friend." But Shultz's friend would have a short tenure. Ardito Barletta resigned just eleven months after taking office. It was not a voluntary departure. Noriega, it would later be revealed, had forced his resignation, probably because he had named a commission to investigate drug trafficking linked to Noriega as well as the murder of a prominent Noriega critic.

Vice President Eric Arturo del Valle stepped in to become yet another civilian puppet president, dependent on Noriega. The ham-handed ouster of Ardito Barletta and the brutal killing of Noriega's critic, Hugo Spadafora, marked a turning point in US-Panamanian ties. Over the next few years, relations would steadily deteriorate. Washington had given Noriega tacit free rein to do business with Colombian drug traffickers and maintain cordial ties with Havana. By 1986, however, Noriega's behavior and actions in the eyes of official Washington outweighed his value.

Perceiving his second-in-command, Colonel Roberto Díaz, to be a threat, Noriega forced his retirement in June 1987. That was followed by Díaz publicly accusing Noriega of stealing the 1984 election and of ordering Spadafora's murder. The accusations sparked violent street protests and opposition calls for an end to the Noriega regime. But Noriega hung on.

By this time, the Reagan Administration had decided to have Noriega removed from power. The formula for doing so was a mix of persuasion—having administration officials make Noriega understand that his rule was no longer tenable—and aid to internal opposition forces, as well as tightening of economic screws.

Congress, too, weighed in to oust Noriega. The US Senate on June 3, 1987, passed a resolution asking the Panamanian government to remove Noriega from his post. The Panamanian Defense Forces (PDF) responded by organizing a mob attack on the American embassy and expelling Ambassador Arthur Davis. The following month, the Reagan Administration ordered an end to joint military exercises and cut off economic aid. For the first time, an administration official, Elliott Abrams, Assistant Secretary of State for the Bureau of Inter-American Affairs, went on the offensive. In a speech following the attack on the embassy, he assailed Noriega for maintaining fraternal ties with Cuba and Nicaragua.

In another first, Noriega faced criminal charges. Two US grand juries in January 1988 indicted him and 16 associates on charges of drug and weapons trafficking. The Miami and Tampa indictments accused Noriega of exploiting his position as head of the defense forces to allow Colombian criminal organizations to use Panama to ship substantial amounts of cocaine and marijuana to the United States. Yet, the Reagan Administration continued to maintain diplomatic relations with the regime.

Since January 1986, I had been a correspondent in *Time*'s Washington bureau. My beat was the State Department. In my new position, I cultivated dozens of sources; some were senior State Department and Drug Enforcement Administration officials. Others were Congressional staffers who dealt with foreign policy issues. One was Michael Kozak, Deputy Assistant Secretary of State for Inter-American Affairs, a veteran diplomat with wide-ranging experience, including assisting in the Panama Canal treaty negotiations.

I encountered Kozak one afternoon in early March 1988. Diplomats, such as Kozak, who knew of my on-the-ground experience in Central America and Panama were more easily accessible to me than, say, staffers in the Bureau of European Affairs. I told him he appeared haggard, hoping he would open up. My gambit worked. Kozak sighed, smiled and shook his head. He invited me into his office and said he would reveal something to me, but that I would have to treat it as background information, not attributed to him by name but only as "an administration official." These were standard ground rules for officials who wanted information made public.

Kozak told me he had just returned from Panama, where he met with Noriega to discuss his resignation. I wasn't entirely surprised because there were signs that the administration was searching for ways to have Noriega removed. Noriega appeared open to stepping down, Kozak said, but no agreement had been reached.

At the end of our short interview, I asked Kozak if he would keep me apprised of how his future meetings with Noriega went. He agreed, and Kozak kept me generally informed during our periodic meetings. In one interview he said that the Bush Administration was offering Noriega safe exile in Spain and the quashing of all criminal charges. The dictator had amassed an estimated fortune of $300 million, the proceeds from his criminal activities. I asked if the dictator would be allowed to keep some of this money. Kozak said he could not answer that question. However, as a logical matter, he would have to be allowed to retain a portion of the money to support his life in exile. Noriega's handpicked president, Manuel Solís Palma, would remain in office but call new elections.

Then in late March 1988, Secretary of State George P. Shultz went public with a deal offering Noriega safe passage to exile in Spain. But by May, Noriega was still active in Panama. On May 7, presidential elections were held, pitting longtime Noriega critic Guillermo Endara against Carlos Duque, who was backed by the PDF. When it became apparent that Endara and his running mate Guillermo Ford had won, the Noriega-controlled electoral board invalidated the election. Board officials cited interference from unnamed outside forces as the reason for its decision. Foreign election observers, among them former President Jimmy Carter, had concluded the election was stolen. A May 9, 1989, a *Times* story said in part, ". . . an independent sampling of the vote showed that the opposition coalition, led by Guillermo Endara, had won by a 3-to-1 margin."

Raucous street protests followed. Demonstrators were set upon by pro-Noriega Dignity Battalions, some of whom beat Endara and Ford with clubs and iron bars. Photos of the bloodied men were published worldwide and made the cover of *Time* magazine.

In the ensuing chaos, the National Council of State in August announced a provisional government headed by a former attorney general. He promised to organize new elections in six months.

Increasingly, Noriega was turning to Cuban advisers and counterintelligence agents to hold onto power. Clinton Adlum, posted to Cuba's Interest Section in Washington, frequently sought me out. I had for some time known he was an intelligence agent, and we traded information. He stressed that despite Noriega's deep flaws, he and the PDF were valued allies. I surmised that Panama was an excellent source of American goods denied to Cuba under terms of the US embargo. Adlum would not explain the details of the relationship, but State Department officials told me that Noriega and his Cuban friends were sharing intelligence on American activities in the region.

Many months later, I learned that Cuban counterintelligence officials in the days before the US invasion of Panama had intercepted telephone conversations of American soldiers based in Panama, who talked of something big in the works. The Cubans accurately concluded that an invasion was imminent and warned the Panama Defense Forces.

Noriega had ruled ruthlessly, but from the shadows. Now he was given to public shows of defiance and fierce denunciations of American intervention. During one demonstration, he brandished a machete.

In early April, I met one last time with Kozak, following yet another meeting with Noriega. Kozak was pessimistic an agreement would be reached. "He [Noriega] tells me he is a prisoner," said Kozak. Quoting Noriega, he said, "'Look, the men who are close to me won't let me leave. They demand that I stay right where I am.'" Reportedly, Kozak gave Noriega a May 25th deadline to accept a deal for exile in Spain. The deadline passed and the die was cast.

The noose was tightening around Noriega. PDF Major Moisés Giroldi led a coup against him on October 3. It was easily snuffed out, and Giroldi and nine comrades were shot. Protected by Dignity Battalion members, Noriega briefly addressed reporters, who asked who was behind the coup. "The Americans did this! The piranhas did this. They want to finish Panama!" Noriega shouted back.

Seemingly anticipating what was to come, on December 15, 1989, Noriega said that the Bush Administration, through constant psychological and military "harassment," had "invoked the powers of war" against Panama. American troops had carried out military exercises that Noriega deemed provocative. The legislature the same day declared that "the Republic of Panama is in a state of war for the duration of the aggression unleashed against the Panamanian people by the US Government." Noriega declared himself the "Maximum Leader."

On December 20, the day of the invasion, the White House inaccurately asserted that the incursion was in part launched after "Noriega declared a state of war with the United States." It was a lie that is still repeated today.

On the eve of the invasion, the United States had 12,000 troops stationed in Panama. Given the outright hostility that now existed between the Panamanian regime and the United States, an armed conflict seemed inevitable. The spark was a December 16th incident. Four US servicemen driving in a civilian car were halted at a PDF roadblock. According to American military officials, the men sought to leave when their car was surrounded by an angry mob that included PDF soldiers. The PDF alleged the men were armed and spying. Panamanian soldiers fired on the vehicle, killing one of the servicemen and wounding another. An American military officer and his wife were also detained by PDF officials. They were allegedly assaulted. The officer's wife was hospitalized, and Panamanian soldiers purportedly threatened her with sexual violence.

I was attending a *Time* Christmas party on December 19 when Bureau Chief Stanley Cloud got a phone call from a Defense Department official notifying him that *Time* was one of several news organizations selected to accompany troops on a combat mission going abroad that night. The destination was not disclosed. Defense, in the interest of giving the media access, had a so-called "pool" of news organizations that would be included in combat deployments.

Cloud asked me if I wished to go along. I declined for one important reason: There was no doubt that the destination was Panama.

I correctly anticipated that Noriega's Dignity Battalions, who wore civilian clothes, would take to the streets. American soldiers would not hesitate to gun them down. Invading American forces would consider them enemy combatants. As a Latino on the streets of Panama City, I knew I would be highly vulnerable. What was to distinguish me from a Dignity Battalion member who just happened to be unarmed?

The only prudent course would have been to always stay with the troops. But then I would have produced highly filtered stories. Indeed, that is what happened. As for the pool reporters, they were kept away from the action, denying them the opportunity to witness combat.

Operation Just Cause began on December 20 at 1 am with an assault on the Punta Paitilla civilian airport and several PDF targets. The Río Hata airfield was hit, evidently because Noriega had a home there.

With nearly 28,000 troops, including the 82nd Airborne, and more than 300 aircraft involved, it was at that time the largest American deployment since Vietnam. The 16,000 PDF and perhaps 2,000 Dignity Battalion members could at best offer token resistance. I later learned during a reporting trip to Panama that many soldiers shed their uniforms and hid.

President Bush in a televised address to the nation had, in part, this to say: "General Noriega's reckless threats and attacks upon Americans in Panama created an imminent danger to the 35,000 American citizens in Panama. As President, I have no higher obligation than to safeguard the lives of American citizens. And that is why I directed our Armed Forces to protect the lives of American citizens in Panama and to bring General Noriega to justice in the United States." Bush also said the invasion was in response to Panama's drug trafficking and money laundering.

Contrary to most historical accounts, the Bush Administration had long planned an invasion. The shooting of the American soldier was a pretext. The United States Army website states that meticulous military training for Just Cause began in May 1989, a full seven months before the invasion.

By all accounts, the assault was overwhelming and terrifying for many Panamanians. The poor Panama City neighborhood of El Chorrillo, reportedly a Dignity Battalion stronghold, was hit particularly hard.

Noriega fled once the invasion began and remained a fugitive for several days before finding refuge in the Vatican diplomatic mission. American troops blasted the building with loud rock music, in a novel attempt to flush him out. Vatican officials also prodded him to surrender, which he did on January 3, 1990. Noriega was flown to the United States and stood trial for the charges outlined in the 1988 indictment. He was found guilty and sentenced to 40 years in prison.

Guillermo Endara was secretly sworn in at Fort Clayton, a US Army base. First Vice President Ricardo Arias Calderón and Second Vice President Guillermo Ford also took their oath of office. The ceremony held on December 20 at about 2 am became controversial when his opponents said Endara was not a legitimate president because he had not taken his oath on Panamanian soil. Endara replied that the ceremony was held in an unidentified private home.

Ten months after the invasion, I went to Panama to report on the aftermath and get at what really had happened when American military might came crashing down on a miniature nation. The mood in Panama City was uncharacteristically somber when I arrived on November 15, 1990. Burned out and heavily damaged buildings stood as grim reminders of the invasion. I found widespread discontent with the Endara government. It was grappling with the daunting task of strengthening an economy debilitated by years of corrupt governance and the substantial damage Operation Just Cause left in its wake.

"The only thing that changed is that some of my neighbors are dead," said Francisco Torres, a janitor and El Chorrillo resident. "When the Americans attacked, it felt like the world was ending—explosions and fire everywhere. Thank God we weren't hurt, but a lot of people were killed. This government does not talk about that," said Torres. "For the poor like us, life has always been hard. Honestly, I don't have much hope things will change."

Administration officials I interviewed before traveling to Panama described the portly Endara as well-meaning but not particularly well-suited to transform the nation into a stable democracy. I was left with the impression that Endara's rapid and unconventional installation was yet another Washington misstep.

The city of Colón was emblematic of the country's woes. Once a prosperous port of call for cruise ships, Panama's second-largest city had become a collection of rotting tenements, beset by an unemployment rate of some 30 percent, rampant drug use and violent crime. I met with Father Carlos Aziz, Colón's bishop. When I told him I wished to take a walking tour, he warned against it: "You will be beaten and robbed, for sure." I had parked two blocks from his church, but he urged me to move my car on to church grounds so that it would not be stolen. I told Aziz that when I visited Colón in 1984, there was no danger in walking the city streets. "We had Noriega's people to keep some order. That is gone now," he said.

During my five days in Panama in 1990, I tried to pin down the number of dead and wounded caused by the invasion. I had arrived with a variety of estimates in hand. The US Army initially said 516 Panamanians had been killed, but an internal study concluded that the true figure was more likely about 1,000. Depending on the source, somewhere between 300 and 3,000 lost their lives. Twenty-four American soldiers were killed. In Colón, according to Aziz and several residents with whom I spoke, the residents said that more than 80 were killed. Some died in an apartment building that was hit by helicopter rocket fire. The building had a huge gaping hole.

Aziz said locals were trying to put the invasion horrors behind them. At the same time, they were looking to the government for economic help and job creation. "We thought maybe this government would remember us," said Aziz. "Instead, the government says it has no way to help."

At the time, the United States had provided Panama with $130 million off arrears on its $5 billion foreign debt. Another $70 million in direct aid was also received. "What we're giving them is not even equal to direct damages caused by the invasion," former ambassador Ambler Moss told me.

Totally dependent on imported oil, Panama was faced with a global surge in petroleum prices. In the coming year, the nation would be faced with nearly a doubling of petroleum prices, from $20.20 in 1990 to $38.28 per barrel in 1991. "The economy is strangled," said comptroller Rubén Carles.

Operation Just Cause was officially meant to deal a blow to drug trafficking; instead, the flow of drugs continued under Endara. Since the start of the Endara administration, more than 13,000 pounds of cocaine—worth $153 million wholesale—had been seized. "One can only surmise that if this much is being seized, a lot more is moving," said Deane Hinton, the US ambassador to Panama when I was there. Money laundering, which supported the drug trafficking, continued unabated.

However, Endara resisted any move to make banking in Panama more transparent. American officials wanted to have access to accounts they suspected were linked to criminal activity. But Endara's associates claimed that would destroy the nation's banking industry. And he also reimposed the oligarchic practice of handing out jobs to family members and cronies, all of whom were white. The country once again would be run by *rabiblancos*, the wealthy white, as it was during the pre-Torrijos years. Despite their grave faults, Torrijos and Noriega had revolutionized the country by giving jobs to blacks and mixed-race Panamanians.

As for Noriega, he would serve time in American, French and Panamanian prisons. The ex-dictator was to live the rest of his life in prison. His term ended, however, after surgery for a brain tumor, when he died on May 29, 2017, at the age of eighty-three.

Contemporary Panama is on much more solid economic footing than it was in 1990. The nation's annual economic growth rate is among the world's highest. Panamanians are the second-richest Latin Americans, and the Panama Canal currently generates almost $2 billion in revenue each year. But strong economic performance has not translated into broadly shared prosperity, as Panama has the second-worst rate of income distribution in Latin America, according to the CIA's *World Fact Book*. And Panama is still plagued with corruption. The Panama Papers scandal in 2016 proved that Panama's leaders were content to have the nation used as a giant tax haven and money-laundering center. The release in 2015 of more than 11 million files from the Panamanian firm Mossack and Fonseca laid bare a complex web of tax shelters and money laundering.

Operation Just Cause had targeted money laundering, but over the years, the shady industry came to flourish once again. In an ironic twist, the candidate of the Democratic Revolutionary Party, the party Torrijos had founded and Noriega later controlled, was elected president in May 2019. The party is reported to have remade itself into an honest and truly democratic one. In taking office in July, 2019, President Laurentino Cortizo vowed to root out corruption and tackle income inequality.

It is heartening to see Panama transform itself from the oddity it was for so many years: a tiny Latin American isthmus bifurcated by a swath of US territory, home to a thuggish dictator and thousands of American troops. Panama finally gets to be just another Latin American nation striving to move up in the world. That's an achievement that should make Panamanians proud.

CHAPTER ELEVEN
México lindo, querido y sufrido

IT STRUCK WITH FEROCIOUS, horrifying intensity, violently shaking shrubs near us, causing high-rise hotels to sway wildly like palm trees in the wind. The ground beneath our feet vibrated rapidly.

The September 19, 1985, Mexico City earthquake hit at 7:18 a.m. My family and I were outdoors in Acapulco, which suffered minor damage. But the 8.0 magnitude quake in its first few minutes killed several thousand people in Mexico City, destroyed some 400 homes and buildings and damaged thousands more. Some 40,000 would be killed, although the government would put the death toll at 10,000. The epicenter was hundreds of miles from the capital, but the city's mushy subsoil greatly magnified the quake's ferocious impact.

The Mexico City airport was closed, and it took me hours to find a taxi driver willing to take me to the city. I arrived early the next day at the southeastern edge of the capital to find streets buckled and buildings collapsed. As the taxi driver maneuvered to central Mexico City, a scene of apocalyptic devastation greeted us. All across the city, blocks were dotted with buildings rendered into piles of rubble; others were pancaked, floors stacked upon each other. Stunned and in disbelief, I would see worse in the next hours and days. I checked in at the *Time* bureau and coordinated coverage with my colleagues. We had to quickly assess the damage and gather as much information as possible; our deadline was just two days away, and the quake was slated to be the cover story. My first stop was at the Secundaria Número Tres, Héroes de Chapultepec, in the city's center. The three-story high school had collapsed with some 50 students entombed in the rubble. Frantic and weeping parents tugged at enormous pieces of fractured concrete. Some used car jacks in attempts to lift the massive chunks, but it was a futile effort. No professional rescuers were on the scene twenty-four hours after the quake had struck.

When I returned several hours later, soldiers had cordoned off the site. The parents were still frantically trying to move aside debris. The soldiers just looked on. "Why aren't you doing anything to help save the kids? Help these people!" I screamed, gesturing toward the parents. The soldiers were unmoved.

During the day I interviewed dozens of survivors and surveyed at least one hundred sites—apartment and commercial buildings—destroyed or badly damaged. The Hotel Regis, built in 1908, had collapsed, killing seventy-four occupants. At least 560 had died when the Juárez Hospital crumbled; another 160 bodies were never identified.

Quake survivors wandered the streets or gathered at the ruins of their apartments, where family and friends were trapped or dead. They wept, yelled the names of the missing or sat on the ground dazed.

I returned to the *Time* office on the fifth floor of a building on Paseo de la Reforma late in the afternoon to write my story, when the second quake, measuring 7.0 on the Richter scale struck. Having witnessed the first quake's destruction, I was terrified. The building was swaying, its steel girders screeching eerily. Cracks formed on the walls and a large window in my office blew out. I ran out of the office and to the stairway. Everyone else in the office followed. The stairway was filled with many others, all rapidly descending in unison. No one was trampled or tried to shove past others. As I ran, I was convinced the building would come crashing down.

When I reached the street, my knees trembled, and my heart was thumping wildly. Soon the streets were clogged with vehicles headed out of Mexico City. Public transportation, including taxi service, was halted, and so thousands of residents filled the sidewalks. Panic and fear of another earthquake had taken hold.

During the next twenty-four hours, the government would be exposed as thoroughly unprepared for and unable to respond to the disaster—unforgivable considering that Mexico is prone to severe quakes. The Partido Revolucionario Institucional, or PRI, had overseen every aspect of life in Mexico City for some fifty-five years. Now, it was shown to be incapable of mustering even a limited rescue effort. It had just lost its aura of omnipotence.

Many countries offered emergency aid. But President Miguel de la Madrid infamously said, "Mexico has sufficient resources. . . . We appreciate the good intentions, but we are self-sufficient."

Misplaced Mexican pride would cost thousands of lives. "I'm ashamed of my government," foreign ministry official Abraham Montes de Oca told me. "We are incapable of handling this catastrophe but too proud to admit it and accept the help we need."

De la Madrid reversed course the next day, and foreign assistance began to flow. Tragically, it arrived too late for many. Heavy equipment to remove the debris and save survivors was in very short supply. Those trapped could not survive long.

Near a factory that collapsed, I noticed a middle-aged man weeping. I approached him, and he told me his daughter was among the workers.

"A lot of us with family in there were digging them out," he said. "But without equipment, we could not advance much. I could touch my daughter's hand and talk to her. She got weaker and weaker and finally died today."

A team of German rescuers using dogs told me they had detected many survivors in factory ruins. "In our country, we have the necessary equipment to save people," one of the rescuers said, sobbing. "Here, there is nothing. We are seeing people die who should have been saved."

With the government paralyzed, Mexico City residents quickly organized aid efforts. The rich, middle-class and poor, in an unprecedented show of people power, for several weeks distributed food, clothes and blankets to the thousands left homeless.

The government's death estimates seemed low compared to the devastation I saw. It turned out there was an effort to obscure the real figures. A chauffeur I had hired told me there was a rumored mass gravesite just outside the city. We headed towards Puebla, then took a dirt road to the reported site. Seeing soldiers deployed, we stopped and walked toward them. With their backs toward us, we were undetected. I saw small dirt piles in two lines that covered about 150 yards each. There were wood scraps tied together to form crosses, marking the mounds as graves.

A woman stood in front of one, she was shaking, moaning and weeping, looking to the sky. I walked to her, and she embraced me, burying her face in my chest. "My little boy is in there," the woman said, pointing to the grave. "He was just five. Why didn't God take me instead of him?"

I was overcome by sadness. She and I stood hugging each other for a long time. I had no words to comfort her.

Next, the driver and I walked to a large clearing. What I saw shocked me. Two rectangular pits, each about one hundred feet by thirty feet, had been dug and partially filled with mangled corpses. A white powder, probably lye, covered them. Within minutes, a large army truck backed up and dumped more cadavers and pieces of human bodies into one of the pits.

Suddenly, two soldiers ran toward us and demanded to know who we were. I told him and asked why people were being deposited in mass graves. Rather than answer, they ordered us to leave.

No other journalist or anyone I know who was in Mexico City at the time knew about this clandestine gravesite.

During the next two weeks, I roamed Mexico City. To the best of my knowledge, no effort was made to rescue residents who may have survived inside dozens of devastated apartment buildings. I had the misfortune of seeing hundreds of bodies laid out in the Social Security's baseball stadium. They were covered with cloths; survivors converged there in search of missing family and friends. I also saw dozens of bodies pulled from the rubble. One image hit me the hardest. An elderly woman, white with dust and limp as a rag doll, was extracted. Two women who apparently knew her screamed in anguish.

The odor of rotting corpses, faint at first, became intense after a few days. Many people wore surgical masks. I lost my sense of smell at some point, likely a psychological response to the stench, and I have yet to recover it.

There were no survivors found inside Secundaria Número Tres, Héroes de Chapultepec, despite the brave efforts of tunnelers called "moles." They found students crushed or crouched under desks where they died slow deaths.

There were about ten destroyed apartment buildings I visited for several days. Neighbors told me no one had come to attempt to search for possible survivors. After about ten days, the debris and corpses were scooped up and hauled away. Survivors who pitched donated tents along streets received little of the mass aid that flowed into Mexico City. Much of what was to have gone to those whose homes were destroyed got skimmed.

The political fallout marked the beginning of the end of the PRI's uninterrupted rule. The PRI and government were synonymous. It was a party that was all things to all people; it controlled most facets of Mexican life. But in failing to protect and aid Mexicans at a critical time, it was plain the party was criminally incompetent. Many Mexicans who had depended on the PRI for jobs and social programs it provided now saw that they themselves could manage in a crisis. The PRI was useless and hardly the party to lead Mexico into the future.

From its creation as the National Revolutionary Party in 1930, the PRI had held an authoritarian grip on all levels of Mexican politics. Its rise marked the demise of military rulers in favor of political rulers. The military would not involve itself in political matters and the once-powerful Catholic Church would be forced to stick to clerical affairs. Opposition parties were permitted but were feeble, except for the conservative National Action Party, or PAN. Under the PRI's rule, cults of personality did not exist. Presidents, handpicked by their predecessors, by law, were limited to one six-year term. The party's political orientation, ranged from leftist to conservative, depending on the nation's mood.

Government workers, millions of unionized workers and peasant organization members all were *Priistas*. The press was tightly controlled through bribery and the fact that the government was the only provider of newsprint.

I had previously covered two presidential elections, interviewing hundreds of voters. Most said resignedly they had voted or were about to vote for the PRI. "The PRI never loses" was a familiar refrain.

చొన్నా

Immigration has long been a point of conflict between Mexico and the United States. Traditionally, it involved the illegal entry into the United States of Mexican immigrants. These same immigrants, however, have been welcomed by a wide range of employers. Starting in 2016, the nature of undocumented immigration began to change. Largely replacing Mexicans, other migrants, residents of the Northern Triangle—Guatemala, Honduras and El Salvador—have been streaming north. The region ". . . ranks in the top 10 worldwide for homicide, corruption, drug trafficking and gang violence. Non-state actors perpetuate insecurity, forcibly recruit individuals into their ranks and use sexual violence as a tool of intimidation and control," according to a United States Institute of Peace study. The report also noted that when the civil wars ended, crime skyrocketed, and American aid was allocated. "A significant amount of these funds was allocated to the war on drugs, rather than for security, peace and development," the report found.

Never did I imagine that the wars I reported on would leave such a horrible legacy.

In the summer of 2003, I reported on a heavily trafficked area of the Mexico-Guatemala border. One of my first contacts was the district director of Mexico's National Migration Institute, Sergio Toledo. He watched bemusedly as dozens of Central Americans, perched on inner tube rafts, floated leisurely across the Suchiate River that divides Mexico from Guatemala and stepped into Mexican territory.

"I would need 200 agents just to stop this," he said. He made no move as the illegal entrants from Tecun Uman, Guatemala, hurried past him.

"I have twenty-six agents," he said. "Including the other sector, we have just a little more than 200 officers to patrol 500 kilometers. In Mexico City, they say the army is supposed to be helping us."

Some 100 yards downriver, ten Mexican soldiers washed clothes, ignoring the steady raft traffic.

Most of those who were sneaking into Mexico were headed for the United States, and Mexican officials, responding to heightened US concerns about terrorism, vowed to reinforce their border security. But Mexico's southern frontier was as porous then as it had been when I first visited twenty years earlier.

"We have not found any terrorists coming in," said Roberto Espinoza, chief of immigration enforcement for the border between Guatemala and the Mexican state of Chiapas. "But we can't say for sure that none are coming in." Noting that much of the frontier is covered by dense tropical vegetation, he added, "It is dangerous for us to go in there. We are unarmed, and there are armed gangs all over who rob and kill anyone, especially the migrants."

There were some one hundred criminal bands in the area, ranging from large smuggling operations to robbers who preyed on immigrants, according to Mexican officials. They said that even modest smuggling rings depended on a network of guides, corrupt officials and safe houses that reached into the United States.

While the US-Mexico border was studded with motion detectors, imposing fences, spotlights, night-vision cameras, aircraft and all-terrain vehicles, Mexican officials had only pickup trucks and raw manpower. Meanwhile, the number of illegal immigrants deported from Chiapas—almost all Central Americans—had risen ten percent, to about 62,400, from the same time in 2002. But there had been no corresponding increase in the number of immigration agents assigned to Chiapas, said Espinoza.

"We conduct joint operations with the federal police and the army," he said, "but those are not frequent. The truth is that with the little equipment and manpower we have, we are being overrun."

Plainly, the unregulated immigration flow was a problem many years in the making. Even in 2003, economic conditions deteriorated sharply in the Northern Triangle.

"I would not have thought of leaving my country just two years ago," said Paulino Romero, a 20-year-old dairy worker from Olancho, Honduras. But earning the equivalent of $18 a month and faced with rising living costs, he was crouched in a train yard in Tapachula, Mexico, with other Central Americans.

Mr. Romero and perhaps 200 other immigrants were about to begin a 1,500-mile trip to the U.S. border aboard an ancient freight train called "The Beast." The odds were that he—and hundreds of thousands of others who begin the journey from the southern border each year—won't reach American soil, Mexican officials said. Some would be nabbed by Mexican immigration agents or soldiers posted along the route, while others would be robbed, beaten, raped or killed by Mexican thugs and Central American gang members. Many more risked dying or suffering crippling injuries from falling off moving trains.

Mexican authorities and immigrant advocates wryly noted the intense publicity generated by the migrants' deaths in the United States. "It is tragic when people die" crossing the US border said the Rev. Ademar Barilli, a Catholic priest who built the Migrants' Home, a shelter in Tecun Uman for immigrants who have been robbed or injured. "But here, there is no question that two to three times as many migrants are killed or die here each year. The problem is the authorities don't have the time or resources to track down those who are reported missing. We constantly hear of people being killed in the jungle, and nobody can investigate."

One night, members of Grupo Beta, Mexican federal agents charged with protecting the immigrants and encouraging them to return home, explained to bedraggled migrants the perils that lay ahead. I interviewed Gabriela Coutiño, Beta's public affairs officer. She said, the average fee to be smuggled from home to a destination in the United States was $2,000 (Today it is about $5,000.).

"Usually, the migrants have to hock their homes or borrow money from loan sharks," she said. "If they don't or can't pay the loans, they lose their houses or else their families back home are beaten or killed."

Many can't raise enough money, so they make the trip without smugglers. Such was the case of Gerardo González, 22, who was traveling with his wife and sister-in-law.

"You are taking big risks by having these women with you," warned Julio César Cancino, operations supervisor for Grupo Beta. "The gangs can easily overpower you, and I hate to think what would happen to the women."

Yet when the train jerked into motion, they and dozens of other migrants quickly lodged themselves between boxcars. Mr. Cancino roughly grabbed one of the men, preventing him from boarding. After a few quiet words, he sent the man on his way.

"He is one of the most brutal of the robbers," Mr. Cancino said. "What he and others do is infiltrate the groups of migrants and later beat, rob, rape or kill them."

Inside the House of the Good Shepherd, Alma Cruz, 30, of Tegucigalpa, smiled wanly at the sight of children playing in the dimly lit shelter for injured migrants. Ms. Cruz's experience graphically underscored the hazards of riding a freight train. On the night of February 8, 2004, she and scores of other migrants sought to board The Beast. Ms. Cruz said her hands slipped from the slick iron ladder at the rear of a boxcar.

"I felt a very hard blow, but I couldn't tell where I had been hit," she said. "I was on my back and then suddenly I felt the worst pain you can imagine. That is when I saw that my legs were gone. . . . The train took them."

Bystanders drawn by her shrieks rushed to her aid, then flagged down a car. "I never lost consciousness. I was just consumed by pain and the terror that I would die and leave my little girls," said Cruz, who had two daughters, ages 5 and 2, left with her mother in Tegucigalpa. Cruz was waiting in hopes of receiving prosthetic legs. The shelter depends entirely on donations.

Across the border in Tecún Uman, a small group of nuns and social workers were battling another phenomenon spawned by the flow of immigrants: prostitution and a sharp rise in HIV and AIDS. Roughly 600 prostitutes worked in tumbledown bars and brothels or prowled the streets in the border area.

"What greatly worries us is that the number of prostitutes keeps growing and the ages of the girls keep dropping," said Consuelo Berrocano, a nun who regularly visits the prostitutes. She seeks to draw them out of the sex trade and into occupational programs at a shelter called the House of Women.

"Now we are seeing local men who have been with prostitutes infecting their wives and girlfriends with HIV," she said. "This could turn into an epidemic."

In 2017 and 2018, there were some 30,000 new cases of HIV/AIDS reported in Mexico. The rate of infection has remained constant since 2003.

ↄ෮ↄ

Wayne Cornelius, director of the Center for US-Mexican Studies at the University of California, San Diego, called me over excitedly. "I want to introduce you to the future president of Mexico."

The man he presented that day in May 1981, was about five feet, five inches tall, slight and had a bald pate. Soft-spoken Carlos Salinas de Gotari did not look or act presidential. After serving as Mexico's budget secretary, he would be tapped as the PRI presidential candidate and take office in 1988. However, a computer crash on election night led many to believe the mishap was an act of electoral fraud that denied leftist Cuauhtémoc Cárdenas the presidency

Salinas announced that he would "modernize" Mexico, which involved privatizing much of the economy and creating the Federal Electoral Commission, an independent organization to monitor elections. That duty had been in the hands of the interior ministry. Salinas also successfully negotiated the North American Free Trade Agreement (NAFTA).

What my initial meeting with Salinas showed me is that Mexico is constantly surprising. I had misjudged the short bald man. He not only put Mexico on the path to modernization, despite his administration being plagued with corruption and political assassinations, including that of his successor Luis Donaldo Colosio.

In Washington, my State Department and Drug Enforcement Agency sources told me that Salinas was using his brother, Raúl, as the front man for corrupt schemes, including substantial money laundering. Today, Salinas and former president Enrique Peña Nieto are the most unpopular men to have led Mexico.

Vicente Fox, whom I interviewed several times, was the PAN candidate for the 2000 election. He spoke passionately and movingly about the need to root out corruption and stimulate the economy. His election marked a political watershed. For the first time in seventy years, the president-elect was not a PRI member. As assistant managing editor of the *Dallas Morning News*, I directed news coverage of the event. I was certain that Mexico would undergo historical change. The conventional wisdom, which I accepted, was that the PRI was dead.

Instead, Fox simply followed the neo-liberal policies the PRI had begun. His successor, also from the PAN, Felipe Calderón, was elected over leftist Andrés Manuel López Obrador by a margin of 0.56 percent. López rejected the results, alleging there had been electoral irregularities. When his demand for a full recount was rejected, and amid various legal challenges, López declared himself president, and his supporters held street protests for months. There reached a point when, whatever the merits of his allegations, López appeared mentally unbalanced. Once more, I wrote off a future leader.

Calderón distinguished himself by declaring war on the narco-mafias. This pleased Washington but set off a conflict that caused the deaths of 60,000 during his term.

Back from the dead, the PRI, declaring itself new and improved, nominated as their 2012 candidate Enrique Peña Nieto, who went on to defeat López, running once more. Peña oversaw the substantial expansion of the auto industry and the creation of two million new jobs. On the other hand, corruption proliferated, drug violence continued and the government was found to have spied on journalists. The Open Justice Society found that there were "reasonable grounds" to believe that both the Mexican army and drug cartels had committed crimes against humanity. The group accused Peña and Calderón of not only failing to prevent the abuses but covering them up as well.

Andrés Manuel López Obrador is now president. A leftist, he was elected because he promised greater economic and social justice, an end to corruption and an attack on the drug plague by moving away from crime-fighting and toward investment in social programs. He opened the presidential mansion to the public, while he continued to live in his modest Mexico City home.

At this writing, his approval rating above 60 percent is now falling due to his inability to fulfill many of his promised reforms. And, he has shown himself to be more of a fiscal conservative than his electoral rhetoric suggested.

Starting in 1960, I have watched Mexico cope with economic crises, social upheavals and widespread violence. I have traveled to every Mexican state, some repeatedly. I covered local and national elections in which blatant fraud, including ballot-box stuffing, was common. Elections now are clean and fair.

I have also witnessed the growth of its middle class and economic development. I have seen it maintain its unique culture while welcoming many millions of American tourists.

Mexico's young today are involved in the push for greater democracy, respect for human rights and social justice. No longer is emigration to the United States the default route to economic security.

Mexicans are among the world's hardest working people, and they have helped make the nation among the top ten most popular tourist destinations. Despite the violence, weak rule of law, income disparity and the marginalization of indigenous Mexicans, Mexico has the look and feel of a nation on its way up, no longer paralyzed by authoritarianism, massive corruption and shoddy government.

The United States no longer holds the gleaming promise of prosperity for Mexican emigrants. The American Dream, even for Americans, is more elusive than ever. For Mexicans with scant education and no English fluency, no American Dream exists.

After a few years of not being in Mexico City, an assignment took me back to the capital. Disembarking at the airport, I was overjoyed. I was back home, I thought. It is hard to describe the utter comfort and warmth I feel at being in a nation populated by people just like me, Mexicans. It is liberating to be just another person and not an ethnic oddity, a second-class citizen. If I am treated rudely, I know it has nothing to do with race. In the United States, I am left to wonder if rude treatment is a reaction to who I am or just the act of a discourteous person.

My long involvement with Mexico, including four years living in Mexico City, make me believe that my ancestral homeland in the coming years will realize its potential as a nation that will offer many more of its people a safe and just society.

Mexico will be a country where people want to forge their lives and not flee to the United States chasing elusive prosperity.

Afterword

———

THE KIDS PLAYFULLY running back and forth in front of my grandmother's adobe house were a strange and puzzling sight. It was a blazingly hot El Paso afternoon in 1956, but the boys and girls seemed oblivious to the weather and were enjoying games of tag and hide and seek. Accustomed to Los Angeles summers, El Paso's heat seemed to me unbearably infernal.

I was a scrawny six-year-old left in the care of my maternal grandmother, Sara Gándara Real y Vásquez. She rarely smiled and was consistently aloof. Being alone with her in the house on San Antonio Street was disquieting. My mother was born in that house in the city's Second Ward, or *Segundo Barrio*, as Mexicans called it. The neighborhood was the common point of arrival for emigrating Mexicans.

A few minutes earlier, drawn by the children's laughter, I stepped outside hoping I would be invited to play. But then I quickly drew back. The kids were speaking Spanish! I recognized the language because my grandparents and parents spoke it. But the children's loud, rapid-fire Spanish was practically incomprehensible. Our frequent family outings to nearby Ciudad Juárez exposed me to Spanish, a language I found normal in a Mexican city. But these Spanish-speaking kids were in the United States. Why did they persist in using the language of Mexico? Had they chosen not to speak English, or could they only speak Spanish?

I was also taken aback by their lack of clothing. They wore nothing more than underwear and were barefoot. In Los Angeles, kids my age would never venture outdoors clad only in briefs and without shoes or sandals.

I retreated into my grandmother's rambling house and stared at the kids laughing and shouting. I vaguely identified with them because they looked like me. But the language barrier made them unapproachable.

"Why don't you go play with the kids?" my grandmother asked in a tone that struck me as more of a command than a suggestion. I thought of telling her that I didn't speak Spanish. She always addressed me in English, likely because she knew my Spanish was sketchy, at best. Still, I decided she would think less of me had I told her I didn't speak more than a few words of the language. So, I replied that it was too hot.

"Take off your pants and shirt," she said, "and you won't feel the heat." I had to answer truthfully. "I'm not used to playing outside dressed like that. We wear trunks or shorts where I live."

"Well, this is a poor neighborhood," she said in a steely tone, "and that's how poor kids play here. Go outside and have fun."

I meekly said I would much prefer to stay indoors and watch the kids. She walked off without saying anything. Plainly I had displeased her. As a monolingual English speaker, I realized that not speaking Spanish had denied me the chance to escape my grandmother's dreary living room.

I have not shared this anecdote with many people. It can easily seem an unremarkable childhood incident. For me, however, it is yet another powerful reminder of how long and convoluted my odyssey has been. From 1956 to the present, the journey has taken me to places I did not know existed, confronted me with countless obstacles and many experiences common to Latinos seeking to make their way in the United States.

I have lived a life filled with innumerable adventures that were at times sad, enlightening, terrifying, incredible or beautiful. My persistence, resilience and intellectual curiosity led me to meet thousands of people who lavishly enriched my life. Now in my seventh decade, I am encouraged that Mexicans in the United States will increasingly and successfully embrace their dual cultures and identities.

During my time teaching at the University of California, Irvine, I met many Mexican students who were passionate about melding their twin identities and cultures.

The United States sits on the northern frontier of Latin America, a region that is home to 649 million people. No other region so directly impacts the United States more than Latin America. Even as anti-immigration politicians strive to keep Latin Americans at bay, the immigrants trek north. Many millions have arrived in just the last 25 years. There is no reason to expect that trend to end. Border enforcement and laws are ineffective in shutting off the migratory flow. We are witnessing a demographic transformation of the United States, a country whose make-up will be far more Latino and diverse than it is today.

I hope this book has conveyed some overlooked but important history and reminded us that we can hold tight to our ancestral heritage and still be good Americans. My most fervent wish, however, is that my story in some small way serves as an example of what can be accomplished even in the most adverse circumstances.